The Awesome Pow...
of PowerJ

The Awesome Power of PowerJ

TIM HATTON

MANNING
Greenwich
(74° w. long.)

For electronic browsing and ordering of this book, see http://www.browsebooks.com
The publisher offers discounts on this book when ordered in quantity.
For more information, please contact:

> Special Sales Department
> Manning Publications Co.
> 3 Lewis Street
> Greenwich, CT 06830
>
> Fax: (203) 661-9018
> email: orders@manning.com

Library of Congress Cataloging-in-Publication Data
Hatton, Tim
        The Awesome Power of PowerJ / by Tim Hatton.
            p.   cm.
        Includes bibliographical references and index.
        ISBN 1-884777-53-8 (alk. paper)
        1. Java (Computer program language).   2. PowerJ.
    QA76.73.J38H377   1997
    005.2'762—dc21
        CIP

    Manning Publications Co.
    3 Lewis Street
    Greenwich, CT 06830

    Copyeditor: Katherine Antonsen
    Page design/typesetting: Syd Brown
    Cover design: Leslie Haimes

Printed in the United States of America
1 2 3 4 5 6 7 8 9 10 – CR – 00 99 98 97

Dedication:

For Roy Edward Hatton, 1936–1997

contents

5   *Using the PowerJ standard objects*   90

6 Using menu objects   128

PART III: *Extending PowerJ—classes, templates, databases & more* 215

12 Defining and using templates   217

13 Using classes in PowerJ   223

14   *Using databases*   *233*

15 Building applications for the Internet   276

16 Using JavaBeans and ActiveX   300

17

18

19   *Where do we go from here?*   *334*

acknowledgments

Every book is the result of the efforts of many people who worked on it in its various phases. Here are some of the people who helped with this one.

Marjan Bace—the Publisher who gave me a chance to do what I always wanted: to write.

Ted Kennedy—who arranged for manuscript reviews as we went along.

Mary Piergies—who pulled it all together and got it out the door.

The reviewers:

Richard G. Baldwin,

Dave Miller,

Mark Mitchell,

Tonya Pope, and

Kaj Bjurman.

Your detailed and helpful comments have made this a better book.

Jennifer Cullen at PowerSoft, who arranged for access to various versions of PowerJ and generally made things easier.

If I have left anyone out, it is entirely unintentional.

And now a special acknowledgment to the two people who have made it all possible: my mother and my father.

They helped me through college and law school, helped me set up and run my own practice, and provided support for me when I decided to give up the law and learn to program.

While I was preparing the final version of this manuscript for production, my Dad died suddenly. I had been away, teaching a course for Boston University. On the very day I returned home, he suffered a major heart attack. He died four days later without regaining consciousness.

Dad was a master carpenter who would not tolerate errors of 1/16 of an inch. He was happiest working alone, building something from a single piece of lumber. I will always remember my Dad, not as I saw him in the hospital bed, but as he was on a construction site, hammer in hand, building houses in which people will live and raise families long after any software I will ever write has been abandoned. Those houses will remain as his monument.

When someone you love is gone, you think of all the things you wish you had said and done but didn't. In this place let me just say: Dad, thanks for everything you did for me, especially the things that you really didn't want to but did anyway. You left us so soon.

introduction

Welcome to the world of Java programming using PowerJ, a Rapid Application Development (RAD) tool for Java programming from PowerSoft, the makers of PowerBuilder. With PowerJ, PowerSoft does for Java programming what it did for client/server development with PowerBuilder—makes it easy and fast.

With PowerJ, you can write Java programs the very first day, even if your Java experience is limited. This is made possible by an award-winning drag-and-drop programming interface (first used by Power-Soft in its Optima++ C++ development environment), which actually uses a wizard to construct Java language statements for you and pastes those statements into a code-editor window. Since these statements are constructed by PowerJ itself, they are error free.

Of course, you still need to know programming, since you will be required to use flow-control statements such as `if...else` or `while` to control the execution of your code, but the real guts of the Java language are hidden from you.

That is not to say that PowerJ is a beginner's-only environment. PowerJ will serve the needs of every level of developer. Beginners can rely heavily upon the assistance of the drag-and-drop interface, while advanced Java developers can use the code editor to write the code directly. And everybody can benefit from the debugging features and the form design features, which make development using PowerJ a snap.

Who should read this book?

This book is for beginning and intermediate Java developers who want to learn or get up to speed on developing Java applications using PowerJ. It is also for those who do not know Java but still want to be able to deliver Java applications. PowerJ excels at teaching you Java as you go.

Aside from chapter 1, the Java basics chapter, little time is spent teaching you the syntax of the Java language (many books have been written about that), and most of the focus is on how to accomplish a task using the PowerJ product.

If you are a beginning Java programmer, you should start your reading with Chapter 1, the Java basics chapter.

If you are already familiar with both Java and object-oriented programming concepts, you can start with Chapter 2, which is an overview of the PowerJ Integrated Development Environment (IDE). If you are familiar with both Java and the Power++/PowerJ environment (from using Optima++), you can start with Chapter 3 which begins the in-depth exploration of how to use PowerJ to develop Java applications.

So what is Java all about?

It's hard to believe that just a few short years ago Internet access was the domain of relatively few academic organizations and even fewer "computer people." Today, nearly 40 percent of the American people are on the Internet in one form or another.

So, what has made the Internet so popular? In a word, multimedia. It is the promise of wonderful multimedia content, delivered right to your home or office, on demand, that fueled the print and broadcast media's hype of the Internet and attracted all those new users.

The trouble is, until just a couple of years ago, the ability to easily create and deliver that content did not exist. The ability to move massive amounts of data across small copper wires at modem speeds served as a severe constraint to the development of real multimedia broadcast capabilities and still does (although the problem is beginning to be solved). But the available bandwidth was only a small part of the dilemma.

The problem was that there was no development tool that had the ability to run on the many different client computers that end users were using to access the Internet—not to mention the multiple operating systems that were available for each hardware platform.

Enter Java

Responding to this need, the developers at Sun created the Java language. One use of Java is to deliver true cross-platform development capabilities by transmitting a form of the code itself to each client, where it is executed in a virtual machine. The virtual machine is different for each platform, taking advantage of each platform's capabilities. The only thing that remains the same is that the virtual machine can execute the Java code that is sent to it. The code is the same for all clients.

Of course, all this is possible using methods other than Java. Programs can be written for the Common Gateway Interface (CGI) that can do anything a Java application can do. But there are differences and drawbacks. One is that CGI programs execute on the server and only the result of that execution is sent to the client. Also, CGI has the reputation of being difficult to learn.

More than pretty graphics

But if Java were just a language for delivering multimedia content, it is doubtful that it would be as popular as it is. The fuel that is now feeding the Java fire is its use as a multitiered, business application development language. Java applets and applications are being used to deliver business-related content over the Internet. These applications play off Java's strength as a multiplatform development language. Businesses can write real-time database-driven applications and use Java's cross-platform support to deliver those applications via the Internet to users worldwide—no matter what network they use, no matter what hardware, no matter what Web browser. With Java, you write it once and deliver it to many locations, without change.

Why learn Java?

Java is the hottest language to hit the computer industry in the past ten years. Fueling the fire to make Java hot is the phenomenal rate of growth of the Internet. As the Internet continues to grow at a rapid pace, demand for Java development will also continue to increase exponentially.

Although Java is a general-purpose language that has uses far beyond the Internet, it is mainly its use on the Internet that is driving Java's growth. For traditional applications there are other, more entrenched languages.

But being a C++ derived language makes Java difficult to read, understand, and write for many developers. Several products have been released from the major players in the industry to enable RAD for the Java developer. Microsoft's Visual J++ and Symantec's Café are examples.

Each of those products was a step in the right direction, but they failed to deliver the full promise of Java-based RAD to the many programmers who do not know Java. PowerJ is different. Its unique interface finally delivers RAD Java development to everyone.

Why learn PowerJ?

The PowerSoft Corporation (now part of Sybase) developed one of the most successful products of the 1990s: PowerBuilder. PowerBuilder was the first product that delivered true RAD for the client/server programmer. With its unique data window architecture, PowerBuilder all but cornered the market on client/server development. Now PowerSoft will try to do it again with PowerJ, its new Java RAD tool.

PowerJ is derived from PowerSoft's Power++, which is a full-blown C++ development tool. Most of what is discussed in this book will be familiar to those who have programmed using Power++. In fact, both products use the same user interface.

Why use PowerJ to develop your business applications?

As more and more shops enter the Java world, managers are increasingly faced with the decision regarding what environment to use to develop their Java programs. PowerJ should be given serious consideration.

Why? Mostly because of its ease of use. Java is new in terms of programming languages. While you may have C++ programmers on staff or you may have PowerBuilder programmers on staff, it is unlikely that you will have Java experts on staff. What you probably will have are some developers who are proficient in other languages and have learned Java on the side. They know the basics of Java and they know programming constructs, but they are not really Java experts.

Since you probably need to get your Java programs written and deployed sooner rather than later, you are faced with the need to either train your staff extensively before beginning development or to hire new, Java-proficient developers. PowerJ will give you the best of both worlds. With PowerJ you can bring your existing developers up to speed on Java at the same time they are delivering real-world Java applications.

The more they use PowerJ, the more they will learn Java. The key is to build your smaller applications first and move into the more complex applications as your developers gain knowledge. Shops that attempt to use a new language to completely rewrite their business processes in one shot seldom succeed unless they go outside for help.

Source code

All source code for the examples presented in this book can be obtained directly from the *The Awesome Power of PowerJ* descriptive pages on the Manning Publications Co. Web site. The URL *http://www.manning.com/Hatton2* includes a hyperlink to the source code files.

Author online

Purchase of *The Awesome Power of PowerJ* also includes free access to a private Internet forum where you can make comments about the book, ask technical questions, and receive help from the author and from other PowerJ users. To access the PowerJ forum, point your Web browser to *http://www.manning.com/Hatton2/forum.* There you will be able to subscribe to the forum. This site also provides information on how to access the forum once you are registered, what kind of help is available, and the rules of conduct on the forum.

Finally, a note about using the mouse

Since PowerJ is a drag-and-drop environment, you will use the mouse extensively. So there will be many times when I tell you to click something or to drag something and drop it somewhere else. When I say click something, I mean use the left mouse button. When you need to use the right mouse button, I always will say to right-click. Double-clicks always mean use the left button. When I say drag something, I mean click it with the left button and move the mouse to the new location and then release the left button.

Of course, if you have a left-handed mouse all this is reversed.

With all that in mind, let's get started on our way to learning Java programming with PowerJ.

Part I

The basics

Before you begin working productively in any new environment you should take the time to acquire a grasp of the basic fundamentals upon which that environment is based. PowerJ is no exception to this rule.

PowerJ is based upon Java, and while it is true that you can write Java applications in PowerJ using the drag-and-drop programming system that it employs, you will not get the most out of the environment unless you have a good understanding of Java. For purposes of this book, all you need to know are the basics of the Java language and those are covered in chapter 1—Java Basics.

Chapter 2 teaches you what you need to know to use PowerJ itself. You will learn what the most frequently used windows are and how to open them. You will learn how to manipulate object properties using the Object Inspector and the Properties dialogs. And you will get your first look at the Reference Card and drag-and-drop programming. Once you complete this chapter you should be able to move around in the PowerJ IDE with ease.

In chapter 3 we build upon the concepts we learned in chapters 1 and 2 by building a couple of programs designed to exercise your knowledge of the PowerJ IDE.

Java basics

1

In this chapter we will discuss the following:

- Syntax of the Java language
- Basic object-oriented programming techniques
- Java classes
- Java variables
- Java flow-control statements

The growth of the Internet has been phenomenal and, as of this writing, it has begun to pervade our society. Not a single day goes by without some newspaper article or radio or television show making mention of the Information Superhighway. The Internet played a pivotal role in the last presidential election, when President Clinton promised to build a bridge to the twenty-first century. On election night the Internet slowed to a crawl, as users jammed the servers to get the latest up-to-the-minute results.

The popular growth of the Internet is due primarily to the content provided by the World Wide Web (the Web, WWW). In fact, although the Internet is much more than just the Web, you will find that when people refer to the Internet they are in fact referring only to the Web.

So what has made the Web so popular? Mostly the nifty interactive content that it provides—the ability to see moving pictures and animations, as well as hear sound. This is what attracts users and enables the content providers to reach large numbers of people with their messages. The major news delivery services such as CNN and MSNBC distribute their content on the Internet. You can listen to sporting events from all over the world, and the day is near when you will be able to watch them, too.

Although the full promise of this multimedia content has not yet been realized, each day brings new advances and better content.

Another driving force in the growth of the Internet has been the use of tools designed for developing Internet programs to deliver business-related content. Businesses that wish to make their goods, services, and information available to the public online have adopted the Internet as the medium for delivery of that content. And rightfully so. Why develop your own online networks when one already exists with protocols that are supported by all the major operating systems and hardware platforms?

But it is that very diversity that makes development for the Internet difficult. Once your business places content on the Internet for access online, you lose control over what operating system or hardware platform is being used to access your programs. User A may be in Ohio running Windows 95 on an Intel-based processor, while user B is in Massachusetts running a Mac, not to mention the different flavors of UNIX that are out there, any one of which may need to access your business' content on the Internet.

Java is the language that allows you to deliver that content without regard to such considerations as operating systems or hardware. That is not to say that there aren't other methods of performing the same task using other languages. But it is a fact of life that Java made this type of development much, much easier.

1.1   *Java's portability*

Java is an interpreted language that will run on any platform for which there is an interpreter available. In other words, if you write Java code, it will run under any system for which there is a Java interpreter available that supports Java, whether that system is running under Win95, NT, UNIX or the Mac. You can place your Java code on a network server and no matter what client machine downloads and executes the code, it will run as intended.

Note

This works because Java code is compiled into byte code rather than machine code. Machine code is specific to certain processor/ operating system combinations. Byte code can be platform independent.

The interpreter for Java is referred to as the Java Virtual Machine (JVM). The JVM is a specification for a theoretical machine that exists only in the RAM of the computer executing the Java application. Most popular Web browsers today come equipped with a JVM for the platform upon which they are intended to run. Most operating system vendors either have, or will have, plans on incorporating the JVM into the operating system itself. In the future, the JVM will almost certainly become a standard component of any system.

1.2   *Java is more than Web-based multimedia and business content*

All this is not to say that there are no other uses for Java; there are. Java is one of the leading languages in the new "thin-client" revolution. In thin-client computing, the applications that the end user runs every day are located on the server and only loaded into the client machine's RAM at run time. This is exactly what Java does. This kind of code distribution eases the pain of maintaining applications in a multiuser environment by allowing the application code to be centrally located. If an update is necessary, that update need only be loaded onto the server and it becomes instantly available to every user.

Recognizing that larger corporations have tired of investing tens of thousands of dollars in yearly maintenance for each PC in their organization, many software providers have jumped on Java as the solution. By utilizing Java versions of common applications such as word processors and spread dialogs (Microsoft has promised a Java version of their Office Suite), companies can begin to take advantage of the savings involved in serving applications from a central location. The hardware vendors are not far behind: New machines are now on the market that strip much of the complexity from PCs (small or no hard drives, etc.) while optimizing them for use in a networked environment.

1.3   Java is object oriented

Java is an object-oriented programming language. While Java is derived from C++, the developers decided to eliminate many of the constraints of that language. The Java developers decided to "start over" and created a language that has the look and feel of C++ and actually extends that language's object-oriented features but at the same time eliminates some of its more obvious limitations and hard-to-understand features.

1.4   Learning Java

The remainder of this chapter gives you an overview of the Java language. This overview is not to be taken as a treatise on Java itself or even as a good method of learning the language. The sole purpose of this discussion is to give you the background necessary to use PowerJ with some understanding of what is going on. As you use PowerJ, your grasp of Java will increase.

It is possible to use PowerJ and to write some fairly sophisticated Java applications without really understanding Java. That is the beauty of the PowerJ environment. However, what will make the great PowerJ programmers stand out from the good PowerJ programmers will be their basic understanding of Java and the ability to open a code editor and write Java code that cannot be developed using the drag-and-drop programming interface used by PowerJ.

1.5 Java classes

As with any object-oriented development package, Java relies upon objects. An object is an instance of a class. Therefore, you can say that the basis for all Java programming is the class.

A class is code that provides the blueprint for everything an object is and does. You will learn more about PowerJ's implementation of classes and objects in chapter 13. Right now, let's try to develop a basic understanding of exactly what a class is. We will talk more about objects and classes in general in section 1.6.1.

A class consists of data and methods. The data of the class are held in class member variables. These are variables that are defined in the class code.

In general, the actual values of the data elements of a class are hidden from the user. In other words, classes are defined so as to disallow the ability to directly access any of the classes' data elements. Instead, you access the data of a class through methods provided for that purpose. Methods consist of code that allows the user to interact with the data of a class.

1.5.1 Relationship between classes and objects

Now that we have a basic explanation of the concept of a class, let's see if we can define the mainstay of the object-oriented programmer—the object.

1.6 What is an object?

To begin to gain an understanding of object-oriented programming, you should become very familiar with the concept of an object. While the definition of an object may be technical, you can also think of an object as a software model of a real-world object. You can look all around you now and see many examples of real-world objects: your house, your boss, and your car are all examples of objects that you see all the time.

Definition

A software object is a software package of variables and related methods.

So what do these objects have in common? Well, they all exist in a certain state and they all have certain behavior associated with them—for example, your boss may have the behavior of arrogance associated with him or her, while your house has the behavior of air conditioning associated with it. Your car has all sorts of behavioral aspects from speed to braking and cornering capability. Examples of the state of these objects is whether the house is messy or clean or whether your boss is bearded or clean-shaven, has hair or is bald.

One of the ways that an object can behave is to change its state. An example of this is when your boss decides to shave or get a haircut.

Objects in software are no different from objects in the real world. They are defined by their existence in a certain state at a particular time and by their behavior. A software object maintains its state in variables and implements its behavior with methods.

Now that we have an idea of what objects are, perhaps we can come up with a working definition of a programming object.

Note

Throughout this book and in other references you will see the words *functions* and *methods* used interchangeably. These two terms are functionally identical.

Most object-oriented programming consists of the process of modeling real-world objects in software—for example, if you were programming an Indy car racing simulator, you would model the car in software in such a way that it mimics its real-world counterpart. But if that is all object-oriented programming could do, it would be severely limited. What kind of world would we live in if computers were limited only to modeling things that actually exist in real life?

Fortunately, that is not the case and you can use programming objects to model abstract concepts that do not actually have a real-life counterpart.

You can, for example, create an object that models the behavior of a typical employee taking vacation time and use the methods of that object to track real-life employees (most of whom are not typical) as they take their real-life vacation days. The rules that the object uses to calculate vacation time do not exist in the real world as concrete objects. They are abstractions only. However, the computer does not care. An object is an object to the software world.

Definition

A programming object is a collection of variables and related functions.

Figure 1.1 illustrates a common visual representation of a software object.

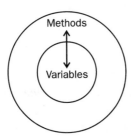

Figure 1.1
Visual representation of a software object

Everything that the programming object knows (state of existence) and can do (behavior) is expressed by the variables and methods contained entirely within that object. A software object that modeled your real-world Indy car would have variables that indicated the car's current state: Its speed is 210 m.p.h., acceleration is 1.5 Gs, and its current gear is the fifth gear.

So what happens when you want to change the state of the Indy car? If you want to slow down to 200 miles per hour, you use the brake. If you want to speed up to 220, you use the accelerator. Not surprisingly, it works the same way in the programming object that models our Indy car. If you want to slow the speed of the object car, you call a brake method, which acts just like the brakes on the real-life counterpart: They slow you down. If you want to speed up, you call a method that acts like pushing on the throttle and you speed up. What the methods do is interact (change) the values stored in the instance variables for speed. Other code in the application will react to that change in the value of the variable and make the car appear to slow down or speed up.

So what about things that an Indy car can't do—for example, it can't fly. Consequently there are no variables or methods that control the altitude of the car. Anything that you do not wish your object to do is excluded from the variables and methods that you, the programmer, provide the object.

As you can see in figure 1.1, the object's variables and methods interact internally. Methods surround and hide the object's variables from other objects in the program. Hiding the object's variables in this manner is called encapsulation. To set the speed of our Indy car, we don't directly alter the speed. We can only change the speed by using the brake or accelerate methods that are provided for that purpose.

1.6.1 Objects versus classes

By now you should have realized that the definitions of objects and classes are very similar. For this reason, the difference between classes and objects is often the source of some confusion. When dealing with real-world objects, it is easy to tell that the object and class are two different concepts—the car (object) and the blueprint for the car (class) are two very different things. But in programming the distinction is blurred.

Definition

A class is merely a definition. An object is a particular instance of a class. You can create many objects from one class, just as you can create many cars from one set of blueprints.

1.6.2 Instances of classes

The act of creating an object from a class definition is called creating an instance. When you create an instance of an object, the computer looks at the class (the definition of the object) and creates the data and methods in memory. This becomes the object that you manipulate during the course of your application.

1.7   *What is inheritance?*

The act of creating an object based upon a class definition can be done in several different ways. One way would be to copy the class into a separate class and then make changes to the new class. This would be the case if we first copied all of the class car into separate classes called Indy and Mustang and then altered the attributes of the new class so that each car was different. Then, when we created an object from the class, we would create the object based on the Mustang class when we wanted a Mustang and upon the Indy class when we wanted an Indy car.

But if we did that we would wind up with a lot of classes, each containing duplicate blueprint information from the base class. If you want to make a change to the base class, guess what? You have to track down each and every one of the new classes and make the same change in them. There has to be a better way, right?

The better way is called inheritance, and it is the most powerful tool of the object-oriented programmer.

In the world of the object-oriented programmer, objects are defined in terms of classes. If you know what an object's class is, you already know a lot about that object. If you know that an object is of the class window, you know that it has a title bar and a border and that you can resize it by dragging the border to the new size (of course these attributes may be altered in a particular implementation of the class, but generally you know that a window can have these attributes). A window can be resizable or not. It can have a border or not. But it is still derived from the general class window. Every different type of window that is derived from the general window class is called a subclass or a descendant of the parent class.

Let's return to our car example for a moment and make these concepts a little easier to understand. As we discussed, we often have many different objects that are derived from only one class. Indy is only one type of car. Mustang would be another type.

Although these two types of cars are radically different in appearance, they do share many attributes, and these attributes are shared with cars of all other types—for example, both Indy cars and Mustangs have brakes and accelerators.

If you continue to think along this path, you will find that there are attributes that are shared by all objects of type car. You are well on your way to inventing the concept of a class. If you think of a car as containing all the attributes that are common to all cars, regardless of their type, you have invented the class car. All cars such as Indy and Mustang can now be thought of as objects of type car. And all objects of type car have in common all the attributes of the base class car.

To implement our Indy car as a software object, we would first create a class called car and we would give this class all the variables and methods that will be common to all cars. (See figure 1.2.)

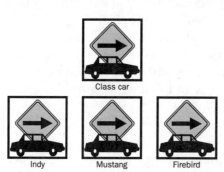

Class car

Indy   Mustang   Firebird

Figure 1.2
Class car and instance variables

The values for instance variables are provided by each instance of the class. So, after you've created the class car, you must instantiate it (create an instance of it) before you can use it. When you create an instance of a class, you create an object of that type, and the system allocates memory for the member variables declared by the class. Then you can invoke the object's methods to make it do something. Instances of the same class share the same instance method implementations (method implementations are not duplicated on a per-object basis), which reside in the class itself.

Now let's apply this principle to the world of object-oriented software. You can see that there are many objects in software that are of the same type. Examples of this are command buttons, list boxes, windows, and so on. Those objects are some user-interface objects with which we are all familiar. Every command button has the same basic attributes as any other command button, and every window has the same basic attributes as every other window. They may look different, but every window and button can be boiled down to the basic attributes they share with every other window or command button. The boiled-down version of the window or button is the window class or the button class. In other words, the class is a blueprint or plan for creating all objects of that type.

Each subclass inherited from a class will inherit its state of existence (in the form of member variables) from the superclass (parent class). Indy cars and Mustangs share the same variables as found in the superclass car. Also, each subclass inherits methods from the superclass. Indy cars and Mustangs share the same brake and accelerate methods as the class car.

But if subclasses were limited to the same variables and methods as their superclasses, they would be of little use. In that case every car would be identical. So in an object-oriented world, subclasses can add variables and methods to the ones they inherit from the superclass. Indy cars can have more gears than a Mustang and higher limits of acceleration. Also, you are not limited to just one layer of inheritance. The inheritance tree, or class hierarchy, can be as deep as needed. Methods and variables are inherited down through the levels. In general, the further down in the hierarchy a class appears, the more its behavior will deviate from the base class.

1.7.1 *The benefits of inheritance*

Subclasses provide a method of creating specialized implementations of the base class. Through the use of inheritance, programmers can reuse the code in the superclass many times. If you wish to make a change to the behavior that is common to the entire class hierarchy, then you need to make that change only to the base class and all other subclasses will automatically reflect that change. Your base classes should implement generic behavior, while your subclasses refine that behavior to fit particular needs.

1.8 *Classes and objects provide encapsulation and polymorphism*

Encapsulation (also known as information hiding) is one of the most powerful tools of the object-oriented programmer. Encapsulation provides the main basis for the object-oriented programming concept of reusable code. Since an object is self-contained, it can be reused without change in a variety of programs or situations. Since all that is required to use an object is knowledge of its functions or methods, you can take the Indy car object from our racing simulation and place it in a NASCAR simulation where it can compete with car objects of that type.

Encapsulation also assists in making code more maintainable. If you want to make a change to the characteristics of the Indy car, then you access and change only the Indy car object. No other object in the application needs to change (unless you delete or add a method to the object that requires a change in a calling object; in well-designed objects these sweeping changes are seldom required).

Classes in Java are also polymorphic (one of the basic principles of object-oriented programming). When you define methods in a base class and inherit from that class to form descendant classes, you can define methods of the same name at the descendant level. These methods may accept arguments different from those required for the ancestor method and may perform a task in a different manner. When you instantiate the descendant (create an object from it) and call the method against that object, Java will execute the method at the descendant level rather than at the ancestor level. This is referred to as overloading and is the textbook example of polymorphism.

1.9 *Object-based programming versus object-oriented programming*

Notwithstanding adherence to the three defining principles of object orientedness, the main thing that you will notice about object-oriented programming is that it is object based. A good development environment (and the PowerJ environment is certainly that) will shield the developer from many of the guts of object-oriented programming. In other words, when you create an object, it automatically follows certain rules of encapsulation without your having to think about them. But, as you follow along in this book and perform the tasks and exercises that are set out for you to use in learning how to program using PowerJ, you should train yourself to think in an object-oriented manner.

1.10 *The AWT classes*

Since most user interfaces consist of the same objects, windows, buttons, list boxes, and so forth, the makers of Java defined a set of base classes that delivers the functionality of each of the user-interface elements you need to assemble into a completed program. These base classes are called the Abstract Windows Toolkit (AWT). There are two versions of AWT: one for Java 1.02 and one for Java 1.1. PowerJ includes both AWT class libraries, so you can use them when programming for either version of Java.

1.11 *Event-driven systems*

It is also necessary to learn a little about event-driven programming in order to understand the basics of PowerJ. Applications written in PowerJ are usually event-driven.

The Windows operating system is an event-driven system, and all Windows applications are driven by the same sets of events. An example of an event is when the user clicks on a button. When that happens the button's clicked event is fired. If you look in the documentation for the Windows SDK, you will see that most of the user-interface objects (buttons, menu items, list boxes, and so forth.) have the same kinds of events. There are clicked and double-clicked events and item-changed or edit-changed events (fired when the user types something in a field). When working with these standard objects, most of your programming is merely putting code in these events to perform some action when the user (or sometimes Windows itself) causes the event to happen. The online Help system of your development environment also contains a complete listing of all objects and the events that they recognize.

Java's AWT classes respond to all the standard events. Some of them are renamed from what you will see in other languages—for example, the click event of a command button is called the action event. As you learn PowerJ you will pick up the new event names.

1.12 *Do I need to know object-oriented programming?*

Object-oriented programming is the new way of life for programmers. It is used extensively in almost all new development projects, and almost all new development environments are object oriented (or at least object based).

Do you need to know the basic concepts of object-oriented programming? Yes, definitely. Do your applications have to be 100 percent pure object-oriented programs? Definitely not.

What you will do is pick and choose the object-oriented features that make sense for your application. You will find that encapsulation always makes sense, because it makes the code easier to maintain after it is written. Inheritance makes sense for commonly used objects such as buttons, list boxes, and windows, but, it makes less sense for complicated user-interface elements that are extensively modified between one implementation and the next.

PowerJ provides the best of both worlds, since it allows for easy class development and inheritance and also provides an easy method for writing reusable code without using inheritance. This other method is called a template, and we will learn about templates in chapter12.

The only real way to learn object-oriented programming is to read the many books and articles that explain how it is done and then practice it by using it where you can.

1.13 *Elements of the Java language*

Java is a language that is derived from C++. It follows a lot of the rules and syntax of that language—for example, C and C++ programmers will find the ; statement delimiter very familiar, as well as the { } for blocking segments of code.

It is way beyond the scope of this book, which is designed only to teach you about the PowerJ interface and how to use it to create Java programs, to teach you the Java language. You do not have to know the Java language to get started in PowerJ. If you want to become a great PowerJ programmer, known throughout the universe for your PowerJ prowess, then you will find it necessary to learn the Java language extensively.

The following sections should give you the basics to understand how to code in PowerJ.

1.13.1 *Java variable types*

Java supports a full range of variable types:

byte

short

int

long

float

double

char

boolean

In their raw state, these are referred to as the primitive datatypes. In addition to the primitive datatypes, Java also implements data typing in the form of classes. These classes store a variable of the specified datatype, plus additional methods for manipulating that data—for example, the integer class contains methods for converting the int variable it encapsulates into a string. We will learn about some of these standard datatype classes in chapter 7.

1.13.2 *Scope of variables*

When you declare a variable in Java, it obtains a scope. The scope of the variable depends upon the point of the code in which it is declared.

A variable's scope is only within the block of code in which it is declared. That means that a variable may only be referenced within the block in which it is declared. A block is a segment of code that opens and closes with curly braces. The following is an example of a block of code.

```
Class button {  // beginning of button block
   Public static void main (Int Args [ ] ) {  // beginning of main block
   int x ;
   . . .
   } // end of main block
Public void method ( ) { // beginning of method block
   char y ;
   . . .
   } // end of method block
      } // end of button block
```

In the code above, int x has been declared in the main method and can be referenced only within the block for the main method. If you try to reference int x from the method block, an error will occur. The same is true for char y, which can be referenced only from the method block.

1.13.3 *Access modifiers*

You may also control a variable's scope through the use of access modifiers. This is how you hide the actual member variables of a class and require them to be manipulated through methods rather than directly. The Java access modifiers are as follows:

Public variables are accessible by anyone.

Protected variables are accessible only by functions defined within them and also from any classes descending from the class and from within other classes in the same package.

Private variables are accessible only within the class in which they are defined.

If an access scope is not specified, it defaults to private.

1.13.4 *Variable names*

You refer to a variable in your program code by its name. There are many variable naming standards, but the most commonly used states that variable and method names begin with a lowercase letter, while class names begin with a capital letter.

In Java, a variable name has the following attributes.

- It must be a legal Java identifier comprised of a series of characters.
- It must not be the same as a keyword.
- It must not have the same name as another variable whose declaration appears in the same scope.

Variables may have the same name as another variable whose declaration appears in a different scope.

1.13.5 *Operators*

Any programming language depends upon its operators to get work done. Java supports a full range of operators that allow you to manipulate variables in almost any possible manner.

Operators perform some function on either one or two variables. You can divide Java's operators into these six categories: arithmetic, relational, conditional, bitwise, logical, and assignment.

1.13.6   *Flow-control statements*

As with any language, a Java program's execution is controlled by the use of flow-control statements. In other words, flow-control statements govern the sequence in which a program's statements are executed. Java supports a full range of flow-control statements as shown in the following chart.

Statement	Keyword
decision making	if...else, switch-case
loop	for, while, do-while
miscellaneous	break, continue, label:, return

If you are a programmer, you will already be familiar with these statements. They are the mainstay of any programming language. If you are not a programmer, stop immediately and study a basic programming text to become familiar with the type of logic that you need to write programs in any language.

What follows is a review of the basic flow-control statements, so that programmers who are not familiar with the syntax of C/C++ or Java can get started learning that syntax.

Branching statements

Java supports a full range of statements designed to branch your code's execution depending upon a test for condition. These include the `if...else` and `switch` statements.

The if...else statement.   Java's `if...else` statement provides your programs with the ability to selectively execute other statements based on some criteria—for example, suppose that your program printed a statement based on whether the day of the week is Monday. A segment of code to implement this might look like this:

```
if (Monday) {
  System.out.println("Today is Monday");
  }
  else {
  System.out.println("Today is Not Monday");
  . . .
  }
```

This is the simplest version of the `if...else` statement: The statement governed by the `if` is executed if some condition is true. If the statement is not true, then the code in the `else` block is executed. Generally, the simple form of `if` can be written like this:

```
if (expression)
    statement
else
    statement
```

This particular use of the `else` statement is the catchall form. The `else` block is executed if the `if` part is false. There is another form of the `else` statement, `else if`, which executes a statement based on another expression. The form of that statement is as follows:

```
if (expression)
    statement
else if (expression)
    statement
else
    statement
```

An `if` statement can have any number of companion `else if` statements, but only one `else`.

The switch statement. Use the `switch` statement to conditionally perform statements based on some expression. The basic form of the switch statement is as follows:

```
switch (integer expression)
    case value1: (statement)
    case value2: (statement)
    ...
    default: (statement)
```

Suppose, for example, that your program contained an integer named day whose value indicated the day of the week. Suppose also that you wanted to display the name of the day based on its integer equivalent. Here is how you would use a switch to perform that task.

```
int day;
...
switch (day) {
case 1:  System.out.println("Sunday"); break;
case 2:  System.out.println("Monday"); break;
case 3:  System.out.println("Tuesday"); break;
case 4:  System.out.println("Wednesday"); break;
```

```
case 5:  System.out.println("Thursday"); break;
case 6:  System.out.println("Friday"); break;
case 7:  System.out.println("Saturday"); break;
   default: System.out.println("No Day"); break;

}
```

The `switch` statement evaluates its expression, in this case the value of day, and then executes the appropriate `case` statement. If no statement matches, the `default` is then executed. Of course, you could implement this as an `if` statement, but that would be unwieldy.

Deciding whether to use an `if` statement or a `switch` statement is a judgment call. The decision on which to use should be based on readability and other factors. It is usually better to use the most readable code.

Each `case` statement must contain a break. The `break` statements cause control to break out of the switch and continue with the first statement following the switch. The `break` statements are necessary because `case` statements fall through. Without an explicit break, control will flow sequentially through subsequent `case` statements.

If necessary, you can use the `default` statement at the end of the switch to handle all values that aren't explicitly handled by one of the `case` statements.

Looping statements

In addition to branching statements such as those just discussed, Java supports a full range of looping constructs. These include the `while` statement and the `for` statement.

The while statement. Generally speaking, a `while` statement performs some action while a certain condition remains true. The syntax of the `while` statement is as follows:

```
while (expression)
   statement
```

In English this would read as: While the expression is true, take the action(s) contained in the statement.

A statement can be one statement or it can be a statement block. A statement block is a series of legal Java statements contained within curly brackets (`{` and `}`).

The for statement.   Use the `for` loop when you know the constraints of the loop (what causes the loop to end). `For` loops are often used to iterate over the elements in an array, or the characters in a string, such as this:

```
int a [ ]
   int i;
   int length = a.length;
   for (i = 0; i < length; i++) {
   . . .
   x = a [ i ]

} // of course this code does nothing but illustrate the point.
```

You know when writing the program that you want to start at the beginning of the array, stop at the end, and hit every element. Thus, the `for` statement is a good choice. The general form of the `for` statement can be expressed like this.

```
for (initialization; termination; increment)
   statements
```

The do-while statement.   Java also provides another loop, the `do-while` loop, which is similar to the `while` loop except that the expression is evaluated at the bottom of the loop.

```
do {
   statements
} while (boolean expression);
```

The return statement.   The `return` statement is used to break out of a branch of code and return some value to the calling routine.

1.14 Initializing objects from class definitions

Since Java is class based, you will need to understand how to create objects in your applications based upon the class definitions. This is known as creating an instance of the class.

You create an instance of the class using the new keyword—for example, if you want to create an instance of the graphics class (which allows you to draw graphics on a form) you would do the following.

```
import java.awt.graphics;
graphics g = new graphics();
```

This will call the constructor for the graphics class, which will return an instance of the class into the object g. From that point on, when you call methods of the graphics class, you issue the call against the graphics object g.

```
g.fillRect(100,100,100,100);
```

You can create more than one instance of a class—for example, you can create the g object as above and then create another instance using this code.

```
graphics g1 = new graphics();
```

This will create a graphics object named g1, which is also of the type graphics. Objects created in this manner have the same scope as any other variable.

1.15 Enhancements to Java 1.1

Java 1.1 offers many enhancements over Java 1.02. These include the following:

- Unicode support allows you to build multilanguage programs.

- Security and signed applets allow you to access the client computer in ways that were forbidden in Java 1.02. JDK 1.1 provides a tool that can sign Java ARchive (JAR) files, which can contain classes and other data (such as images and sounds).

- Appletviewer allows any downloaded applets in JAR files signed (using the tool) by a trusted entity to run with the same full rights as local applications.

- AWT enhancements enhance performance in the AWT classes, including printing, scrolling, and pop-up menus.

- JavaBeans

- Remote method invocation allows you to create distributed Java-to-Java applications, in which the methods of remote Java objects can be invoked from other Java virtual machines—even those running on different machines.

- Java Database Connectivity (JDBC) is a standard SQL database access interface. This includes an ODBC bridge which allows connection to ODBC databases.

Currently, most browsers and JVM implementations do not support Java 1.1. However, as more and more new JVMs become available through browser updates and operating system upgrades, you will be able to take advantage of these new features when writing your Java programs.

1.16 *Summary*

Java is a popular language, and there are many resources available on the Internet that will help you learn Java. Appendix A contains references to some of these sites.

But the best way to learn any language is to work in it. As you follow along in this book, you can use PowerJ as your learning tool. Build applications and review the sample applications that ship with PowerJ. Build and modify the samples we examine herein.

Above all, don't be afraid to experiment.

PowerJ basics

In this chapter we will discuss the following:

- How to navigate through the PowerJ environment
- How to work with different versions of Java
- How to create a simple form and place objects on it
- How to open and use the Reference Card
- How to use PowerJ wizards and windows

PowerJ uses an Integrated Development Environment (IDE), in which all your activities, from designing windows to writing code, are done inside one single application window. This can be compared with other development environments where you use a resource-editor program to create windows, a text editor to write code, and then a command-line compiler to compile your application. All modern development environments, especially those in use under the Windows operating system, use the IDE approach and PowerJ is no different.

Where PowerJ may be a little different, especially to those who are familiar with PowerSoft's other product of note—PowerBuilder—is that its IDE does not use the Multiple Document Interface (MDI) standard. Instead, each part of the IDE is a window in its own right. This is sometimes referred to as a multiple window interface. This is the interface used by Visual Basic (until recently, when they adopted an Explorer-style interface) and Delphi.

Note

It is interesting to note that Microsoft has redesigned Visual BASIC 5.0 away from the multiple window interface and toward the new Windows Explorer look. Most Microsoft development products are being redesigned that way. It will be interesting to see if others follow suit.

2.1   Starting PowerJ

When you start PowerJ, it will initially display only the main toolbar window and a blank Form Design window. As you work in PowerJ, you will invariably open other windows and arrange them in whatever manner you find suitable. PowerJ imposes no restrictions upon which windows you open or where you place them.

Figure 2.1 shows the PowerJ IDE running over the Windows 95 desktop. Displayed in the IDE are the main PowerJ menu, toolbar and Java component palette, the Object Inspector window, the Form Design window and the Object List window. The following sections will discuss each of these in turn.

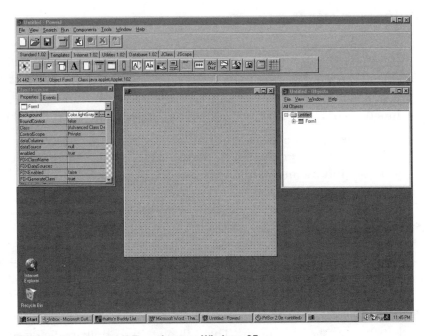

Figure 2.1   PowerJ IDE running over Windows 95

2.1.1 *The main PowerJ window*

At the top of the screen shown in figure 2.1 is the main PowerJ window. This is where you will control most of the functionality of PowerJ. The window is divided into several parts. From top to bottom these are the main menu, the toolbar, the Java 1.02 palette, and the status bar. Each of these will be discussed in the following sections.

Figure 2.2   Main menu bar

2.1.2 *The main menu*

The main menu bar of the PowerJ window offers menu items that help you design, create, and test your application (see figure 2.2). When you point to a menu item, the status bar at the bottom of the PowerJ window will display a helpful explanation of the item. You can easily learn the functions of items by running the mouse over them without clicking.

Examples of items you will find on the menu include commands to start a new project or to build your project files into an application. You will also find the menu items you use to open other PowerJ windows as you create your program.

2.1.3 *Toolbar*

The toolbar appears immediately below the main PowerJ menu bar. It offers even easier access to the most commonly used commands, such as the one to run your program (the running man icon).

You can elect whether or not to display the toolbar by using the Toolbars item of the View menu. That will open the Toolbars dialog shown in figure 2.3.

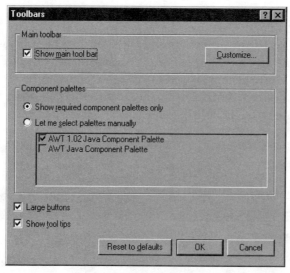

Figure 2.3
Toolbars dialog

In addition to deciding which, if any, toolbar to display, you can select whether to display the large or small icons or to use the tooltip help.

Full customization of the toolbar is available by using the Customize button from this dialog and manipulating the toolbar using the second dialog that appears (see figure 2.4).

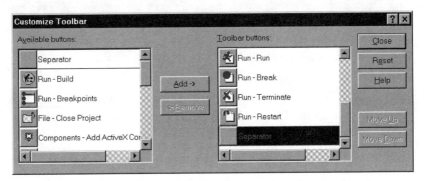

Figure 2.4   Customizing the toolbar

You can see the name of any toolbar button by placing the cursor over the button and leaving it there for just a moment. The name of the corresponding button will appear in a small box called a tooltip.

2.1.4   *Java component palettes*

The next rows of icons are the Java component palettes—a set of buttons that corresponds to the objects you can place on a form. There are two different sets of Java components—hence the need for two different palettes. This is because there are currently two major implementations of Java in use. Java 1.02 is the latest release of the original Java language. Most existing Java programs are written in that version and most of the Java Virtual Machines (JVMs) in use on end-user machines support that version.

A new version of Java was recently released: Java 1.1. It may be a while before support for Java 1.1 reaches universal acceptance, so you will still write most of your code in Java 1.02. The two versions are incompatible since a Java 1.02 virtual machine will not run a Java 1.1 application. Since most JVM implementations available today are Java 1.02, you will be using these components most often.

If you try to use a Java 1.1 object in a Java 1.02 application, you will receive an error message, as shown in figure 2.5.

Figure 2.5   Error message

You will get a similar message if you attempt to place a Java 1.02 component on a Java 1.1 form. By default, PowerJ starts up with a Java 1.02 application project. Later on we will learn how to change this and create other project types.

Tip

By default, PowerJ displays only the component palette that matches the version of Java you are currently using. You can change this by using the toolbars dialog. It is wise to leave this setting as is in order to avoid confusion. If you want to show both toolbars at once, open the toolbars dialog and choose "Let me select palettes manually." This will enable the two check boxes and you can then select either, both, or neither of the toolbars.

The icon for each component gives an indication of its use. If you are unsure what the icon represents, simply place the cursor over the component icon and wait a moment. A tool tip will display the information.

To add an object to a form, click a component button and then click on the Form Design window. This places an object of the selected type on the form.

When you place an object on a form in this way, the object is given a default size. You can resize the object by selecting it and dragging it by its resize handles. Figure 2.6 shows an applet form with a command button object placed upon it—selected and ready to resize as needed.

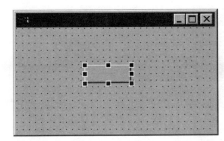

Figure 2.6
Applet with command button object

2.1.5 Status bar

The status bar appears at the bottom of the main PowerJ window. When the mouse points to the Form Design window, the left part of this bar first shows the current position of the cursor in dialog units, then the name of the object that the cursor is over, and, last, the class of the object over which the cursor appears.

The right part of the status bar displays information about other actions that PowerJ performs—for example, it tells you when PowerJ initializes files for a new project.

2.1.6 Form design window

Most of the work in designing a Java application is put into designing the user interface. Users interact with a Java application mostly through forms. A form is a window that contains other objects such as command buttons and text boxes. You use forms to create all your program's windows, dialog boxes, and so on. The Form Design window that appears below the main PowerJ window lets you arrange objects on the form and adjust the form's size as you design the user interface of your program. (See figure 2.7.)

The grid of dots on the Form Design window helps you judge the size and position of objects on the form. The dots do not appear when you run your program.

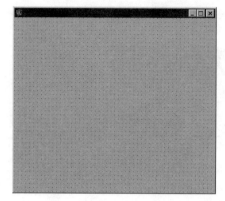

Figure 2.7
Form Design window

2.1.7 *Object inspector*

The Object Inspector window (figure 2.8) allows you to view the properties of the object that is currently selected. You access the Object Inspector window by choosing it from the View menu item.

When you have a form or object on a form selected, the Object Inspector window will show a list of the object's properties and their default values. To change the default value, simply click on it and change the value as desired. Most of the properties have several selections, e.g., true or false, while a few have a text-entry box associated with them into which you can type the value desired (the text attribute is an example).

Figure 2.8
Object Inspector window

Using the Object Inspector window is the easiest way to set the initial conditions of the objects in your applications.

2.1.8 Object list window

If you want to see a list of all the objects in your application, you can select the Object List window under the View menu (see figure 2.9). This will display a list of all the objects in your application using a tree view much like Windows Explorer or File Manager. If you drill down on a form object, you will see a list of all the objects currently on that form.

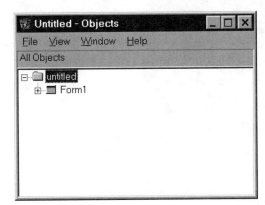

Figure 2.9
Object List window

If you right-click on an object, a pop-up menu will appear that allows you to access PowerJ functions associated with objects of that type—for example, selecting Properties from that menu will display a dialog that varies by object and that allows you to alter some of the attributes for that object type (see figure 2.10).

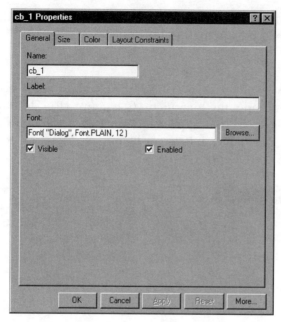

Figure 2.10
Properties dialog

Note

The dialog that is displayed here is not as comprehensive as the Object Inspector window. You can open the Object Inspector window by clicking More on the property dialog or you can make the Object Inspector the default property editor by using the Options dialog's Environment tab.

One important thing to note about the Object List window is that you can use it to open objects in your application—for example, double-clicking on Form1 will open a Form Design window for Form1 editing.

2.1.9 *Targets list window*

The Targets List window, available as a selection under the View menu, allows you to view the build targets of your application (figure 2.11). You can also use the default options portion of the tree to set some of the compiler options. We will study build options in more detail in chapter 18. There are many different types of targets. Which one you will use depends upon the type of application or applet that you are writing.

- Java applet

- Java application

- Java classes

- Java CAB

- Java—JAR

- Java—ZIP

- Java WWW server application

- Java Dynamo server application

- Various Jaguar CTS programs

- Web application

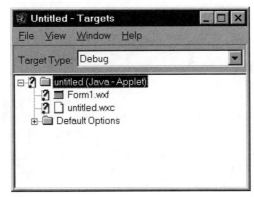

Figure 2.11
Targets list window

We will discuss the differences in these types of target programs in chapter 10.

By default, PowerJ starts with a Java 1.02 applet. If you want to change to another target type, click Tools...Options and use the Start-up Tab to select the new target type (see figure 2.12).

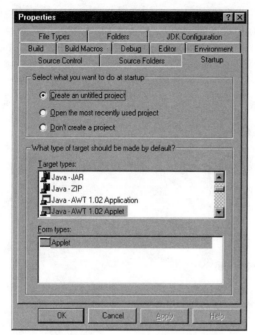

Figure 2.12
Selecting a new target type

From that point on, clicking File...New Project or restarting PowerJ will create a project with that type of target.

2.1.10 Files list window

All of your objects in a PowerJ application exist in the form of files. These files are combined to form your complete project. The Files list window (figure 2.13) will show you the name and location of every file in your application. You may delete files from your project with this window and also use it to open the objects that the files represent.

Figure 2.13
Files list window

Warning

Deleting files in this manner may prevent other parts of your application—those that reference the object contained in the deleted file—to fail. Take care when deleting files in this manner.

2.1.11 *Classes list window*

The Classes list window (figure 2.14) allows you to view the class hierarchy of your application. We will study this window in more detail in chapter 13.

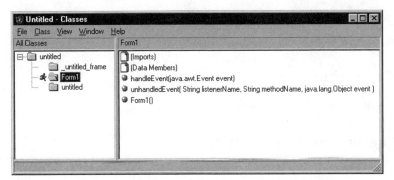

Figure 2.14   Classes list window

2.2 The code editor

The code editor is where you will write your Java code to make your applications do what they need to do. The code-editor window shown in figure 2.15 is displaying the action method for a basic command button (cb_1). Whatever action you want to occur when the command button is clicked will be placed between the curly braces in this method.

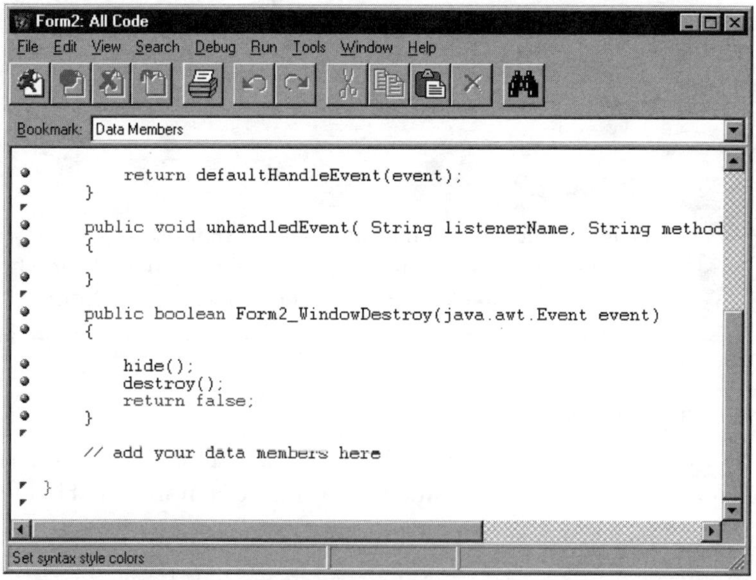

Figure 2.15   Code-editor window

We will be working extensively with the code-editor window as we progress through this book.

2.3 The on-line help system

PowerJ contains full on-line Help support. To access the on-line Help all you need to do is hold down the shift key and press F1. This activates Help that is sensitive to the window that currently has focus.

Help may also be accessed from the Help menu on the menu bar.

2.4   *The reference card*

Unique to PowerJ (and its C++ counterpart, Power++) is the concept of the Reference Card (figure 2.16). The Reference Card is PowerJ's implementation of drag-and-drop programming. Need to add items to a list box? You can use the Reference Card to drill down to the correct statement, build the correct syntax (without errors!), and paste it directly into your code. This tool is what makes PowerJ the wonderful environment that it is and allows even novice Java developers to get up to speed at developing complex applications swiftly. We will see the Reference Card in action throughout this book.

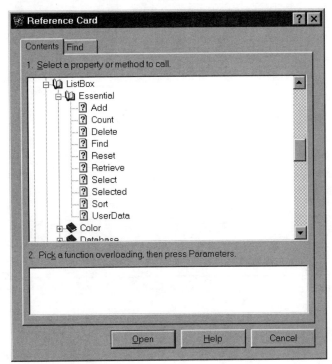

Figure 2.16
Reference Card

This completes our overview of the basic windows with which you will be working as you learn PowerJ. Beginning with the next chapter, we will start to examine how to use these windows to build applications.

2.5 *Summary*

This chapter taught us how to work with the PowerJ IDE. We discussed the two versions of Java supported by PowerJ and how to switch between them. We also looked at how to create a simple project, add a form to it, and place objects on the form. We took our first look at the Reference Card and drag-and-drop programming. We briefly discussed some of the PowerJ wizards and windows.

Your first programs

Now that we know a little about the PowerJ interface, it's time to learn how to use that interface to build two simple applications. This chapter will show you how to create applications in PowerJ, using the PowerJ IDE, and will introduce you to drag-and-drop programming using the Reference Card.

The first example is a to-do list and the second will be familiar to many C/C++ programmers: the "Hello World" application.

3.1 Types of applications

As discussed previously, there are several different types of Java applications you can create with PowerJ. The following sections will discuss each of these different types.

3.1.1 Java applets

A Java applet is an application that is intended to run inside a Web browser. A Java applet should look and behave the same no matter which browser you use to run it.

3.1.2 Java applications

A Java application is a stand-alone Java program that runs directly in the target machine's JVM. No browser is required.

3.1.3 Web applications

A Web application includes both a Java applet target and a Web server extension. Web applications are an easy way to organize the different parts of your PowerJ applications.

3.1.4 Java web server application

This is sometimes called a servlet. This creates an ISAPI servlet for Microsoft's ISAPI Web server

3.1.5 Dynamo server applications

This is an application that targets Net Impact Dynamo running in connection with a Web server.

In this book we will build mostly applets and a few applications. You will find that most Java code in existence today is applet code, which is downloaded from the server and run inside a Web browser. We will use Java1.02 as the target JVM, although the techniques we use are fully translatable to writing Java 1.1 applications.

3.2 *Steps to creating a program*

As with most modern development systems for graphical environments, there are three steps necessary to create a program using PowerJ. First, you design the user interface. This consists of the controls and objects that the user will see and interact with while running the application. Then you specify default property settings for the objects you have displayed. And, finally, you add code to deal with user actions, to make the application perform its intended task.

For the purposes of this first exercise, building a Java application with PowerJ, we will be creating a simple to-do list program consisting of a text field, a list box, and a couple of command buttons. The object is to be able to enter a to-do list item in the text field and, when you click one of the command buttons, move the text into the list box. The other command button will serve the function of deleting whatever item in the list is currently selected. If you want to delete an item, you highlight the item in the list box and click the Delete button. This program will be a Java 1.02 application.

To get started creating the to-do list program, you must first create a new project. You do this by clicking File...New Project. When you do that, PowerJ will create a new project and give it one form.

But look, what PowerJ has created is a Java 1.02 applet project and what we want is a Java 1.02 application project. This is one annoyance of PowerJ. Instead of giving you a project wizard that lets you specify what the default target type of the project should be, it just creates a project based upon whatever type you had last set as the default.

To change the default you must open the options dialog under the tools menu as shown in figure 3.1.

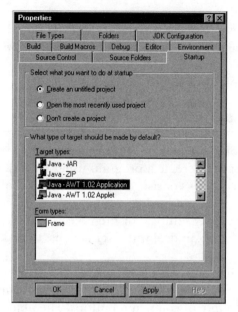

Figure 3.1
Changing the default

There you can tell it to create a Java 1.02 application. Then, when you click File...New, you will have the proper target type for our first program.

3.2.1 Designing the user interface

The first step in developing a PowerJ application is to design the user interface. If you are developing a large mission-critical application, this would be done on paper during many hours of end-user Joint Application Design (JAD) sessions. However, for small applications such as this and for prototypes, you can design the application directly in PowerJ. Designing a user interface in PowerJ is simple. You just click on the interface component from the Java component palette and then click on the Form Design window at the location where you wish to place the control. This will place a standard-sized component on the window.

If you want to size the component as you place it (you can always resize it anytime you want), all you need to do is click on the component on the Java palette, and then click on the position where you want the component to appear on the window. Instead of releasing the left mouse button, drag the mouse to outline the size of the component as you wish it to appear. You will see an outline as you do this, so you will know what size you are making it. When you have it sized correctly, release the mouse button and PowerJ will create a component with the size you want.

3.2.2 *The to-do list window*

We want to place the following components on our window.

- List control
- Text field
- Two buttons

3.2.3 *Adding the list control*

We now want to add a list box to the form. To do this, take the following steps:

1 Click the list box button on the Standard page of the Java component palette.

2 Move the cursor to the Form Design window, pointing to where you want the list box to appear (you do not have to make your window appear exactly as it does in figure 3.1—that is just a guideline). You will notice that the cursor changes from an arrow to a crosshair. The position of the crosshair at the time that you click the left mouse button will establish the position of the upper left-hand corner of the component.

3 Either click and release the left mouse button or hold down the left mouse button and drag the cursor diagonally across the form. While you are dragging, a rectangular outline shows you the size that the list box will be. Then release the left mouse button. You will now see a list box on the window.

If you are not satisfied with the position of your list box, you can move the list box by dragging it. An outline of the box will be displayed as you drag.

You can also change the list control's size. If the list control is not selected, click the list control to select it and display resizing handles on the control's corners and edges. Then drag one of these handles to adjust the size of the list control.

3.2.4 Adding the text box

The next step in designing the form is to add a text box. There are two different types of text boxes—the text area and the text field. We will discuss the differences in chapter 6. For this application we will use a text field. You will follow similar steps in adding the text field as those used in adding the list control.

1 Click the text field button (Textfield) on the Standard page of the Java component palette.

2 In the Form Design window, drag diagonally below the list control to create a text field.

The window now has a list control and text field.

If need be, you can change the size and position of the text field in the same manner as you changed the size and position of the list control.

 Tip

The Form Design window's grid of dots makes it easier to line up objects on the form.

3.2.5 Adding the buttons

Next, add two buttons to the form in the same manner as you added the list control and the text fields. Once you have added the first button, you may add the second by either repeating the same steps or by right-clicking the first button and clicking Copy and then right-clicking on the form and clicking Paste. PowerJ will duplicate the button. If you use the copy-and-paste approach, you may receive a warning about the button name. PowerJ is simply notifying you that another object existed on the form with that name and that the new object is being renamed.

When you are finished designing the form, it should look similar to that shown in figure 3.2.

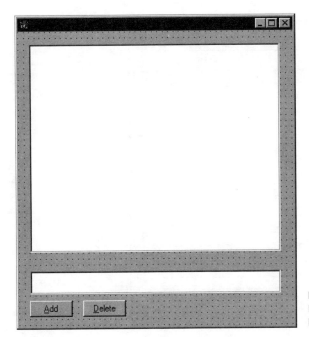

Figure 3.2
Designing the form
is completed

3.2.6 *Testing what you have done so far*

It is always a good idea to test as you go along, so you should now run the applet to see the default behavior of the controls that you have added. To do that, take the following actions:

1 In the Run menu of the main PowerJ menu bar, click Run. You can also click on the Run button on the toolbar. PowerJ will compile the program for execution. Progress messages will be displayed as the process occurs.

2 When the program has finished compiling, the program window appears containing the objects you placed on the form. At this point the program should appear similar to that shown in figure 3.3.

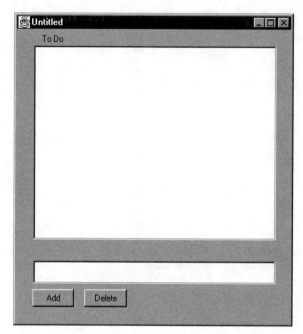

Figure 3.3
Compiling the program
is completed

3 Experiment with the new program. Notice that you can enter text in the text box and press the command buttons, but the list box does not change.

4 Close the new program by clicking the Close button on the right of the title bar. Of course, at this point the application's objects perform no functions.

3.2.7 *Setting the tab order*

When you experiment with this form, you may notice that you can tab from control to control; however, the order in which you tab will depend upon the order in which you placed the controls on the form. Since this is probably not a logical order, you may want to change it. You can do so by right-clicking the form and clicking Edit Component Order. This will display the Component Order Editor dialog, as shown in figure 3.4.

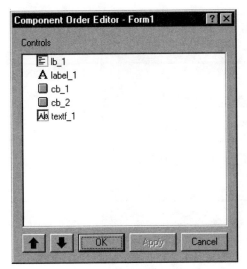

Figure 3.4
Component Order Editor dialog

To change the order, select the component and click the arrow keys to move it up or down.

3.2.8 *Specifying object properties*

The next step in creating a program is to alter, as necessary, the properties of the objects you placed on the form. Properties of objects affect the appearance and behavior of the objects.

3.2.9 *Labeling the buttons*

At this point you have blank buttons. It is a very good idea to put some text on the buttons to show your users what the button will do when clicked. To do that, take the following steps:

1   Use the right mouse button to click the button and click Properties to display the property dialog for the button. The property dialog for buttons is shown in figure 3.5

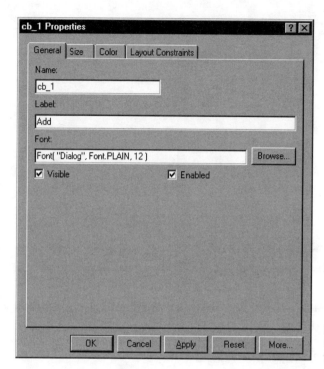

Figure 3.5
Properties dialog
for buttons

2 On the General page, click in the Label box, then type the text which you wish to appear on the button. One button should say Add and the other button should say Delete.

3 Click OK.

The button is now labeled with the text you typed. You can repeat the process to label the Delete button.

You can manipulate other properties in this manner. As we go through the exercises in this book, you will become very familiar with the property dialogs for the various components.

3.2.10 *Adding code*

The last step in creating this program is to write code that will be executed when a user clicks each of the buttons. When this happens, the program should take the following actions.

When the user clicks the Add button:

- Retrieve the text from the text field.
- Add the text to the list control.

When the user clicks the Delete button:

- Delete the highlighted entry from the list control.

Writing the code to perform these tasks is fairly straightforward when you use the drag-and-drop programming interface provided by PowerJ. The first step is to open a code editor to the action event of the Add button. To do this, right-click the Add button and click Events...Action. This will open up a code-editor window to the appropriate event, as shown in figure 3.6.

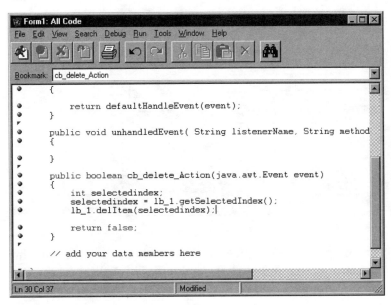

Figure 3.6   Code-editor window

The first code that executes must obtain the value the user has entered in the text field. To use drag-and-drop programming to write this code, just position the code editor so that you can see the Form Design window, and then drag the text field from the Form Design window into the code editor window and drop it in the action event for cb_add (just ahead of the line that reads):

```
return false;
```

This will cause the Reference Card to open. The Reference Card will display the text field choices, as shown in figure 3.7.

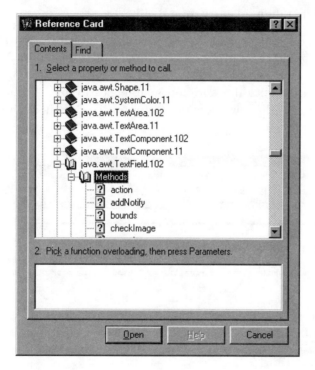

Figure 3.7
Text field choices

Open up the Methods tree and look for the getText() method. Highlight that method and click Parameters. This will open the Parameters wizard, as shown in figure 3.8.

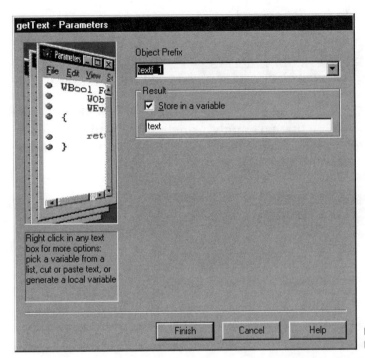

Figure 3.8
Parameters

Make sure that the "Store in variable" check box is selected and that an appropriate variable name is entered in the field below. Then click Finish. The following code will be placed in the code-editor window.

```
java.lang.String               text;
text = textf_1.getText();
```

Notice that we have made a slight mistake here. We failed to give the text field a descriptive name before writing code against it. However, this presents no problem to PowerJ; just go rename the text field using its Properties dialog and then look at your code editor. If you renamed the text field `textf_todo` the code editor will now have the following:

```
java.lang.String               text;
text = textf_todo.getText();
```

Pretty cool, huh?

3.2.11 Adding to the list control

The next step is to write the code that adds the item to the list control. To do this using drag-and-drop programming, simply repeat the steps above but drag the list control instead of the text field. Drop the list control in the code editor below the code we just placed there but ahead of the return. Then find the `addItem()` methods. Notice that there are two. Choose the one that takes only a single string as the argument. Click parameters to open the Parameters wizard and "write" the code just as you did for the text field (see figure 3.9).

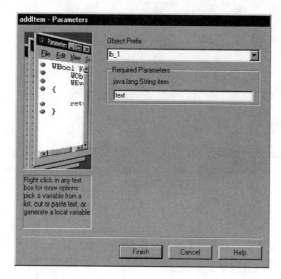

Figure 3.9
Parameters

Notice that this version of the Parameters wizard asks you to enter a string item as the required argument. You should type in the name of the variable that you used to store the value from the text field. When you have done this and clicked Finish, the code editor should now contain the following code.

```
java.lang.String                text;
text = textf_todo.getText();
lb_1.addItem( text );
```

You probably will want to rename the list box.

This code is fine, as far as it goes. But we do need more. What happens when the user clicks Add and there is no text entered in the text field? Since this is not a desirable condition, we need to place code in this event to prevent this. The proper way to do that would be to determine whether there is a value in the text variable prior to calling the `addItem()` method. We need to use an `if` statement.

```
if (text.length() > 0)
    {
        lb_1.addItem( text );
    }
```

This code will determine whether something has actually been entered in the text field (and stored in the text variable) prior to invoking the `addItem()` method. The easiest way to add this code is to type it into the editor window.

Note

The preceding code uses the `length()` method of the standard Java string class. For a full discussion of the methods available on the standard Java components, see chapter 5.

3.2.12 *The delete button code*

Next, you will want to put code in the Delete button's action event that will delete the currently selected item from the list box. The following code will perform that task.

```
int                     selectedIndex;
selectedIndex = lb_1.getSelectedIndex();
lb_1.delItem( selectedIndex );
```

Whether or not you use the Reference Card and drag-and-drop programming to reach this result is irrelevant and I will leave it to you. You will find that as you learn Java, or if you are an experienced Java programmer now, you will use the code editor to enter code directly rather than using the Reference Card. Once you reach that level, the Reference Card's usefulness remains for writing code involving obscure methods that you seldom use.

3.2.13 Sprucing up the user interface

Now you can add some enhancements to the user interface. A couple of label objects can be put in place over the list control and the text field to indicate to the user what data are displayed or entered there. You could enable and disable the Add and Delete buttons, depending upon the contents of the list control and text field at any given moment.

3.2.14 Still not complete

Of course, we still are far from a completed application. There is no way to store information entered in the list for display in future sessions. And the list itself is barebones—there is no way to enter date or time information other than as part of the string itself and no way to see enhanced details about the individual to-do items.

3.2.15 Testing the application

You are now ready to test the code. To do that you take the same steps you took to test the user-interface elements.

1 In the Run menu of the main PowerJ menu bar, click Run. You can also click on the Run button on the toolbar. PowerJ will compile the program for execution. Progress messages will be displayed as the process occurs.

2 When the program has finished compiling, the program window appears containing the objects you placed on the form.

3 Experiment with the new program. Notice that you can edit text in the text field and press the command button and the text is copied from the text box to the list box. You can also test to see that nothing happens when there is no entry in the text fields. Test the delete functionality by highlighting an item in the text box and clicking Delete.

4 Close the program by clicking the Close button on the right of the title bar.

You have now created your first working Java application using PowerJ!

3.3 Building the application

Before your applet can be distributed to others, it must be built. To build your application, click on Build under the Run menu. What the result of the build process will be depends upon the type of target being built. We will discuss target types in more detail in chapter 10.

Building a program differs from running it from the Run menu. When you run from the Run menu, the program is being executed within the PowerJ environment. You have access to the debugger and other features of PowerJ. When you build a program, PowerJ creates a set of program files for distribution to other machines. These machines may not even have PowerJ installed. When the program is executed on the other machine, it will be running inside that machine's JVM.

3.4 Saving your project

Every project is a group of files that together make the program. This includes one or more targets and the source files used to create each target. Target files are files that are created during the compile process. These files may come in a wide variety of types, and each type will be discussed in turn in later chapters.

Note

Since there are many files associated with a single PowerJ target, you must keep each target in a separate folder. This prevents the files for one target from overwriting the files for another.

You can save the project you have just created so that you can run it again or modify it sometime in the future.

Every project has an associated project file, which lists information about the project. PowerJ project files use the extension *.wxj*. When you save a project, you must first name a folder for the project and then name the project file.

1   On the File menu of the main PowerJ menu bar, click Save Project. This displays the contents of the Projects folder in your PowerJ folder, as shown in figure 3.10.

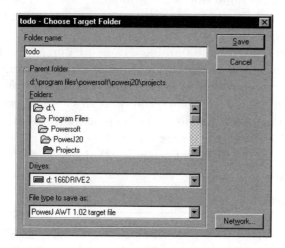

Figure 3.10
Projects folder

2   Under folder name, type the name to-do and click Save. This creates a folder, called to-do, for the project and opens a dialog to prompt you for the project file name, as shown in figure 3.11.

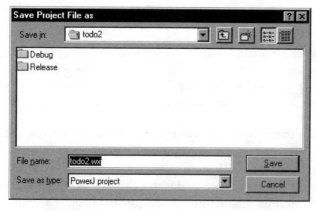

Figure 3.11
Save project file as . . .

3   Under file name, leave *to-do.wxj* as the project file name.

4   Click Save.

PowerJ will create a project file named *to-do.wxj* in the new folder named *todo* along with other files and folders of the project. You can now open the project at any time by clicking File...Open on the main PowerJ menu.

3.5 Enhancements to the project

There are many enhancements that can be made to this project. One of these is to implement some form of error trapping (what happens if the user clicks the button while there is no text in the text box?). Another would be to prevent duplicate values from being entered in the list box. You might also want to have the ability to remove items from the list box. These are good items to use to experiment with PowerJ before proceeding to the next section.

3.6 Creating an applet

Let's take a look at another, very simple application. Only this time let's create it as an applet for a Web browser. We will recreate the ever-popular "Hello World" application familiar to most C programmers.

Note

Don't forget to open the Options dialog from the Tools menu and change the default application type of Java 1.02 applet.

Create a new project by clicking File...New Project on the main menu bar. This will open up a blank Form Design window.

To create our "Hello World" application we want to place the text "Hello World" in the center of our form. To do that, click on the label component from the Java component palette and place the label on the window, near the center.

Next, right-click the label and select Properties from the pop-up menu. This will display the label Properties dialog, as shown in figure 3.12.

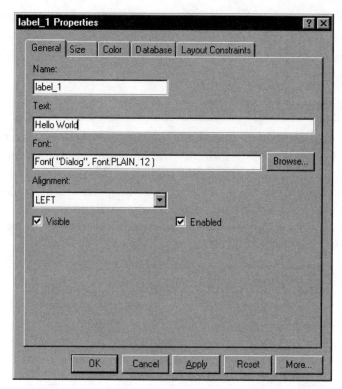

Figure 3.12
Properties dialog

Type "Hello World" in the text property and select Center from the Alignment drop-down. This centers the text you typed inside the dimensions of the label. When you click OK, you will see the words "Hello World" displayed in the Form Design window, as shown in figure 3.13.

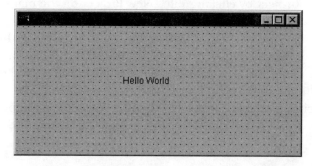

Figure 3.13
Form Design window
(small font size)

We don't want that tiny text, so let's open the Properties dialog for the label again and change the font size. Click the button labeled Font to display the font selection dialog, as shown in figure 3.14.

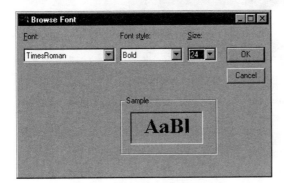

Figure 3.14
Font selection dialog

Change the font to Times New Roman Bold 24. Then exit all the dialogs. Now you are ready to run the application. When you do so, it will look like the screen shown in figure 3.15.

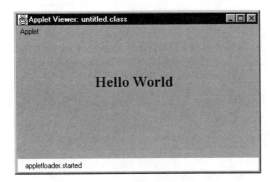

Figure 3.15
Form Design window
(larger font size)

At this point the applet is running inside the Applet Viewer. Applets are designed to run inside a Web browser. To help you create the HyperText Markup Language (HTML) needed to display your applet, PowerJ will create a sample HTML file in the Projects folder. To run the compiled applet in the browser, copy the applet files and the HTML file to a single directory and double-click the HTML file. You can also run the applet in the Web browser from within the PowerJ IDE. To do this, click

Run...Options under the Run menu and select "Use of Web browser" on the General page. (See figure 3.16.)

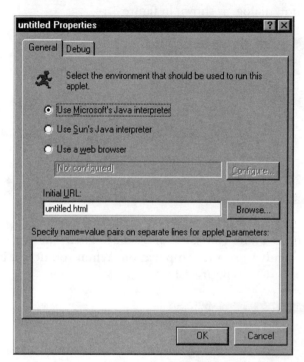

Figure 3.16
Options under the Run menu

Click the Configure button to select the browser (see figure 3.17) and click OK dialogs. Then select Run.

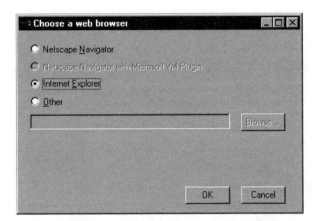

**Figure 3.17
Options under the
browser menu**

Here is our applet running in Microsoft's Internet Explorer (see figure 3.18).

**Figure 3.18
Applet running in
Microsoft's Internet
Explorer**

OK, so I admit we cheated. We didn't really write a classic "Hello World" program where we were responsible for creating the window and drawing the text on the window's surface. But the point is, we didn't have to. PowerJ hid all that ugly work from us. Now isn't that much better than writing all that code?

Now, on to more advanced topics and real-world applications.

3.7   *Summary*

In this chapter we learned how to create a simple form-based applet in PowerJ. Our applet contained some of the standard components, and we learned how to manipulate their properties to control their initial appearance. We then discussed how to use the Reference Card and drag-and-drop programming to write the code needed to make our applet perform its intended task. Finally, we learned how to run our applet in the development environment (for testing) and how to run it inside a Web browser.

Part II

Putting PowerJ to work

Once you understand how PowerJ works and can move around the IDE, it's time to put that knowledge to work. We begin with a more in-depth look at the PowerJ IDE and the drag-and-drop programming concept in chapter 4 and then move on to discuss the standard components that ship with PowerJ (both the Java components and some that are exclusive to PowerJ) in chapter 5.

In chapter 6 we learn how to build menus for our frame windows and how to write code to make them work.

Chapter 7 takes us back to the Java world when we look at the standard datatype classes that make Java easier to use than C/C++.

Of course, the purpose of PowerJ is to write computer programs and to do that we have to write code. Chapter 8 looks at the Code Editor and takes our closest look yet at drag-and-drop programming and the Reference Card system.

Chapter 9 takes a closer look at how to work with the different types of forms and windows used in Java programming and how to use the PowerJ Form Wizard to incorporate them into your programs.

PowerJ programs consist of targets combined into projects. In chapter 10 we take a look at the different types of targets and projects available to you.

Perhaps the component that most separates a good environment from a great environment is its ability to help you debug your programs. PowerJ includes a full-featured debugger and chapter 11 teaches you how to use it.

Working in PowerJ

In this chapter we will do the following:

- Take an in-depth look at the PowerJ IDE
- Look more closely at some of the wizards and windows that you use when working with PowerJ
- Learn more about the Reference Card and drag-and-drop programming

Now that we have learned some PowerJ basics and have a couple of projects under our belt, let's take a look at some of the other features of PowerJ that make it a great coding environment.

PowerJ is a fully integrated visual development environment that allows you to build applications based upon forms. Using drag-and-drop techniques, you design a form to appear the way you want, and then add necessary code to make the form's controls work as desired.

 Note

PowerJ Conventions—In PowerJ there are usually many different ways to perform the same task. This chapter does not attempt to show you all the different methods you can use to perform a task— rather it shows the easiest or fastest method (in my opinion).

4.1 Using the form design window

In PowerJ, you will most often work with the Form Design window to build and maintain the forms that make up the user interface of your application. You use the Form Design window to do the following:

- Size the form
- Set the initial property values for the form
- Add other controls to the form and set their initial properties

When you run your program, the form will have the same appearance you have given it using the Form Design window. The Form Design window is shown in figure 4.1.

Figure 4.1
Form Design window

4.2   The form grid

By default, the form is marked with a grid of dots to help you position objects. These dots will not appear when the program is running. You can toggle the grid on and off by right-clicking the form and selecting Properties. Navigate to the Grid tab shown in figure 4.2 and then uncheck the "Display the grid" check box.

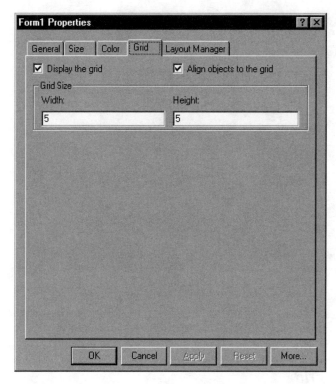

Figure 4.2
Grid tab

You may also change other grid settings.

4.2.1 Grid Size

The width and height boxes are used to set the distance between the dots in the grid. The distance is measured in dialog units, which are designed to be less device-dependent than pixels. In other words, two dialog units will appear approximately the same distance apart no matter what the screen resolution.

4.2.2 Aligning objects to the grid

On the grid page there is also a check box entitled "Align objects to the grid." If this box is marked, all objects on the form have their size and position adjusted to align with the grid. In other words, every object on the form will have its size and position adjusted so that its corners exactly coincide with grid dots. If this box is unchecked, PowerJ does not adjust the size and position of objects on the form.

If you wish to have the maximum amount of control over the position of objects you place on the form, you should either turn off the "Align objects to the grid" option or decrease the number of dialog units in the height and width of the grid. Turning off this option allows objects to be placed at any location on the form, while decreasing the spacing of the grid decreases the amount that an object's size and position must change before it is aligned with the grid.

4.3 Resizing the form window

The Form Design window behaves just like any standard Windows window: You can resize it by grabbing the border with the mouse cursor and then dragging the mouse until the window is the desired size. The window will be the same size when the program is running as it is in design mode.

4.4 Creating a new form

When you create a new PowerJ project, PowerJ will create one form. Depending upon the type of application you have selected as your default (more about projects and the defaults in chapter 9), the form may be of a different type. The default form, out of the box, is an applet.

4.5 Types of forms

There are four different basic types of forms: the applet, frame, dialog and modeless dialog. A dialog is a form that is opened to obtain information from the user and is closed once the user has filled in that information. A dialog will always stay on top of other forms in the application. A modeless dialog is a type of dialog that does not always stay on top. Other form types you will see in the Form Wizard are merely descendants of these types (which are themselves inherited from a common ancestor—the container).

4.6   Adding new forms to the project

To add a new form to your project, click File...New...Form. This will open the Form Wizard, shown in figure 4.3.

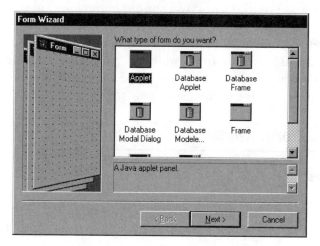

Figure 4.3
Form Wizard

Select the type of form and click Next. This will display the second page of the Form Wizard as shown in figure 4.4.

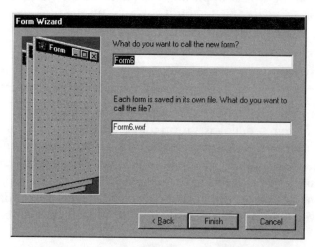

Figure 4.4
Form Wizard (page 2)

Here you select the form name and the file name for the form's code. The form name should be something descriptive, such as frm_Main for the main program window or frm_Contact for a window that displays contact information from a database.

Warning

You should always give a form a descriptive name. If your forms are given the names form1, form2, and so on, then you will find that the classes PowerJ will build for your form will also have the names form1.class, form2.class, and so on. Now this is no big problem if you have the only PowerJ application in the world. But suppose your server administrator requires that all classes be stored in a common directory and ten other developers also left their form names as the default? See the problem? The solution is to always name your forms; it takes very little time.

Once you have selected the form name, the file name will be filled in with a name reflective of the form name, such as *Frm_Main.wxf*.

After the Form Wizard closes, you will see a design window for the newly created form.

Note

The Form Wizard will display different pages for different form types: for example, if you selected one of the database dialogs, you will see pages that enable you to select the database and create a query. We will look at those pages in chapter 14.

4.7 *Opening and closing forms*

Since your application may consist of several forms and you will use a separate Form Design window for each form, you may need to open and close Form Design windows in your project in order to be able to make sense of your desktop.

4.7.1 *To close a form design window*

You may close an open Form Design window in the same way that you close any other open window in Windows: simply click on the Close button in the upper righthand corner. If the type of form you are working with does not have a close button, then you can use the close item on the system menu in the upper lefthand corner. If the form doesn't have a Close button or a system menu, you can close it using the keyboard by pressing Alt-F4.

The window menu of the main PowerJ menu bar contains a list of all open Form Design windows.

4.7.2 *To open a closed form design window*

There are many ways to open a closed Form Design window. The easiest is to display the Object window by selecting its menu item under View. The Object window will display a list of all forms in your application, whether these forms are open or closed. To open a form, right-click its name in the Object window and then click Open.

4.8 *Changing a form's properties*

As with any object, a form has a set of properties that controls the appearance and behavior of the form when it is displayed. When you create a form, PowerJ sets the form's properties to default values. If you wish to change these settings you can do so using the form's property dialog.

4.8.1 *Setting a form's properties*

To change the settings for the properties of a form, you can access the form's property dialog. To do this all you need to do is right-click a blank area of the form (one that has no components placed upon it). The pop-up menu that appears will contain an item for Properties. Clicking the Properties item will display the form's property dialog, as shown in figure 4.5.

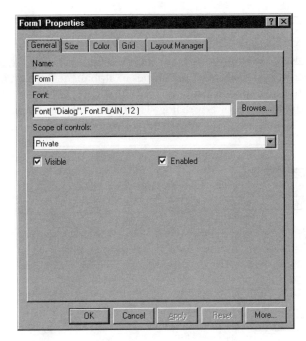

Figure 4.5
Property dialog

Note

The Properties menu item is in bold type. This means that this is the default action for that particular object. Default actions can be invoked by double-clicking the object.

You use the property dialog to set values for any properties you want to change. The different properties are grouped together using tabs. You click the tabs at the top of the main area of the property dialog to set the different types of properties. When you have finished altering the properties, click OK. The new setting will now be in effect.

Note

The changes you have made may or may not be visible in the Form Design window depending upon the type of property.

Tip

You can also change properties through the Object Inspector. Since the Object Inspector displays properties in alphabetical order, it may be easier to find a specific property through the inspector rather than through the form's property dialog. The Object Inspector appears in figure 4.6, which shows the properties for a standard text box.

Figure 4.6
Object Inspector

Note

The types of properties you will see in the Properties dialog or the Object Inspector window will depend upon the type of form. Frames, for example, have title bars and a title property, while applet windows do not.

4.9 Making your forms work

Of course, if all you could do with PowerJ is create blank forms, it wouldn't be much of a tool. In order to make forms into applications, you must add controls or components to the form so that it appears the way you want and performs some desired task. You can also add functions and other properties to a form. The rest of this chapter deals with adding different objects to forms—something we looked at briefly while building our applications in chapter 3.

4.10 *Adding objects to a form*

Before your application will do anything, you will probably have to design a form. You can design forms from within the PowerJ environment simply by adding objects to the blank Form Design window. The objects you can add are located on the component palette.

4.11 *The component palette*

The component palette is a tabbed toolbar, which has icons representing the controls that you can add to a form. (See figure 4.7.)

Figure 4.7   Component palette

The components are divided into categories: Standard, Template, Internet, Utilities, Database, JClass, and JScape. To determine the type of component on the palette (the icons are fairly descriptive but sometimes a little obscure), place the cursor over the button, wait a moment, and PowerJ will display a tool tip showing you what the button means.

You will notice that there are two sets of standard components: those for Java 1.02 and those for Java 1.1. These are provided because, even though Java 1.1 is the most current release, it has not yet been widely adopted by the browser and JVM market. This means that most of your code will be written using Java 1.02 in order to reach the broadest possible audience.

If you try to place a component from one version into an application designed for the other version, you will receive an error message, as shown in figure 4.8.

Figure 4.8   Error message

For that reason, you should leave PowerJ with its default setting, which displays the toolbar for the Java version of the current project target.

4.12 Adding components to forms

To add a component to a form, simply click the button for the type of component you want to add to the form, and then move the cursor to the Form Design window and click the location where you want to place the component. This will add a component with a default size and with its top left corner at the location you clicked.

You can resize the component, if necessary, by dragging the component's sizing handles.

Tip

You can place and size a control as desired in one operation by moving the cursor to the Form Design window, holding the button down, and dragging across the form until the object reaches the desired size.

4.13 Positioning an object on the form

If we were all perfect, we would never place an object on a form in a location from which it must later be moved. However, since this will invariably happen, PowerJ gives you the ability to place an object in one position on a form, and then move it.

4.14 Changing the position of an object on a form

To change the position of an object, just click the object in the Form Design window, and then drag the object to its desired position.

Tip

If you hold down the Shift key and press an arrow key, PowerJ will move the selected object in the direction of the arrow.

4.15 *Changing the size of an object*

You may need to change the size of an object that you have already placed on the form. To do this, click the object in the Form Design window. You will see sizing handles appear on the edges of the object, as shown in figure 4.9.

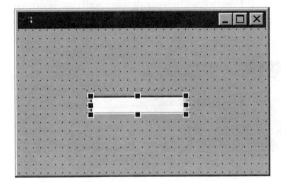

Figure 4.9
Sizing handles

To change the size of the object, drag a sizing handle. The outline of the object will grow or shrink as you move the handle. The outline represents the new size the object will have when you release the mouse.

4.16 *Deleting an object from a form*

It is very easy to delete an object from the Form Design window. Just click it and hit the Delete key on your keyboard. You can also right-click the object and select Delete from the pop-up menu.

If you want to delete several objects, you simply select them by "lassoing" them with the mouse cursor or by holding the Ctrl key while clicking them. Then either hit the Delete key or right-click inside one of the selected controls (clicking outside a selected control has the effect of unselecting them). Then click Delete from the pop-up menu.

Warning

Deleting an object also deletes any event handlers (and code you have written) you may have associated with the object. Once deleted, this code cannot be retrieved. So be careful when deleting objects from forms. PowerJ will prompt you with a dialog to make certain you wish to delete the object, as shown in figure 4.10.

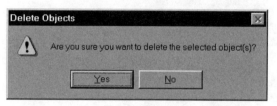

Figure 4.10
Delete objects dialog

4.17 Deleting an entire form

You may also need, from time to time, to delete an entire form from your application. To do this, use the Objects window, as shown in figure 4.11.

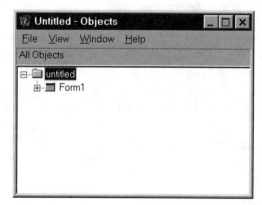

Figure 4.11
Objects window

To delete the form, right-click the name of the form you want to delete, and then click Delete on the pop-up menu.

Note

If the form you delete is used only in the current application, it will be deleted entirely and all associated source files will also be deleted. In the process, all objects and member functions associated with the form, as well as any files associated with the form, are deleted and cannot be recovered. If the form is used for other executables, it will be removed from the selected target, but its source files will not be deleted.

4.18 *Copying an object*

There are many situations where you want the form to contain a set of similar objects—for example, you may want several text boxes lined up with each other in a vertical fashion for data-entry purposes. While you can always simply place as many text boxes on the form as you need, using the standard methods discussed previously, you can also place as many text boxes as you need on the form by placing one text box in the normal fashion and then making as many copies of that text box as you need.

To do this, click the right mouse button on the object you want to copy, and then click Copy. This makes a copy of the object in the Windows clipboard. Then, click the right mouse button anywhere on the form and click Paste. This places a new copy of the object onto the form. You may then move the object to its desired location.

The copy is given an appropriate name based on its type—for example, if the original is named text_1, the copy may be named text_2. You may receive a warning from PowerJ that another object currently has the same name as the object you are pasting. PowerJ will rename the pasted object to avoid the conflict.

The copied object has the same properties and event handlers as the original—for example, if you have defined an action event handler for the original object, the copied object has an identical action event handler, except that it is named cb_2_action instead of cb_1_action (in the case of command buttons). Since it is not likely that you want every button or other object you create in this manner to perform the same task when clicked, you should make your copies prior to creating any code in the event handlers for the objects.

Of course, if you want the objects to behave in the same fashion (e.g., if you are pasting these controls on separate forms rather than on the same form), you should write the code first and then copy the object. In any event, after you have copied controls using this method, you should review the properties and the event handlers of the copied object, just to make sure that they're what you want.

4.19 Cut operations

Cut copies the object to the clipboard, and then deletes it from the form. You can then paste the copied object elsewhere in the Form Design window or in another form.

4.20 Copy, cut, and paste shortcuts

You can use the following standard Windows keyboard shortcuts for copy, cut, and paste operations.

- Ctrl+C   Copies the selected object(s)

- Ctrl+X   Cuts the selected object(s)

- Ctrl+V   Pastes onto the selected form

4.21 Aligning objects

In order to make your form designs pleasing to the end users, you must learn to use precise placement and alignment of objects on the form. You can align objects using the grid, or you can align them by selecting all the objects you wish to align and then clicking the object whose alignment you want to match while holding down the Ctrl key (the sizing handles on this object will be solid rather than hollow). Use the right mouse button to click the solid-handle object, and then click Align. This produces a menu of possible alignments, shown as pictures. Select the type of alignment you want by clicking on its picture. The objects with hollow handles will move to match the object with solid handles.

Note

Selecting multiple objects—you can select several objects at once by holding down the Shift key and clicking each object you want to select. The first time you Shift+click an object, it receives solid sizing handles. When you Shift+click a new object, the new object receives solid sizing handles and previously clicked objects receive hollow sizing handles. Once you have selected a set of objects, you can align or resize them using the techniques mentioned here.

4.22 *Matching object sizes*

You can also change the size of one object to match another by first selecting all the objects whose size you wish to change by "lassoing" them with the mouse. Then click an object whose size you want to match while holding down the Ctrl key. You will see solid sizing handles on this last object. Use the right mouse button to click the solid-handle object, and then click Same Size. This produces another menu of possible choices to match sizes in various ways (height, width, both). As with the menu alignment, this menu shows possible sizing operations with pictures. Click the type of sizing you want. The objects with hollow handles will change size to match the object with solid handles.

4.23 *Working with object properties*

Most object-oriented programming tasks concern themselves with the manipulation of objects' properties in response to user input. In other words, when the user interacts with the program, the properties of the object, or objects, that are on screen at the time will change in response to his or her actions.

4.24 *Changing an object's properties*

Every form and object has a set of associated properties. These properties affect the appearance and the behavior of the object. Each different type of object has its own set of properties.

It is the setting and altering of these properties at design time and run time that make the application work. The properties of each object are set to their default values. The properties you set at design time define how the object will appear when the program is initially started. You can change the default values at design time using the Properties dialog for each object. A Properties dialog for a button (which we have used before) is shown in figure 4.12.

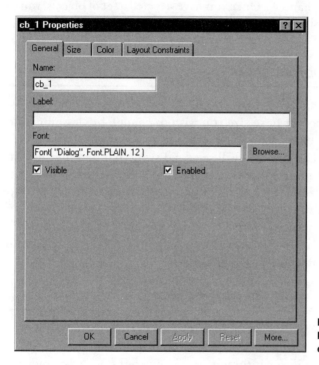

Figure 4.12
Property dialog for a command button

4.24.1 Accessing the properties dialog

You can access and alter properties of an object in two ways, which we discussed briefly earlier. You can use the right mouse button to click the object whose properties you want to change, and then click Properties to display the Properties dialog for the object (as shown in figure 4.12), or you can click the control for which you want to see the properties and then click View...Object Inspector to bring up the Object Inspector window as shown in figure 4.13.

Object Inspector	
Options	
Properties	Events
▢ cb_1	▼
background	Color.lightGray
Class	[Advanced Class Definition]
enabled	true
font	Font("Dialog", Font.PLAIN, 12
foreground	Color.black
Height	14
label	
Left	85
Name	cb_1
ResizePercentages	Rectangle(0, 0, 0, 0)
Top	80
visible	true
Width	40

Figure 4.13
Object Inspector for a command button

The Object Inspector window will display all the properties for the currently selected object, in alphabetical order. By using the Object Inspector, you can gain access to all the object's properties, while the property sheets usually display only the more commonly used properties. As you work with PowerJ, you will learn which properties are on the property dialogs and which need accessing via the Object Inspector. You may also elect to keep the Object Inspector window open at all times. The properties displayed in the Object Inspector window will change as different objects gain focus.

Tip

Use the Object Inspector as you set properties. You can change objects simply by clicking on another object in the Form Design window without having to close the Properties dialog and reopen it.

Note

The changes you have made to an object's properties may or may not be shown in the Form Design window—for example, if you turn off an object's visible property, the object remains visible in the Form Design window, so you can see that it is still part of the form and have access to it at design time. However, when you run the program, the object will be invisible.

4.25 *Changing an object's name*

When you place an object on a form, PowerJ automatically assigns it a name. These names are prefixed with the type of object (e.g., cb for command button) and then an _ and the number of that type of object on this form (the first command button is cb_1, the second is cb_2, and so on.). These names are hardly descriptive, and, for easy readability of your code, you should give them another name (e.g., cb_close for a Close button). The name of the object is a property of the object and can be changed using the Object Inspector or property dialog for the object.

If you change the name of an object, PowerJ changes the names of all associated event handlers. In other words, if you change the command button's name from cb_1 to cb_close, PowerJ automatically changes the button's action event handler from cb_1_Action to cb_close_Action. We discussed this in the previous chapter.

However, beyond that, PowerJ also changes all references to the object in your code—for example, PowerJ will automatically change:

```
cb_1.setVisible( true ) ;
```

to

```
cb_close.setVisible ( true ) ;
```

Tip

PowerJ will only change the name of the object in the code for the current form. For that reason, if you are going to change the name of the object, you should do it as soon as the object is placed on the form rather than after code is written in other forms or classes to manipulate the object's properties. The longer you wait to change the name of an object, the more possibility there is of an error. PowerJ will not change the name of the object in lines that start with // (C++ style comments), quoted strings, and user-defined structures that contain elements with the same name as the object.

4.26 Adding and modifying event handlers

Event handlers are the heart of event-driven programming. An event handler is where you place the code that responds to user actions and operating system events. Every object may have any number of associated event handlers—for example, a command button will most likely have an associated event-holding code specifying what happens when the user clicks the button. In PowerJ this is called the button's action event handler.

Making your program work is not only a matter of placing objects on a form: You must write code to handle events that you wish the object to respond to. We did just that in the previous chapter when we added code to the action events of the two command buttons to make them add and delete items from the list.

4.27 Creating event handlers

You can define additional event handlers as needed for the functionality of your application.

To create an event handler for an object, simply right-click the object in the Form Design window, and then click Events. You will see a list of commonly used events for that particular type of object. There will also be an entry named More. If you click a specific event in the list of events, you will open the code editor window to the proper event handler. PowerJ will take care of creating all the code necessary to create the event handler itself. All you need to write is the code that actually makes the object perform as intended.

If you click More instead of a particular event, PowerJ opens the Object Inspector on the Events tab, shown in figure 4.14.

Figure 4.14
Object Inspector on the events tab

This lists all the possible standard events that can be triggered on the selected object. Double-clicking any of these events opens a code editor to edit an existing event handler or create a new one.

If an event already has an associated event handler, there will be a check mark next to the event name.

You can define custom events for an object by using the Classes window, which will be discussed fully in chapter 13.

You will find as you develop Java applications using PowerJ that you will regularly use the same events over and over again while ignoring almost all others—for example, you will almost always define a clicked event for a command button but will almost never use the create event.

Of course, once you have events defined for the objects you are using, you still need to place code in the events to make the object behave as it should in response to user actions. This is done using the code editor window and drag-and-drop programming techniques, discussed in chapter 6.

4.28 *Summary*

In this chapter we took an in-depth look at the PowerJ IDE, learning how to use it to create Java programs quickly. We learned how to use wizards to create forms and targets, and we learned how to make those forms work together by writing code using the Reference Card and drag-and-drop programming.

In the next chapter we will take a closer look at the standard PowerJ components and their properties.

Using the PowerJ standard objects

In this chapter we will discuss the following:

- Standard components
- Common properties and events
- Properties and events that are unique to each component
- When to use the components

90

The PowerJ interface was designed from the ground up to make programming a snap. Designing a PowerJ application consists mostly of using the standard components available on the PowerJ component palette to assemble the application into a coherent whole from prewritten objects. This chapter reviews each of the standard components available in PowerJ and discusses how you can use them to build a form-based application. In this chapter, we will not look so much at what kinds of things you can build with the components but more at how they work. We will look at the properties and methods that are common to many of the components and then, when appropriate, at properties and methods that are unique to certain components.

5.1   The standard components

The PowerJ component bar, shown in figure 5.1, contains most of the tools you will use to build your form-based applications.

Figure 5.1   PowerJ component bar

There are 20 standard components available to you. From left to right on the component bar, these are as follows.

1   Button

2   Check box

3   Choice (drop-down list box)

4   Label

5   List

6   Menu bar

7   Panel

8   Scroll bar

9	Text area
10	Text field
11	Server socket
12	Socket
13	Group box
14	Masked text field
15	Multiline label
16	Paint canvas
17	Picture box
18	Picture button
19	Tab control
20	Grid control

5.2   Two Javas are better than one

As mentioned previously, there are two versions of Java currently in use: Java 1.02 and Java 1.1. Java 1.1 is the newest version, but JVMs Java 1.02 is currently installed on more systems. Even though Java 1.1 is newer, you will probably write programs for Java 1.02, at least in the near future.

Every Java 1.02 component has a Java 1.1 counterpart. Since Java 1.02 is still the mainstream version, we will discuss those components here, noting differences in the two where necessary.

5.3   Many objects have common properties

As we have discussed, most of your programming tasks will revolve around setting the initial properties of objects at design time and then changing them at run time in response to user actions. We will start our review of the standard component objects by looking at some of the properties shared by most, if not all, of them. In the next few sections, we will look at properties that are unique to a particular object, as well as discuss when you should prefer the use of one object type over another (e.g., when to use text fields instead of text areas).

5.3.1 *The label property*

Probably the most often used of the common properties is the label property. The label property is simply a string used as a label for an object. The formatting and positioning of the label will appear differently for each different type of control. An example of this is that the label of a command button is displayed on the button itself, while the label of a label control is displayed inside the label control. And on some objects the label is not seen at all but is merely a value that you can use in behind-the-scenes coding. In other programming environments, the label property is known as the text property. The name has changed but the function has not.

To set the label property, you use the General tab of the object's property dialog. We have already seen the property dialogs for several of the components. Most of them are similar.

You may also change the display font of the label. To do this, click the Browse button. This will display the font selection dialog shown in figure 5.2, from which you are able to set the font name, style, and size.

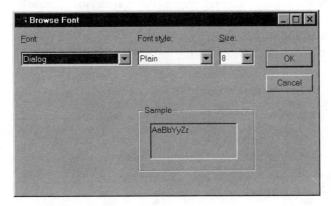

Figure 5.2
Font selection dialog

Note

The label property can also be manipulated using the Object Inspector window (see figure 5.3).

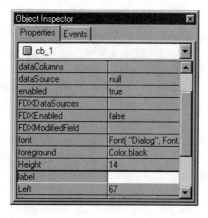

Figure 5.3
Object Inspector

5.3.2 *The visible property*

Another of the common properties available in most objects is the visible property, which controls whether the user can see an object on the form. For example, you may decide that a group of check boxes should not be visible until the user performs some action. You would manipulate the visible property to achieve this task.

PowerJ objects are visible by default when placed on a form. If you want the object to be invisible initially, you must change this by using the General tab of the Properties dialog for the object.

Note

When you turn off the visible property for an object, the object remains visible in the Form Design window. The object will not be visible when the program runs.

5.3.3 *The enabled property*

The enabled property controls whether the object actually responds to user actions. If you set the enabled property of a command button to false, the button still appears on the form, but nothing happens if the user clicks on it.

When an object is disabled, its appearance is changed as a visual clue to the user that the action associated with that object is not currently available. The usual method of doing this is to have the text string associated with the object "grayed out."

When an object is originally placed on a form, the enabled property is set to `true` by default. If you want the object to be disabled when the form is first started, use the General page of the object's property dialog to set the enabled property to `false`. While your program is running, you can change the enabled property from `true` to `false` by using the `setEnabled()` method (on most objects) or the `enabled method()` (depending on whether you are using Java 1.02 or 1.1). This method has the following standard syntax:

```
object.setEnabled (true);
```

5.3.4 *Color property*

PowerJ is designed to write applications for a graphical, visual environment. Since this environment is color, almost every object will have an associated color property. In fact, almost every object will have two associated colors: a foreground color and a background color. A text box, for example, has the inside of the box filled with the background color, while the text is displayed in the foreground color.

You change the color property of an object by using the Color tab of its property dialog, as shown in figure 5.4.

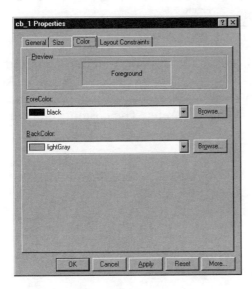

Figure 5.4
Selecting the color tab

The Color tab contains two drop-down list boxes, which contain the common system colors. At the top of the tab is a preview showing what the object will use for foreground and background colors with the current selection. If the user does not want to set a color that appears in the drop-down list box, he or she may click the Browse button, which will open the standard Windows custom colors shown in figure 5.5.

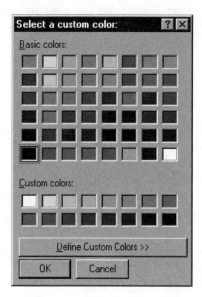

Figure 5.5
Custom colors

To select a color, simply click in the column from the colors at the top of the color dialog and click OK. If you don't see a color that you like, you may mix your own color by clicking on Define Custom Colors and using the mouse to mix the color that you prefer. The custom colors dialog is shown in figure 5.6.

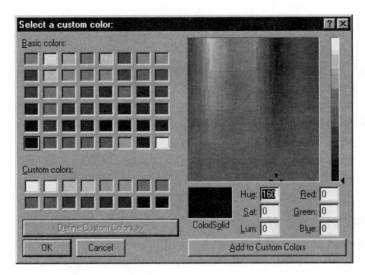

Figure 5.6   Custom colors dialog

When you have the color as you want it, click the Add to Custom Colors button and that color will be saved for future use.

5.3.5 *The object name property*

When an object is placed on a form, PowerJ automatically assigns the object a name, which consists of a prefix indicating the type of object and a number indicating the numerical sequence of this object on the current form. The first command button you place on a form will have the name cb_1, while the second command button you place on a form will have the number cb_2.

You can find a complete list of prefixes used by PowerJ in the appendix.

When you write PowerJ code to manipulate properties of an object at run time, you do so using dot notation. Dot notation consists of the name of the object, which is assigned by PowerJ, to the left of the dot and the method or property that can be manipulated to the right of the dot—for example, the following code changes the label property of a command button to the value "OK."

```
cb_1.setLabel ("OK");
```

Since the name of an object is simply a property of the object, you may change it from the default assigned by PowerJ. To do this you can use the object's property dialog. Simply type the name of the object in the edit field labeled Name and click OK. From that point on you must refer to the object in code by its new name.

When naming an object, it is always wise to follow some sort of naming convention. Naming conventions usually consist of prefixes, which tell you what type of object you are dealing with, and an underscore followed by a descriptive name. While PowerJ will assign a command button the name of cb_1 if the function of the command button is to close the form, the proper name that should be given to the button is cb_close.

5.3.6 *Additional common properties*

In addition to the properties we have just discussed, each object contains additional common properties. These properties include database access (which will be discussed in chapter 14).

PowerJ's drag-and-drop programming interface and its learn-as-you-code approach make it easy to learn the properties of any given object. Just use the Reference Card and the Object Inspector to view the methods properties for any object. You will find that you learn quickly as you use PowerJ and that you will become familiar with the properties that are most commonly used while others will always require that you look them up.

5.4 *Run-time-only properties*

Some objects have properties that cannot be set at design time. The only way to set these properties is to write code to manipulate them at run time. An example of this is if you want to initialize a text area with a multi-line text string (strings assigned to the text property at design time can only contain one line). Some of these run-time-only properties are quite useful, and one, the focus property, is discussed in the following section.

5.4.1 *The focus property*

In order for an object to receive input from the user, it must have focus. Only one object on a form can have focus at a particular moment—for example, when the user types at the keyboard, the text that he or she types will appear in the text box that has focus.

Focus is usually set when the user clicks inside the object with which he or she wants to interact. It is possible to programmatically force focus to a particular object in code by calling its `getFocus()` method. `getFocus()` will force the object upon which it is applied to have the focus.

5.5   *Component review*

Now that we have reviewed the properties that are common to most of the standard components, it is advisable that we begin a component-by-component review.

Where appropriate we will discuss properties that are unique to each of the standard components and also give you an indication of when to select one component over another component in designing the user interface. We will also note whether the component is a native Java component, derived from *java.awt*, or a PowerSoft component, derived from *powersoft.powerj.ui*.

5.5.1   *The selection tool*

At the left of the standard component bar, you will see an arrow button indicating the selection tool. Although this is not a component, it does serve a useful purpose and deserves mention here.

When the selection tool is depressed, moving the cursor over the form allows you to click on the form or on the component you want to select. Selecting any other component button will depress that other component's button and raise the button for the selection tool. If you then move the cursor over the form, you will notice that instead of seeing an arrow, you will see a crosshair. The crosshair indicates that this is the location at which you will place the selected component. If you change your mind and do not wish to place the component you have selected, just move the cursor back to the component bar and depress the selection tool.

5.5.2   *The button (java.awt.button)*

We will begin our review of the standard components with a look at the button. In Windows-speak this object is known as the command button, but Java refers to it simply as the button.

The button is one of the two objects you will use most often (the text box is the other). Buttons are used to allow the user to trigger some event or some action—for example, you will display a button with the label Close for the user to click when the he or she wishes to close the form. Likewise, a button with the label of Save could be used to save changes the user made to other objects on the form in a database.

Perhaps the most commonly used property for a button is the label property we discussed in section 5.3.1. The label property can be used to set the string, which comprises the label of the button, such as Save or Close. We have seen this in action in our to-do list application, where we labeled our buttons Add and Delete.

Another commonly used property is the enabled property, which will determine whether or not the button will respond to user input. A button that is enabled is clickable, while a disabled button cannot be clicked (or selected using an access key). Additionally, a disabled button appears to be dimmed or "grayed out" on the form. It is appropriate to disable buttons when their action is not permitted due to the status of the program at the time.

Button events

The button has the full range of standard events, such as the create and destroy events fired whenever the button is created in memory and when the button is removed from memory, the mouse enter event (occurs whenever the mouse moves over the button), and other mouse-related events (such as mouse drag and the `GetFocus` and `LoseFocus` events.

In general, the most important event you will concern yourself with on a button is the action event. This event is fired when the user clicks the button with the mouse, when the button has focus and the user presses Enter, or when the user types the keyboard access key combination for the button. The action event is where you want to place code that performs the required functionality when the button is clicked, as we did with the to-do list application.

Note
The event names used in this book are the Java 1.02 event names. Some events have been renamed in Java 1.1. The names are similar, so translation is not difficult. For example, the action event in Java 1.02 is called the Action_Performed event in Java 1.1.

5.5.3 *The check box (java.awt.Checkbox)*

Check boxes are often used to obtain option settings from the user. A check box can have two states—checked or unchecked—which indicate whether the option associated with the check box is on or off.

Figure 5.7 illustrates a design form with two check boxes.

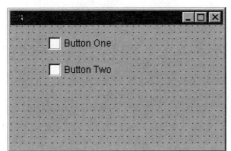

Figure 5.7
Design form with two check boxes

Check boxes may be bound to a database from which their checked value may be determined at run time or may have their values set at design time.

Check boxes have several properties that are unique. These properties include the checked property, check box groups, and check box events.

The checked property

The checked property indicates the status of the check box when the form is initially displayed. You may also manipulate the checked property at run time in your code by using the function `getState()` and `setState()`. In this manner, you may determine whether the user has checked or unchecked a box, and your code may branch accordingly—for example, the following code determines the status of the checked box and will perform some action depending upon whether the checked box is checked or unchecked.

```
boolean    state;
state = checkbox_1.getState();
if (state)
    {
        //perform action if checked
    }
```

```
else
{
     //Perform action if unchecked
}
```

Check box groups

Check boxes are often used to enable a user to pick between mutually exclusive choices. In other words, in a group of check boxes the user may make only one choice. In order to force this exclusive behavior on check boxes, they must be part of a check box group.

To create a check box group, open the Properties dialog for the first check box that you wish to become a part of the group. On the General tab you will see a drop-down list box for group. Since there are no groups defined, this list box will be empty.

To define a group, click New. This will open the Add Group dialog, where you can enter a group name. Once you specify a group name, click OK to return to the Properties dialog. Make sure that the group name you entered is selected in the group field and click OK. (See figure 5.8.)

Figure 5.8
Add group dialog

You will notice that the appearance of the check box has changed to that of an option (radio) button, as shown in figure 5.9

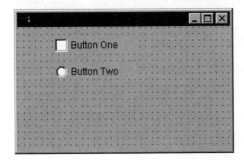

Figure 5.9
Option (radio) button

To add the second button to the group, open its Properties dialog. You will notice that the group name now appears in the drop-down list. Select it and click OK. If you run the form, you will see that clicking on one check box will automatically deselect the other (if it was selected).

You can have more than one group on a form.

Check box events

The check box has the full range of standard events associated with it. You will find that the action event is really all you need to meaningfully interact with the check box in code. The action event is fired whenever a user clicks the check box. You may use the action event to set a form-level variable to hold the status of the box, or you may perform some action each time the box is clicked.

5.5.4 *The choice control (java.awt.Choice)*

The choice control (also known as the drop-down list box or sometimes the combo box) is a control that performs the function of list boxes but takes up much less room on the form.

When the user selects an item from the list, its value is automatically copied into the text box displayed when the control is in its normal, not dropped down, state. This allows the user to easily see the current selection. This is standard behavior for a graphical computing environment such as Microsoft Windows (bet on the fact that most of the applications you write will be run under that operating system). The user will undoubtedly be familiar with that behavior.

Figure 5.10 illustrates a design form with a choice placed upon it.

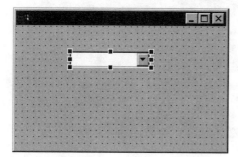

Figure 5.10
Design form with choice

Choice control properties

In addition to the properties common to all objects, the choice control can also be bound to the database using the data source, data columns, and the bound control properties. Other properties of the choice control, the ones you will use most often, are concerned with adding or deleting items from the list or determining the item that has been selected.

Adding items to the list

It is easy to add items to the list at design time. All you need to do is access the property dialog for the choice control and use the Item tab, as shown in figure 5.11.

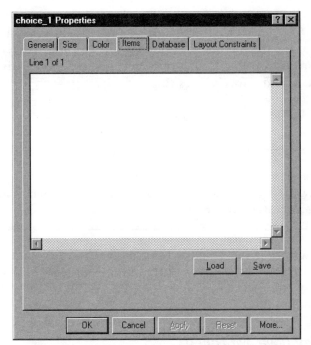

Figure 5.11
Adding items to the list

To add items to the list all you do is type them in. You may also retrieve items from a text file by clicking the Load button and selecting the file. Once items are entered, you may save them in a text file by clicking Save.

Of course, a popular method for loading items is to use the database functionality to retrieve items at run time. You may also need to add items on the fly at run time. The code below shows how to do that using the addItem() method).

```
choice_1.addItem( "Item Three" );
```

Of course, what you are mostly concerned with is how to determine what selection the user has made from the list. Read on.

Version makes a difference here

Unlike many other areas of PowerJ programming, where the version of Java you are working with makes no difference, the choice control behaves differently under Java 1.02 than it does under Java 1.1.

In Java 1.02, selecting an item fires a `ListSelect` event and deselecting an item fires a `ListDeselect` event. After one of these events has occurred, you can use the methods provided by the control to determine which item is currently selected. The following code determines the text of the selected item and stores it in a string variable.

```
java.lang.String                selectedItem;
selectedItem = choice_1.getSelectedItem();
```

Note

You may also retrieve the index value of the selected item using the `getSelectedIndex()` function.

When working with Java 1.1, selecting or deselecting an item triggers an item event. You can use the standard methods to determine which items are currently selected. Additionally, Java 1.1 triggers an action event when the user double-clicks an item.

5.5.5 *The label control (java.awt.Label)*

The label object is used to place text on some part of a form. An example of this is when you wish to place text immediately above or to the left of a text field showing a description of what the text field contains. We used a label control when we created our "Hello World" applet.

The only property you will find useful in a label control is the text property (actually this should be known as the label property to be consistent with other objects—I assume the name change was to avoid confusion). This is generally set at design time and not changed at run time. Label controls are fairly static. Label controls do have the full range of events associated with them—for example, you may decide to perform some action when the user clicks on a label (in the action event), although this is rare.

5.5.6 *The list (java.awt.List)*

You use a list control to present the user with a list of choices. Unlike a choice, the list always appears on the form so that the user can see more than one of the items from which he or she may select. Items in the list are usually shown in a single column, as illustrated in figure 5.12.

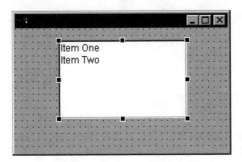

Figure 5.12
List items

List Controls come in two flavors.

1 Single selection list

2 Multiple selection list

The difference is that in a multiselection list control, the user may select more than one item. You determine whether a list box is in multiple select mode by checking the multiple mode check box on the General tab of the property dialog.

Single selection lists

In a single selection list control there are several ways for users to select an item from the printed list. The user may click the item or highlight the item by clicking in the list box and using the arrow keys to navigate.

When the user clicks on one item and then on another item, the first item is automatically deselected. This is because the nature of a single selection list control allows the user to select only one item from the list.

List control properties

List controls can draw their data from a database by using the data source, data column, and bound control properties. We will discuss these properties in chapter 14. You may also specify the items in a list control at design time by using the Items tab of the list control properties page. In this way, list controls are identical to choice controls (see section 5.5.4).

List controls also have a count property, which enables you to ascertain the number of items in a list. The following code performs this task.

In Java 1.02:

```
int num = lb_1.countItems();
```

In Java 1.1:

```
int num = lb_1.getItemCount();
```

Adding items to the list at run time

You add items to the list at run time using the addItem() method in the same manner as for a choice control.

Clearing the list

Another useful method associated with list controls is clear(). You may use the clear() method to remove all the entries from the list—for example, the following code will clear all entries from the list control:

```
lb_1.clear();
```

To determine the value the user has selected, use the getSelected-Item() function, which returns a string containing the selected item, or the getSelectedIndex() function, which returns the index number of the selected item. This was discussed fully in section 5.5.4. List boxes use many of the same methods as choice controls.

List control events

The event you will use most often when working with list controls is the ListSelect event. It is fired each time a user clicks on an item from the list.

Multiple selection list controls

Multiple selection list controls are very similar to single selection list controls. The only difference is that the user may select any number of items from a multiple selection list control. To select an item in the multiple selection list control, the user simply has to click on it. If the user clicks on a selected item, the item will be deselected.

From a programming standpoint, the difference is that you may have to read and act upon more than one selected item if the list control is in MultiSelect mode.

Making a list control allow for multiple selection is done by setting the multimode property to `true`. This can be done at design time or at run time in code.

```
lb_1.allowsMultipleSelection(true);
```

The major difference in working with multiple selection list controls is the manner in which you obtain the list of selected items. Working with single selection list controls is easier, since only one item may be selected at a time, and that item may be returned using the `getSelectedItem()` function.

When working with a multiple selection list control, the `getSelected-Item()` function will not work when there is more than one item selected (it will return an item if there is only one item selected). Instead, you must use the `getSelectedItems()` function. `getSelectedItems()` returns an array of strings containing the selected items in the list.

You may also use `getSelectedIndexes()` to return an array of integers representing the index numbers of the selected items. These index values can then be passed to the `getItem()` function to return the string values (if that is necessary).

The following code retrieves the selected list from a multiple selection list control and stores its values in an array of strings for further manipulation.

```
java.lang.String[]              selectedItems;
selectedItems = lb_1.getSelectedItems();
```

5.5.7 *The menu bar (java.awt.MenuBar)*

The menu bar object is a single object containing all the items displayed in the menu bar of a form. When you want a form to have menus, place a menu bar somewhere on the form. It does not matter where you place the menu bar object representing the menu—the menu itself will always appear below the title bar of the frame.

The menu bars may only be placed on frames—not on dialog boxes or other forms. For that reason you cannot place a menu bar on the main applet window (the one that is embedded in the browser), since that is not a frame. You can, however, open a frame window from code within the applet window and use a menu on the frame.

We will discuss menus in detail in the next chapter.

5.5.8 *The panel (java.awt.Panel)*

A panel is an object that can contain other objects. It is similar to a form; however, a panel can itself be placed on a form. Panels have properties and events, but in the case of panels that are placed on forms, you will seldom use them.

To use a panel on a form, just place it and size it as you would any other control. Then place any other objects you wish to have contained inside the panel upon the panel itself, just as you would place them on a form. To assist you in placing objects on a panel, you may turn on a set of grid dots, just as you can on a form.

Warning

If you place objects on a panel on a form, those objects become a part of the panel. If you delete the panel from the form, all the associated objects, their event handlers, and code will also be deleted. Be careful not to delete the panel until after you have preserved any necessary code.

5.5.9 *The scroll bar (java.awt.Scrollbar)*

You use a scroll bar to scroll through information displayed in an associated object. You might want to associate a scroll bar with a picture box, for example, so that when a user moves the scroll bar, the picture changes to another viewpoint.

A scroll bar can be either vertical or horizontal. You can set this property at design time using the property dialog, where unchecking the vertical box will render the scroll bar horizontally.

There are very few times where you will want to use an individual scroll bar. Scrolling is generally handled at the level of the individual control— for example, if you are using a multiline text area, when the text is too large to appear within the boundaries of the text box, a scroll bar will appear. The advantage of those scroll bars is that they work automatically without having to write additional code. If you choose to use a separate scroll bar, you will be responsible for writing all code to manipulate its associated control, depending upon the user's interaction with the scroll bar. Several events are provided to perform this task. There are also properties provided to set and determine the current position of the scroll indicator button.

Scroll bar properties

You can think of a scroll bar as representing a range of integer values, from a minimum value to a maximum value. The position of the scroll bar's position indicator is represented as a value in the scroll bar's range—for example, if the range runs from 0 to 100, a value of 50 puts the slider in the middle position of the scroll bar.

The following properties are associated with a scroll bar's position and range.

Minimum.   This is the minimum value represented by the scroll bar.

Maximum.   This is the maximum value represented by the scroll bar.

Value.   This is the current value of the scroll bar.

Visible.   This represents a number indicating the range of values that is currently visible—for example, the scroll bar is associated with an object that can show 20 items at a time. Then visible would have a value of 20.

LineIncrement.   `LineIncrement` is the amount that the value should change if the user clicks one of the end arrows of the scroll bar.

PageIncrement.   The `PageIncrement` is the amount that the value should change if the user clicks in the blank area above or below the scroll indicator.

You can set these values using appropriate methods, as follows.

```
scroll_1.setPageIncrement( 1 );
scroll_1.setLineIncrement( 10 );
```

If you set the increments for a scroll bar, the default event handlers for the scroll bar automatically change the value and move the slider the specified amount in response to user actions.

Scroll bar methods

The scroll bar properties have all the usual `get` methods.

```
int max = scroll_1.getMaximum();
int min = scroll_1.getMinimum();
int val = scroll_1.getValue();
int vis = scroll_1.getVisible();
```

You can set the current scroll position using:

```
int value;
scroll_1.setValue( value );
```

Scroll bar events

Scroll bars have a variety of events that allow you to determine the proper action to take in response to the user's action. PowerJ will alter the properties discussed above in different ways, depending upon the event fired.

ScrollAbsolute.   This event fires when the user drags the scroll indicator to a new position. When this event fires, PowerJ will change the value property to reflect the new position of the scroll indicator.

ScrollLineUp.   This event fires when the user clicks the arrow at the top or left of the scroll bar. PowerJ will then subtract `LineIncrement` from the current value.

ScrollLineDown.   This event fires when the user clicks the arrow at the bottom or right of the scroll bar. PowerJ will add `LineIncrement` to the current value.

ScrollPageUp.   This event fires when the user clicks in the blank area above or to the left of the scroll indicator. PowerJ will subtract `PageIncrement` from the current value.

ScrollPageDown.   This event fires when the user clicks in the blank area below or to the right of the scroll indicator. PowerJ will add `PageIncrement` to the current value.

Using these properties and methods makes programming scroll bars fairly easy, whenever their use is necessary. You will find that you rely more often on "built-in" scroll bars.

5.5.10   Text box

The text box is an area on the form that displays text. Normally, the text box allows the user to enter new text or to edit text already contained in the box. Text boxes may also be "read only," in which case they behave somewhat like a label, which the user cannot edit. Java text boxes come in three flavors.

1   The text area (which is a multiline text box) (*java.awt.TextArea*)

2   The text field (single line) (*java.awt.TextField*)

3   The masked text field (*powersoft.powerj.ui.MaskedTextField*)

This section will discuss text areas and text fields; the masked text field is discussed in section 5.5.12. In this section, when I refer to text boxes I am speaking generically.

Both flavors of text boxes have most properties and methods in common, and we will discuss them as if they were identical (referring to them as text boxes), making note only when there is some difference. Figure 5.13 illustrates a design form showing both types of text box:

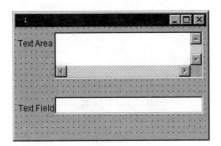

Figure 5.13
Text area and text field

Text box properties

As with all controls, you initially set some properties of your text in your text box by using the text box Properties dialog.

`ReadOnly` creates a text box that does not allow the user to interact with or edit the text in the text box. The `EchoCharacter` property is used to hide the actual text that the user has entered, such as in a password field. You can also use the property dialog to set default text for the text box to display when the form is first opened.

As we will discuss in chapter 14, text boxes can be bound to a database using the bound control data source, database, and data columns properties (found on the Database tab).

Manipulating the text at run time

At run time you will use the `getText()` method to determine which text has been typed in the text box. The `getText()` method has the following syntax:

```
texta_1.getText ( ) ;
```

The `getText()` function returns a string. Likewise, you can use the `setText()` method to place text in the object.

```
texta_1.setText("The text")
```

If you are operating against a text area and want the text to be placed on multiple lines, simply embed a /n at the point where you want the line break.

```
String text;
text = "This is Line One /nThis is Line Two";
texta_1.setText(text);
```

will print:

```
This is Line One
This is Line Two
```

in the text area text_1.

Selecting text

You can programmatically select text in a text box using the `select-All()` and `select()` methods. The `selectAll()` method selects all the text in a text box object, while the `select()` method selects a part of the text in a text box object, delimited by a start point and an end point.

```
int start, end;
textf_1.select( start, end );
```

When the user selects text, you can obtain the selected string using the following code:

```
String str1 = texta_1.getSelectedText();
```

Text box events

The main events you will concern yourself with when working with text boxes are the `KeyUp` and `KeyDown` events and the `GetFocus` and `LoseFocus` events.

These two "key" events are fired any time the user types within the text box. You can use these events to determine the key the user has pressed or the value of the string currently contained within the text box. The only difference is that the `KeyDown` event fires when the key is pressed and the `KeyUp` event fires when it is released.

You may find it more appropriate to ignore the key events and to place code in the `LoseFocus` event. In this way you can obtain the entire string, without the overhead of key-by-key processing. You may even place a command button on a form and retrieve the text when the button is clicked.

5.5.11 *The group box (powersoft.powerj.GroupBox)*

As with a panel, a group box is used to surround other objects. You can use a group box to visually associate controls, such as check boxes and option buttons, that contain related information. Figure 5.14 is a form with a group box surrounding user name and password entry fields.

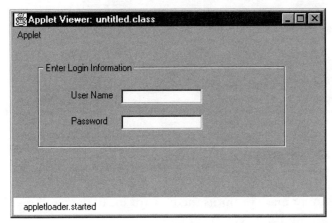

Figure 5.14
Group box

Group boxes also add a 3D look and feel to your forms.

Once you have placed objects on a group box, they are associated with that group box and moving the group box will result in moving all the controls at once, with the relationships between them being preserved. Also, as with a panel, if you delete the group box, you will also delete all associated objects and their underlying code.

5.5.12 *The masked text field*
(powersoft.powerj.ui.MaskedTextField)

A masked text field is a text box used to show a date, time, or number in a standard format. Figure 5.15 illustrates a masked text field showing a date.

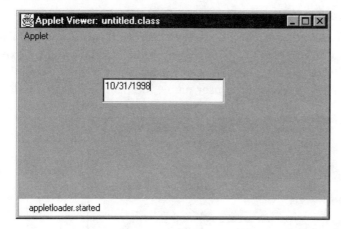

Figure 5.15
Masked text field

Masked text properties

The masked text field has two basic properties that control the mask.

1   The input mask prompts the user for input data and restricts the type of input that can be entered.

2   The output pattern indicates how the masked text field displays data once they have been entered. This is designed to make it easier to read the entered data.

When the masked text field has the focus, it displays its current value using the input mask. This typically makes it easier for the user to enter new input. When it loses the focus, it changes to display its current value using the output pattern.

Note

Output patterns are only supported in Java 1.1 applications.

Additional masked text properties

Masked text fields support all the properties of regular text fields. They also have the following properties to help control their appearance:

PromptChar. This sets the character displayed in the masked text field to show the user where input is required—for example, if you set `Prompt-Char` to an asterisk, the user sees an asterisk in each position where a character should be entered.

InputMask. This is a string specifying the type of input that may be entered. Some of the characters may be literals, which are displayed "as is" when the user enters data. Others are placeholders, which indicate positions where the user will enter data—for example, in a phone number mask.

```
(###) ###-####
```

The parentheses and the - character are literals; the # characters are placeholders representing numerical information.

Table 5.1 shows all the characters that can be used as placeholders.

Table 5.1   Placeholder Characters

Character	Usage
#	A single decimal digit; the user can only enter characters from 0 through 9.
?	A single alphanumeric character; the user can only enter characters from 0 through 9, a through z, or A through Z.
U	A single uppercase letter.
L	A single lowercase letter.
M	A single letter (either uppercase or lowercase).
*	Any single character.

OutputPattern (Java 1.1 only). This is a string specifying the pattern for displaying the value in the box. An output pattern string starts with a single character indicating the type of value. Possible characters are as follows:

D or d — a date.

T or t — a time.

N or n — a number.

S or s — a text string.

An output pattern for a date might be specified with the following code:

```
D:mmm dd yyyy
```

Beep on error.   This causes the computer to beep if the user enters a character that does not fit the `InputMask`.

Use current date.   This causes the field to default to the current date (if a date mask is specified).

Flag output error.   This causes the word "error" to display if the field cannot display the indicated data.

Working with the text property.   As with any other text box, the masked text field's text property holds the value that is displayed within the field. Unlike other text areas, you can access that value in two different ways, depending upon the result you want.

If all you need is the string itself, without any of the formatting characters, then you access that value using the `getText()` method as if it were a normal text box. However, if you need to capture the formatting characters, you use the `getMaskedText()` method.

5.5.13   The multiline label (powersoft.powerj.ui.MultiLineLabel)

The multiline label acts the same as any other label except that the text it contains can span more than one line. All other properties and methods behave the same as for the native Java label.

5.5.14   The paint canvas (powersoft.powerj.ui.PaintCanvass)

The paint canvas is similar to the picture box (discussed in section 5.5.15) in that it is used to hold pictures. The difference is that the paint canvas usually holds pictures that the program draws at execution time, while the picture box displays pictures located in files (such as *GIF* files).

5.5.15   The picture box (java.awt.PictureBox)

You use a picture box to display graphic images such as bitmaps.

Picture box properties

You can use the General tab of the picture box property dialog to set the following properties:

AutoSize.   The `AutoSize` property changes the size of the picture box, automatically, to match the size of the picture.

ScaleImage Property. The `ScaleImage` property changes the size of the picture, automatically, so that it will fit inside the picture box. The picture is scaled appropriately to preserve its proportions.

ImageCentered Property. The `ImageCentered` property centers the picture within the picture box. If this is turned off, the picture is drawn in the upper left corner of the picture box.

You set the design properties of the picture box using the Picture tab of the picture box property page, shown in figure 5.16.

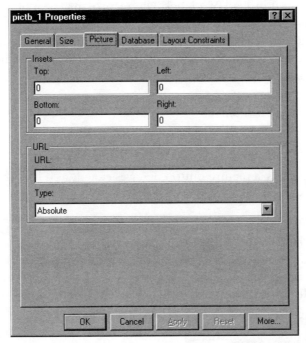

Figure 5.16
Picture box properties

These properties include the following:

Insets. These set the distance between the area available to draw the picture and the edges of the picture box.

URL. This provides a URL indicating where the picture can be found. You can use this to open a file containing a bitmap, or other supported file type, in the picture box. If the URL is unavailable at run time, no picture will be displayed.

Type.   This property sets the type of picture. Choices are `Absolute`, `CodeBased`, and `DocumentBased`. `CodeBased` and `DocumentBased` are only supported for applet targets.

5.5.16 *The picture button (powersoft.powerj.ui.PictureButton)*

A picture button is identical to a regular button except that a picture button has a picture on it instead of a label. The picture may be a bitmap, an icon, or something you draw.

At design time you assign a picture to a picture button using the Picture tab of the picture button's property dialog. This dialog looks just like the one for the picture box. Simply enter the location of the picture file in the URL edit.

You may also set the image at run time using the set image method, which has the following syntax:

```
Pictbttn_1.setImage( Image ) ;
```

In all other respects, a picture button behaves exactly as if it were a regular button (see section 5.5.2).

5.5.17 *The tab control (powersoft.powerj.ui.TabControl)*

You use a tab control to group sets of data on different "pages" within the same form. A perfect example of this concept is the property dialog, which we have discussed throughout this chapter. A design form with a tab control is shown in figure 5.17.

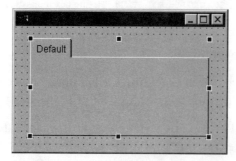

Figure 5.17
Tab control

Setting the number of pages

You can set the number of tab pages displayed by your tab control by using the Pages tab of the tab control property dialog, shown in figure 5.18.

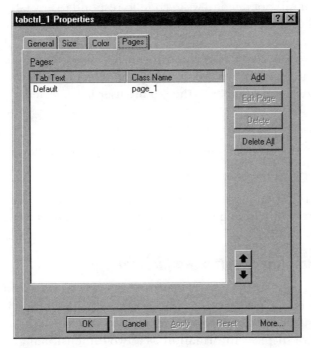

Figure 5.18
Pages tab

Note

A tab control is actually two controls in one—the tab control and the tab form control. Normally, you do not use any properties or events associated with the tab form control. To display the property sheet for the tab control, make sure you click on the tab part of the control.

To add a page, simply type in the text you wish to appear and click the Add button. Notice that this also creates a second tab form control. Each tab page has its own associated tab form control.

You place the controls you want to have displayed on the tab form control when the user selects that tab.

Tab control events

Normally, you will not need to write code to respond to any tab control events. The code generated by PowerJ takes care of switching between tab pages as the user clicks on a tab.

From time to time you may need to know what tab the user has selected. You can perform this task by using the select event. The following code will return the number of the tab the user has selected:

```
int selectedtab;
selectedtab = tabcntrlname.getSelected();
```

Similarly, you can force the selection of a tab by using the following code:

```
tabcntrlname.setSelected(tabnumber);
```

You will find that tab controls are a great way to save programming time and resources by allowing you to build your applications using fewer forms than normal.

5.5.18 The grid control (powersoft.powerj.ui.Grid)

One of the most popular third-party controls for many development environments has been the grid control. Now most development tools include a native grid control and PowerJ is no exception.

A grid control displays information as a two-dimensional grid. The most well-known example of grid controls is spreadsheet programs.

Each column and/or row in the grid may have a heading. There are also scroll bars that allow the user to view all parts of the grid even though it may not all fit on the form. Each individual entry in the grid is called a cell. Figure 5.19 shows a form with a grid control.

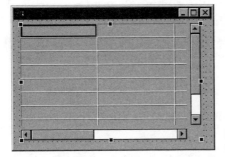

Figure 5.19
Grid control

Grid Properties

A grid control works just like any other control in that you specify properties at design time using the property dialog. However, the grid control is a little more complex, and there are many more properties to be concerned with. Therefore, the grid control property dialog has a few additional tabs. The grid control property dialog is shown in figure 5.20.

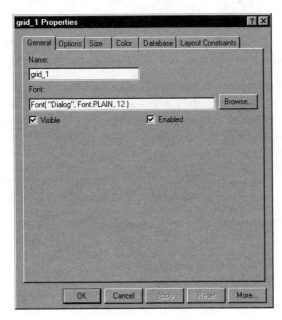

Figure 5.20
Grid control property dialog

The following text discusses the commonly used properties. For any property not covered here, consult the on-line help. We will look at the database-related properties in chapter 14. Here we will concern ourselves mostly with grid manipulation properties and the methods you use to work with them.

The most useful properties are found on the Options tab.

Number of columns.   This option sets the number of columns in the grid control.

Number of rows.   This determines the number of rows in the grid control. By default, the value is set to the largest number than can be supported.

ReadOnly.   If you set this property, the use may not edit any of the entries in the grid control.

LiveEditMode.   By setting this property, you allow the user to edit cells inside the grid itself but only if ReadOnly is not turned on. When the user clicks on a cell, the cell offers all the editing facilities of a normal text box, allowing the user to modify the existing value or enter a new one.

FullRowSelection.   If this is turned on, clicking any cell in the grid selects the entire row containing that cell.

MultiMode.   If MultiMode is turned on, the user may select more than one cell at a time. The user may select several adjacent cells in the same column by dragging the mouse across those cells or by holding down the shift key and moving the arrow keys. If MultiMode is turned off, the user may only select one cell at a time.

ResizableColumns.   By turning this on, you allow the user to change the size of columns by dragging the lines that divide column headers.

ResizableRows.   This allows the user to change the size of rows by dragging the lines that divide row headers.

ShowColumnLines.   This makes the grid control use lines to separate all columns.

ShowRowLines.   This makes the grid control use lines to separate rows.

ShowVerticalHeader.   This allows for header entries at the beginning of each row.

Show HorizontalHeader. This allows for header entries at the top of each column.

HScroll and VScroll. These settings control whether the grid control contains horizontal and vertical scroll bars to scroll through the grid.

CellRanges. The `CellRange` class comprises a range of cells in a grid control. You can use `CellRange` objects to pass ranges of cells to other methods—for example, the `setSelectedCells` method takes a `CellRange` argument holding the range of cells you want to select.

A `CellRange` object specifies a cell range by giving the starting and ending rows of the range, plus the starting and ending columns. The following code shows how to create a `CellRange`:

```
CellRange cr = new CellRange( startRow, startCol, endRow,
endCol );
```

Rows and columns are referenced with integer indexes. The `startRow` and `endRow` values may be equal, meaning that the cell range only refers to cells in a single row. The `startCol` and `endCol` values may be equal (meaning that the cell range only refers to cells in a single column).

Heading labels. You can assign label headings to columns with the `setColumnLabel` method.

```
grid_1.setColumnLabel( 0, "Name" );
```

This sets the label of the leftmost column.

You set row headings like this.

```
grid_1.setRowLabel( 0, "Heading" );
```

This sets the label of the topmost row. Before the labels are shown, they must be enabled using the `ShowVertical Header`.

Working with cells. You can set values into cells using the `setCell` method.

```
grid_1.setCell( rowNumber, columnNumber, value );
```

Note

The cell in the upper left corner is at position 0,0 rather than the more intuitive 1,1.

You use `getCell` to determine the current value of a cell:

```
Object obj = grid_1.getCell( rowNumber, columnNumber );
```

Deleting rows and columns. You can also delete rows and columns by using the various methods provided for that purpose.

```
grid_1.deleteRow( rowNumber );
```

This deletes the given row from the grid.

```
grid_1.deleteAllRows( );
```

This deletes all rows from the grid.

```
grid_1.deleteColumns( pos, numColumns );
```

This deletes a number of columns from the grid. The `pos` argument gives the number of the first column to delete, and the `numColumns` argument gives the total number of columns to delete.

Adding rows and columns. You can also add rows and columns using the following method:

```
Object label;
Vector values;
grid_1.addRow( pos, label, values );
```

This adds a new row to the grid control. The `pos` argument gives the row number for the new row. The `label` argument gives the row heading for the row, and `values` gives a set of values to place in the new row. Both `label` and `values` may be null.

```
grid_1.addColumn( pos, label, values );
```

This adds a new column to the grid control.

Selecting and unselecting cells. The `SelectedCells` property determines which cells are currently selected.

```
CellRange cr;
grid_1.setSelectedCells( cr );
```

This selects the given cell range if the selection policy property permits the cells to be selected.

`getSelectedCells` returns a vector of `CellRange` objects indicating the ranges that are currently selected.

```
Vector crVect = grid_1.getSelectedCells();
```

In this example, each element of `crVect` is a `CellRange` object indicating one range that is selected.

To unselect all the cells that are currently selected, use the following code:

```
grid_1.clearSelectedCells();
```

5.6 *Summary*

This completes our review of the standard components. The easiest way to learn how to manipulate and use the standard components in your application is to practice using them on forms. As you continue through this book, you will see many examples for the use of the standard components.

Using menu objects

6

In this chapter we will do the following:

- Discuss the menu bar object
- Learn how to attach a menu to a form
- Learn how to create menu items and subitems
- Learn how to create cascaded menus
- Learn how to write menu code

128

This chapter demonstrates the use of the PowerJ menu bar object component, which was briefly discussed in chapter 5. Menus form a very useful navigational function in graphical applications. For that reason proper care must be taken that they are well designed in order to provide maximum functionality. PowerJ provides you with all the tools necessary to design good menus for your application. The menu bar is defined in the class *java.awt.MenuBar*.

6.1 Adding a menu object to a form

To add a menu to a form, simply click the menu bar icon on the standard component and click anywhere on the form. You may add more than one menu bar object to a form.

Note

Standard component menu bar objects may only be used in forms that are of type frame. To create a form of type frame, simply select that type when using the Form Wizard to add the new form to the project. Frames cannot be created in applets, and for that reason menus are unavailable in applet projects. Further details regarding the Form Wizard can be found in chapter 10.

Note

It does not matter where on the form you place the menu bar object, since the menu will always appear at the top of the form at run time.

6.2 Menu name property

A menu bar object has only one property (and no events)—the Name property. You set the name property by using the property dialog of the menu bar object, shown in figure 6.1.

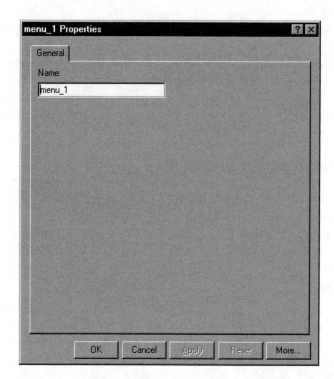

Figure 6.1
Menu name property

As with all objects, instead of accepting the default name, you should replace the number identifier with something more descriptive—such as the name of the form upon which the menu object is placed.

6.3 The default menu

You may wish to add more than one menu bar object to a form. You would do this, for example, if you wish to change between two different menus, depending upon circumstances at run time.

If you elect to have more than one menu bar object on a form, you must specify which of them is the default menu. The default menu will be the one that is displayed when the form is initially loaded.

You specify the default menu bar object by using the form's property dialog as shown in figure 6.2 by simply selecting the desired menu bar object from the drop-down list shown on the Menu Bars page of the property dialog.

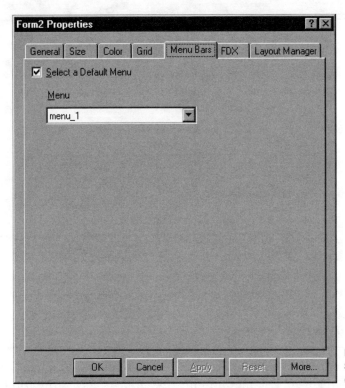

**Figure 6.2
Selecting the
default menu**

6.4   *Adding menu items to the menu bar*

To add menu items to the menu bar, you must invoke the menu editor. Do this by right-clicking the menu on the form and selecting Edit Menu. The menu editor dialog is shown in figure 6.3.

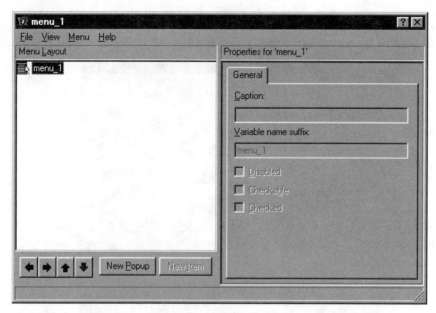

Figure 6.3 Menu editor dialog

6.5 *The menu editor dialog*

The menu editor dialog is where you create the menu items you want to have on your form. The menu items that appear across the top of the form are referred to as pop-up items. To create a new pop-up menu item, simply click the new pop-up button.

On the Menu Layout window portion of the dialog, you will then see the new item with a generic name. Simply type the text you want to have on the menu in place of the name given by PowerJ. Figure 6.4 illustrates the menu editor dialog with several pop-up items defined.

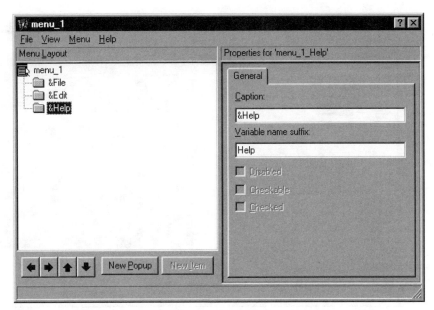

Figure 6.4   Menu editor dialog with pop-up items

6.6   *Adding child items*

To create child items, which will appear when you click on the high-level pop-up item on the menu bar, simply click Menu...New Child Item on the menu editor dialog menu. This will create a child item with a generic name, which you can change to something more appropriate. Figure 6.5 shows the menu editor dialog with some child items defined under the file pop-up menu.

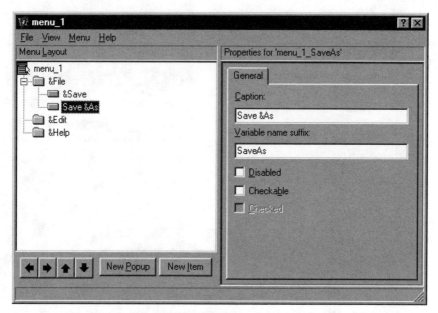

Figure 6.5   Menu editor dialog with child items

The Menu Layout window operates much like Microsoft's Windows Explorer in that it is a simple tree control. At the high level of the tree, place the items you want to have on the menu bar at the top of the form. Lower-level items appear when the high-level items are dropped down or the subitems are cascaded off the drop downs. You may use the arrow keys at the bottom of the Menu Layout window to move items around as desired.

6.7   Setting menu properties

The right side of the menu editor dialog allows you to set the menu item property for each individual item. Simply select the item in the menu layout portion of the dialog and change the property on the right side of the screen.

There are five properties that you can change. These are the caption, which is the text string that the user sees; the variable name suffix, which is created from the name of the menu (the actual name of the menu item is the menu name suffix appended at the end of the menu bar name—for example, if you have a pop-up item at the high level called file, the name of the menu item will be menubarname_file); the disabled property; the checkable property; and the checked property (only if the menu item is checkable).

The disabled property is used to determine whether the menu responds to the user's input. The checkable property is used to determine whether the menu displays a check mark next to it when the user clicks it. If you select a checkable property, the third property is enabled. The checked property indicates whether or not the menu item will display with a check mark initially.

6.8 Accelerator key

Accelerator keys are special keyboard combinations associated with a particular menu item. By typing the keyboard combination, you get the same effect as clicking on the menu item—for example, you may have a menu item under the file menu entitled Save. If you give the saved menu item an accelerator key control "plus S," you can trigger the saved action simply by typing control +s.

6.9 Menu separators

You use horizontal lines to separate child menu items into groups. These lines are called separators. Separators exist only to make a menu easier to read. When the user clicks on one of these lines, no action is performed. To place a separator in your menu, simply click on menu New Separator. The separator will appear directly below the currently highlighted item.

Separators can only be used to separate child menu items.

6.10 When to use menu items

Menu items can be divided into two distinct types. Some menu items perform a function as soon as you click on them—for example, a Save item generally saves the current files without prompting the user for save information, while a Save As item will open a dialog that will obtain file information from the user.

According to interface conventions, menu items that will open a dialog to obtain further information before they will complete their task should be assigned names ending with points of ellipsis (...), which indicates to the user that the item needs to contain more information before it will take action. Of course, menu items that take immediate action will never display points of ellipsis.

However, just because a menu item opens a dialog box does not mean it must have points of ellipsis. An example of this situation is a property menu item which will open a property dialog. The function of the menu property is simply to open a dialog. A menu has completed its function when the dialog is opened and does not need points of ellipsis.

6.11 Deleting menu items

You can delete menu items you have created by accessing the delete function from the menu editor dialog. To do this, simply highlight the menu item you wish to delete and then click Menu...Delete (or press the Delete key).

Deleting a highlighted menu automatically deletes all the items contained below that menu item as well. If you have to delete an item, PowerJ will display a dialog to make sure you really want to delete all the subitems. If there are items you do not wish to delete, cancel the deletion at this point. You may move the item to another menu before deleting the unwanted one.

6.12 Writing menu code

Of course, menu items do not function unless there is code written to make them perform the intended task. Menu items will only respond to one event: the click event. A menu item without a click event performs no action.

To create a click event handler for a menu item, simply select the name of the menu item you want to work with, right-click it, and select Event; then select Click on the cascaded menu. This will open the standard PowerJ code editor, which you have already seen.

The following sections will discuss some examples of code that you may or may not wish to place in your menus or that relate to the manipulation of menu items at run time.

6.13 Enabling and disabling menu items

You may use the `setEnabled()` method to enable or disable menu items during execution. The following code shows how to enable and disable menu items:

```
menu_1_save.setEnabled( true );     // enabled
menu_1_save.setEnabled( false );    // disabled
```

6.14 Checking menu items

You may use the `setChecked()` method menu object to mark a menu item with a check or to remove checks that are already present. The following code will check or uncheck a menu item:

```
menu_1_save.setChecked( true );     // checked
menu_1_save.setchecked( false );    // unchecked
```

6.15 Making the menu item visible or not visible

Use the `setVisible()` method to make a menu item appear or disappear during execution. The following code performs this task:

```
menu_1_save.setVisible( true );     // visible
menu_1_save.setVisible( false );    // not visible
```

6.16 Changing the text of menu items

There are times when you might wish to change the text of a particular menu item to reflect the new program context. An example of this is a word processing application that contains an Undo menu item under Edit. You may wish to change the text to "undo typing" or "undo insert" to inform the user of which action will be undone.

You use the `setText()` method of a menu object to change the text of a menu item. The following code changes the text of a menu item:

```
Menu_1_save.setText("New Caption");
```

6.17 Removing menu items

You may use the `removeMenuComponent()` method to remove an item from a menu. Removing an item does not delete the menu item object from the menu bar object. For this reason you can remove a menu item and then put it back later on.

The following code will remove menu components:

```
boolean success = menu_1_file.removeMenuComponent (menu_1_save);
```

The `removeMenuComponent()` function returns a Boolean value, which is `true` if the function was successful and the menu item was removed and `false` if an error occurred.

6.18 Adding items to menu

To add items to the menu use the `addMenuComponent()` method. This acts as the opposite of the remove menu component. The following code places a menu item on the menu:

```
boolean success = menu_1_File.addMenuComponent( menu_1_save );
```

You should use the function carefully. You may only use this method to restore items that have been previously removed. (It is always best to specify menu items at design time. You may then remove them at run time if they are not needed or remove them from the project if you determine they will never be needed.)

If you fail to specify menu items at design time, it is infinitely more complicated to build the item from scratch at run time. It is not nearly enough to add the newly created item as we did. You must also specify the click event handler for the item or the item will perform no task. For this reason you should always create your items at design time. It is beyond the scope of this book to explain how to create an item from scratch.

If you are writing stand-alone Java applications, you will make use of menus. Remember, before you actually start developing the menu, that proper menu design takes considerable thought. Also, remember that each individual menu item is an object unto itself and as such consumes system resources. Elaborate menus can dramatically slow the time taken to initially display a form.

6.19 Summary

In this chapter we learned how to work with menu bar objects. We learned how to attach a menu to a frame-type form and how to create the menu items and child items the user will see when the program is executed. We also learned how to create cascaded menus and how to write code to make the menu items work.

7

The standard datatype classes

140

In addition to the standard components we have looked at extensively in the previous two chapters, Java (and therefore PowerJ) also includes several standard datatypes. These classes allow you to create datatypes such as strings and integers, which also have methods you can call against them. The string class, for example, contains methods that allow you to manipulate the string by trimming the white space from each end and comparing its value with another string.

The advantage of this is that it makes it easier than it was in the old C language to perform operations on variables. Each of the primitive datatypes (`int`, `char`, `double`, `float`, and so on) has a class counterpart. This chapter takes a look at some of the datatype classes you will use most.

7.1 *The object class (java.lang.Object)*

The object class is the ultimate ancestor of all other AWT classes in Java. It provides several standard methods, which can be called against any of the standard classes derived from it. These methods include `getClass()`, which returns the class name of the object (will return the class name of the descendant it is called against), and the `equals()` method, which you will use to compare objects for equality or to assign the contents of one object to another.

Other methods are provided, but not implemented fully at this level, which means that you must write code at the descendant level for any objects which you inherit from this class and for which you want to provide that functionality. The `toString()` method, which is intended to convert the object's contents to a string class, is an example of a method that is provided but not implemented. If you inherit a new class from the object class and wish to provide `toString()` functionality, you must write code in the descendant to implement the function. The reason that `toString()` functionality must be implemented at the descendant level is that the ancestor has no way of knowing what datatype the descendant will be converting.

Many of the standard classes inherited from the object class already provide `toString()` functionality, and this functionality is defined at the descendant level. This is an example of the object-oriented principle of polymorphism.

7.2 The string class (java.lang.String)

The string class is used to store string constants. It hides from the developer the fact that in Java strings are simply arrays of characters, and it allows the entire value of the string to be accessed without having to resort to character-by-character reading.

The string class contains methods that allow you to manipulate and compare string values far easier than was the case in the old C language, where specialized functions were provided for that purpose. Java's string class encapsulates all the "guts" of the string manipulation functions and hides them from you, rendering programming tasks much easier to perform. Table 7.1 shows the commonly used string class methods.

Table 7.1   String Class Methods

Method	Usage
length()	Returns the length of the string
concat(string)	Adds the string passed as a parameter to the string that the method is called against
toUpperCase()	Changes the string to uppercase
toLowerCase()	Changes the string to lowercase
trim()	Removes white space from the beginning and end of the string
replace(char1, char2)	Replaces all occurrences of character 1 with character 2
equals(string 2)	Compares the string with string 2 for equality. Returns true if the strings are equal.
equalsIgnoreCase(string 2)	Compares the string with string 2 for equality, ignoring the case of the two strings. Returns true if they are equal.
compareTo(string 2)	Determines the "sort" order of the two strings. It returns a positive value if the string is lexicographically greater than string 2, returns zero if the two strings are equal, and returns a negative value if the String is lexicographically less than string 2.
endsWith(string 2)	Returns true if the string ends with the character sequence in string 2
startsWith(string 2)	Returns true if the string begins with the character sequence in string 2

Table 7.1   String Class Methods

Method	Usage
substring(offset) substring(start, end)	Returns a string consisting of the characters beginning at the offset position and ending at the end of the string or beginning at the start position and ending at the end position
valueOf(value)	Converts another datatype, such as an int or Boolean, into a string. Returns the converted value

There are several other methods you may find useful from time to time. You can learn these by examining the class file under your main PowerJ directory or by looking at the on-line help. The methods in table 7.1 are the ones you will use most frequently.

7.3   The StringBuffer class (java.lang.StringBuffer)

While the string class represents string constants (the value cannot be changed once the string is initialized), the StringBuffer class represents fully alterable string variables.

Many of the methods supported by the string class are also supported by the StringBuffer class. These include the length() and equals() methods. Table 7.2 shows the methods are supported by the String-Buffer class:

Table 7.2   StringBuffer Class Methods

Method	Usage
capacity()	Returns the integer value of the capacity of the StringBuffer
ensureCapacity(min)	Makes sure that the StringBuffer has the capacity specified in min (an integer value)
setLength(int)	Sets the length of the buffer to the value contained in int. If the new length is less than the current length, the string is truncated
append(value)	Appends value to the end of the StringBuffer. If value is a nonstring, it is converted prior to the append
insert(offset, value)	Inserts value in the StringBuffer beginning at the position in offset

7.4 *The integer class (java.lang.Integer)*

As with strings, Java and PowerJ also provide you with classes for the numerical datatypes. These classes include the float, long, double, and integer classes. Since these classes share most methods, we will examine in depth only the integer class.

The most commonly used methods of the integer class are shown in table 7.3. They deal mostly with conversions.

Table 7.3   Integer Class Methods

Method	Usage
toString()	Converts the Integer to a string and returns the string value
parseInt(string)	Converts a string value to an Integer and stores the Integer in the Integer class.

7.5 *The point class (java.awt.Point)*

The point class represents a position on a window in x and y locations. The position is accessible using the values stored in the member variables `point.x` and `point.y`.

7.6 *The dimension class (java.awt.Dimension)*

The dimension class contains two member variables, which describe a rectangle in width and height. The member variables are accessible using `dimemsion.width` and `dimension.height`.

7.7 *The rectangle class (java.awt.Rectangle)*

The rectangle class describes a rectangle on the current window. It contains the same height and width information as the dimension class but also contains the x and y location of the rectangle. You can use a rectangle as a group box around controls on a window.

The rectangle class contains several useful methods (see table 7.4).

Table 7.4   Rectangle Class Methods

Method	Usage
reshape(x,y,width,height)	Changes the rectangle's size and position to the new coordinate's width and height
resize(width,height)	Changes the width and height of the rectangle but leaves its coordinates alone
move(x,y)	Changes the coordinates only
translate(incrX,incrY)	Changes the coordinates by adding the increment values to x and y
grow(incrhorz,incrvert)	Changes the size of the rectangle by increasing the width and height by the increment values while leaving the center in place

These functions deal with altering the rectangle's position and size. There are other methods that can be used to determine whether a given point is inside or outside the rectangle, as well as for other purposes. Consult the on-line help for details.

7.8   *Miscellaneous classes*

In addition to the classes outlined above, Java and PowerJ implement several additional classes, which you may find useful from time to time but which are used less often than the ones we have just discussed in detail. These classes are Font, Toolkit, and URL. You can refer to the on-line documentation for more information about these classes.

Proper use of the standard types of classes is essential to getting the most out of PowerJ. The examples we will build later in the book will rely on the classes and their methods where appropriate.

7.9   *Summary*

In this chapter we learned that, in addition to classes that give you standard components with which to build your applications, Java and PowerJ also provide you with classes for each of the standard datatypes. The advantage of using these classes instead of the primitive datatypes is that each class also contains methods that make it easy to work with and manipulate the data.

The code editor &
drag-and-drop programming

In this chapter we will do the following:

- Take a closer look at the PowerJ code editor
- Learn how to customize the code editor
- Learn more about the Reference Card and drag-and-drop programming

No programming environment has yet eliminated the need to actually write code and PowerJ is no exception. To make your coding tasks more pleasant, PowerJ comes equipped with a heavy-duty code editor and a unique drag-and-drop programming interface, which actually teaches you how to program in Java as you develop applications. This chapter discusses the PowerJ code editor and its drag-and-drop programming system.

8.1 The PowerJ code editor

The PowerJ code editor is an extremely advanced editor, which not only allows you to write Java code for your applications but actually helps you write it (when you use the Reference Card system). In fact, you can use the code editor and the drag-and-drop interface to learn Java programming as you write your first applications. You have already seen this in action earlier when we wrote our first applications, and you will use it even more extensively as you continue to program using PowerJ.

8.2 Opening the code editor

Whenever you ask to modify or look at the code in an event handler, the code editor window will open. You can examine an event handler either by right-clicking an object or form and then selecting events from the pop-up menu or you can use the Events tab of the Object Inspector. No matter how you navigate to the event, the same code editor window is displayed (see figure 8.1).

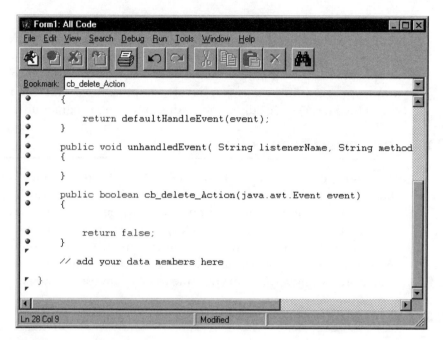

Figure 8.1   Code editor

Figure 8.1 shows the code editor displaying the action event for a button. Notice that the editor already contains code to create the event handler and to return a false value from the event. The initial code for an event is always the same (per object type)—for example, the code for a command button's action event is always as follows:

```
public boolean cb_buttonname_Action(powesoft.jcm.event.ActionEvent
    event)
    {

        return false;

    }
```

Those of you familiar with Java programming will recognize this as a standard function prototype. The function name is a combination of the name of the object and the event to which the function corresponds (in this case action). You can also determine that the function returns a Boolean value (either `true` or `false`).

When you open the code editor, you will notice that the cursor is placed at a point on the line directly below the opening curly brace for the function. This is PowerJ's way of teaching you that this is where you must place your code in order for the function to properly process the event.

You will also see that the editor places

```
return false;
```

at the end of the function. PowerJ will always place a `return` value in a function call to serve as the default `return` value. You will alter this in your code as necessary.

8.3 Color your world

In the bad old days of C (or even COBOL) programming, we coded on a screen editor that displayed everything as green text against the monitor's black background. When Windows took over the development world, things got better. Then we had black text on a white background.

Modern development environments display code in full color and the colors are used to enable you to determine variable types and function types at a glance. PowerJ is no exception and its editor is fully color enabled.

8.4 Coding in color

As you type in your source code, the editor uses color to indicate various elements in your code—for example, if you start to type a character string such as "String," the editor displays the partial string in bright red. When you close the quotes—"String"—the editor changes the entire string to a different color. This reminds you to always enter the closing quote.

By default, the editor displays comments in bright blue; reserved words (as, if, and while) are shown in green. Some code generated by PowerJ is read-only and you cannot change it with the editor. Read-only code is displayed in gray to distinguish it from normal code (gray is the usual disabled text color on most systems). If you don't like this color-coding scheme, the Tools menu of the code editor window will allow you to change the colors for various program elements using the dialog shown in figure 8.2. Color selections made here remain the same for all projects.

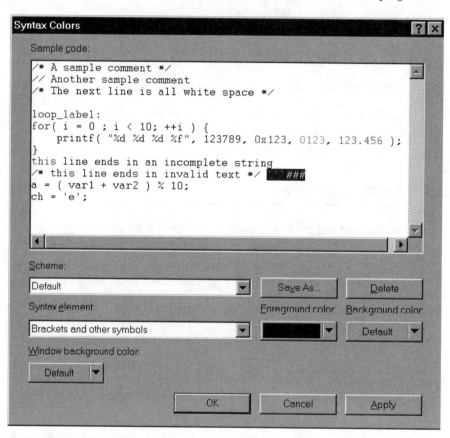

Figure 8.2 **Syntax colors**

8.5 *Saving source code*

When you save your project, the entire project, including the source code, is saved. However, there may be times when you want to save source code as a text file for later use in another project. To do this, use the code editor File...Export menu item to save the current function to a text file. This saves a copy of the function you are editing in a text file.

8.6 *Undo and redo*

The Edit menu contains an Undo command for undoing the most recent editing actions. Using the Undo function several times in a row undoes the same number of editing actions. The number of edits you can undo is only restricted by the amount of memory available.

The Edit menu also contains a Redo command, which repeats the last step you undid. If you use Undo several times and then the use Redo the same number of times, you will get back to where you started.

8.7 *Two editors in one*

The PowerJ code editor comes in two sizes. The default size is the big editor; it shows the code for an entire form. All event handlers currently defined for the form are viewable using the code editor in this mode. You can scroll through the editor using the scroll bar and see all the code currently defined for the form.

Conversely, the small editor mode shows the code for only a single event handler.

Tip

It really makes no difference which mode you use, so choose the one you like best. Always use the big editor mode when you need to do global find/replace operations.

You can pick the editor mode under the Tools menu by clicking Options. On the Editor tab shown in figure 8.3, select "Edit each event with a new editor." This will cause PowerJ to default to the small editor mode.

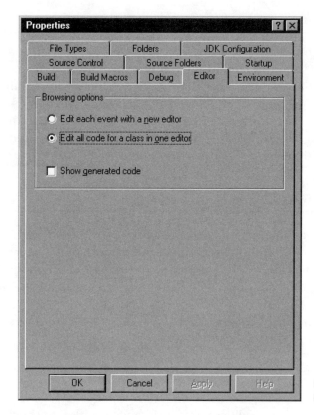

Figure 8.3
Editor tab

8.8 *Drag-and-drop programming*

PowerJ's claim to fame is its unique drag-and-drop programming interface, which we worked with when we built our to-do list. Using the drag-and-drop interface, PowerJ walks you through creating the code to make your objects behave the way you want them to. It is possible to write fairly sophisticated applications using the drag-and-drop interface with very little knowledge of Java coding at all.

Drag-and-drop programming makes it easy to construct Java statements that refer to objects on a form. The following sections are designed to give you a more detailed overview of the use of drag-and-drop programming.

8.8.1 *The reference card*

The heart of the drag-and-drop programming interface is the Reference Card. You use the Reference Card to drill down to the correct statement, build the correct syntax (without errors!), and paste it directly into your code. Although we have used the Reference Card in our initial applications and are familiar with it, let's take a closer look now.

Note

If you do not have a code editor window open, you cannot open the Parameter Wizard from the Reference Card. When you select an entry from the Reference Card, the parameters button is grayed out, so you cannot press it. There is no point in calling the Parameter Wizard if it has nowhere to place the code it constructs.

Open the reference card

To begin to code using PowerJ's drag-and-drop programming, you must first open the Reference Card. There are two ways to do this.

The first approach is to use drag-and-drop programming. To do this, drag the object you want to act on from the Form Design window to the code editor window, where you want to specify an action and drop it there. This approach has the advantage of opening the Reference Card at the point that lists all the actions you can perform on that particular object. Opening the Reference Card in any other manner will require you to navigate to the particular point where you will find the code you need.

You can also open the Reference Card by selecting it from the Help menu.

Note

You can also drag an object from the object window to the code editor to open the Reference Card. Dragging from the object window is often more practical than dragging from a Form Design window, especially if you are running short of space on your monitor.

As you drag over the code editor, the insertion point will move as you drag to show you where code will be added. When you release the cursor, the Reference Card will open and display the selections for the object type you dragged to the editor window. You can drill down through these selections to access the property you want. Figure 8.4 shows the Reference Card open to the choices for the command button and drilled to the Visible property.

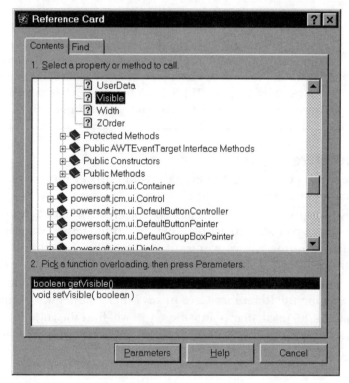

Figure 8.4
Reference Card

Notice that there are two functions listed for the Visible attribute.

```
setVisible()
getVisible()
```

You will often find that these functions come in pairs—one to set the value of the attribute and another to retrieve the value currently stored in the attribute into a variable.

The next step is to choose a function from the Reference Card to open the Parameter Wizard, which helps you create Java code to perform that action. You do this by double-clicking the name of the function you want (you can also single-click it and click the Parameters button, but why move the mouse?). Figure 8.5 shows the Parameter Wizard for the `setVisible()` function.

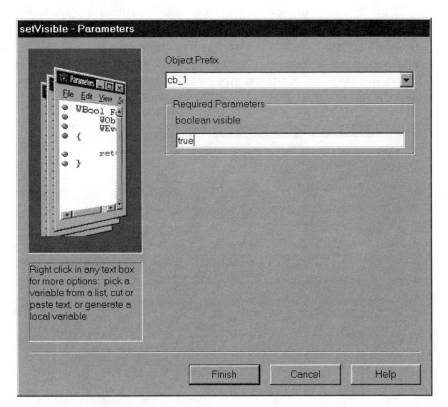

Figure 8.5   Parameter Wizard (setVisible)

You can set the parameter (the function in this case takes only one) to any value or variable as long as the value or variable meets the type requirement (in this case the Boolean has been set to `true`). In many cases, where you pass parameters to functions, clicking in the parameters field will enable a drop-down list of variables from which you can choose.

While it is possible to type this code directly into the code editor window (and experienced programmers will no doubt do exactly that), the beginning programmer can use drag-and-drop programming to create this code with very little typing of code or knowledge of the Java language.

8.8.2 *Methods that return values*

If the method you select returns a `result` value, the Parameter Wizard asks if you want this result assigned to a variable. If you click "Store in a variable," the Parameter Wizard will create a suitable variable declaration as well as a statement that assigns the method result to that variable. If you use `getVisible()`, for example, to determine if a button is visible, the Parameter Wizard displays the following (see figure 8.6):

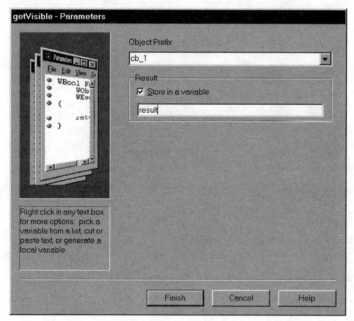

Figure 8.6
Parameter Wizard

The return value from the `getVisible()` function will be stored in a variable called `result`. When you click Finish, the following code is generated:

```
boolean                     result;
result = cb_1.getVisible();
```

Since the variable (`result`) has been created by PowerJ and is of the proper type to receive the return value, no errors are possible.

8.8.3 *The object prefix*

The Parameter Wizard always has an area where you can enter an object prefix. This is where you specify the object that you want to call the method against. When you are using drag-and-drop programming, PowerJ prefills in the object prefix with the name of the object where the drag-and-drop operation is started. You can change this to another object name by selecting that object from the drop-down list.

8.8.4 *Reference card organization*

In addition to helping you learn to code in Java by teaching you proper Java syntax, the Reference Card also helps you learn the Java class structure. It does this by organizing the objects into high-level topics divided by class.

If you open the Reference Card directly from the Help menu, so that it opens at the top of its tree structure, you can better see how it is organized. Each high-level topic is a base Java class—for example, *java.awt*. If you expand the *java.awt* class, you see all the classes that are inherited from *java.awt*—for example, *java.awt.Button*, which defines a basic command button, is shown under the *java.awt* tree structure. Expanding *java.awt.Button* will reveal all the methods defined for the class.

Using the Reference Card in this manner can assist you in learning the Java class hierarchy. The entire class hierarchy is reproduced in the appendix.

8.9 *Summary*

From this quick review of some of the coding features of PowerJ, you can tell that PowerJ truly represents the next generation of development environments. Hopefully, the features included in PowerJ will soon become a mainstream feature in all development environments and make all our jobs much easier.

Working with forms and *9* and windows

This chapter takes a look at various ways of using forms and windows. Since PowerJ is designed around creating graphical applications, this chapter will lay the groundwork for creating the user interfaces that your end users will appreciate and find pleasing. You will also learn how to manipulate the forms' source code files to make project management easier, as well as how to open and close forms at run time. We will learn how to extend the basic forms by adding member functions of our own and discuss how to call those member functions at run time.

9.1   Creating new forms

The basics of how to create a new form are explained in detail in chapter 4 and need not be repeated here. Much of this chapter deals with situations where your application has more than one form.

9.2   Types of forms

There are four basic form types in PowerJ:

1   Applet—used in an application that runs within a Web browser.

2   Frame—used in stand-alone applications. This type of form can have a menu.

3   Modal dialog—a pop-up type window that always has focus. When a modal dialog is open, no other window in the application can get focus. All processing stops (except for that contained within the modal dialog) until it is closed.

4   Modeless dialog—similar to a modal dialog except that other windows may receive focus.

Other form types, such as database frame or database modal dialog, are just subclasses of these four basic types.

9.3   Navigating through forms at design time

If your project contains more than one form, you will need to navigate through them at design time, in order to place the components you desire upon each form. PowerJ provides several different ways to do this.

If the Form Design window for that form is already open, and you can see any part of it, just click on it to bring it to the front. If the Form Design window for the form you want is open, but hidden by other windows, click Window from the PowerJ menu and select the form you want. This will bring it to the top.

If the Form Design window is not open, you can open it by opening the Objects window (see figure 9.1).

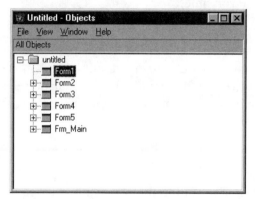

Figure 9.1
Objects window

Right-click on the form you want to open and then select Open. Alternatively, you may open the Files window (under View on the main menu) (see figure 9.2), and double-click on the file name to open the form.

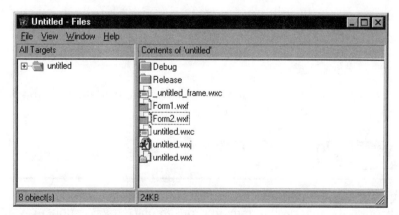

Figure 9.2 Files window

9.4 Setting the main form

The main form of a project is the form that is initially displayed when the application begins running. By default, this is first form created in the project. You can determine which form is your project's main form by opening the Classes window. The main form is marked with an icon showing a running person, as shown in figure 9.3.

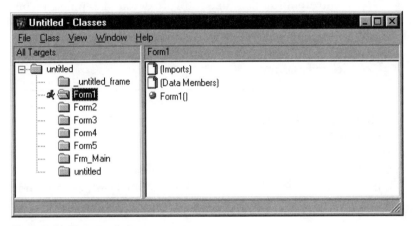

Figure 9.3 Classes window

To change the main form, right-click on the form you want to become the main form and select Main Form from the pop-up menu.

9.5 Form code

All form code is contained within the form's source file. The source file contains the class definition from which the form is instantiated at run time. Events are defined as member functions of a form class—for example, the routine that handles the action event for a command button on Form1 is declared as follows.

```
public boolean cb_1_Action(java.awt.Event event);
```

Since methods and events are members of the form class, they can usually be called from within the form without qualifying the call with the form name. If you issue a `setText()` call from within the form code, the call will operate on the form without having to be qualified.

```
Form_1.setText("New Caption")
```

Note

The event routines for a form are declared as public member functions. However, do not call them directly from code outside the form class. This violates the object-oriented rule of encapsulation. In fact, proper encapsulation would require that the methods be declared as private.

9.6   Adding new functions and events to the form

Although we will talk about classes in more detail in chapter 13, we can take the time here to learn how to add member functions, events, and properties to the form class. That task is performed using the Classes window.

9.6.1 Adding a user function

To add a user function to the form class, just right-click on the form name and select Insert...User Function. This will open the window shown in figure 9.4, where you specify the function prototype.

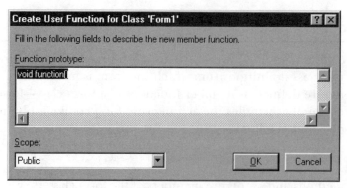

Figure 9.4
Function prototype

The function prototype specifies the return datatype of the function and the number and type of its arguments—for example:

```
public boolean myfunction(int someint)
```

is the prototype for a function that accepts a single integer as a parameter and returns a Boolean value.

You may also specify the scope of the function. The scope controls where in your application it is valid to call your function. Once you have specified your function prototype and clicked OK, a script-editor window will open, as shown in figure 9.5, where you can write the code needed to make your function work as desired.

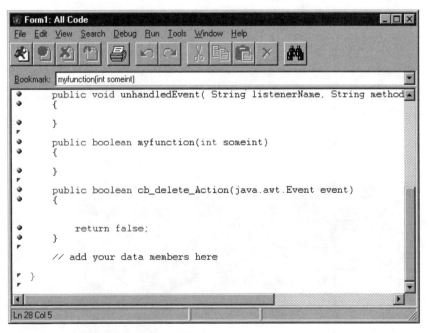

Figure 9.5   Script-editor window

9.6.2 *Adding a new property to a form*

Properties make up the data of a form—in other words, a property is simply a variable that exists in the form class. You can add new properties by right-clicking the form name in the class window and clicking Insert...Property. This will open the Property Wizard, shown in figure 9.6. This is where you specify the name of the property and its datatype.

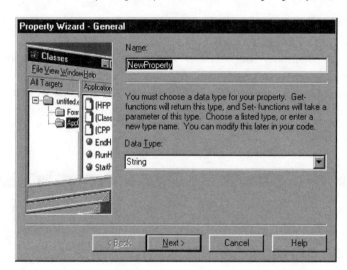

Figure 9.6
Property Wizard

Once these values are filled in, clicking the Next button will take you to the second page of the Property Wizard, as shown in figure 9.7.

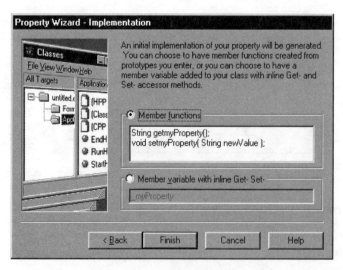

Figure 9.7
Property Wizard
(page 2)

This page presents you with two choices. The first is to create two member functions in the form class, the getPropertyName() and set-PropertyName() functions. The second choice is to create a member variable in the form class with inline get and set functions. Since almost all of the Java classes are implemented using the getPropertyName() and setPropertyName() methods, it is highly recommended that you choose that approach.

Clicking Finish will generate the code needed to add the new property, and a new code-editor window will open to allow you to add the code that implements the desired functionality (see figure 9.8).

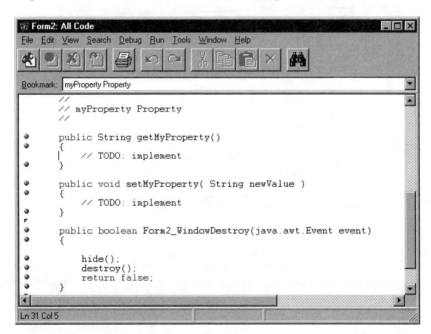

Figure 9.8   Code-editor window (property)

In chapter 13 we will learn what code to place in these methods in order to implement the desired functionality.

9.6.3   *Adding new methods*

Sometimes you want to add a new method to a form but not associate it with a form variable or property. You might do this, for example, if you need to perform some calculations on data. You would create a function that accepts as arguments the data upon which it is to work and returns the result of the calculations.

To add a new method to your form class, just right-click the form name and click Insert...Method. This will open the Method Wizard, as shown in figure 9.9.

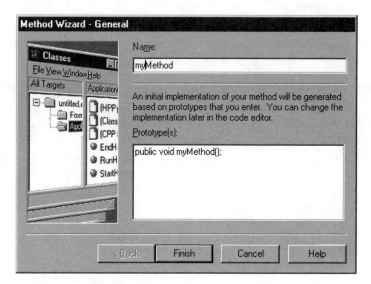

Figure 9.9   Method Wizard

Here, you specify the name of the method and its prototype. Clicking Finish will open a code-editor window ready for you to write the code that makes the method perform its task (see figure 9.10).

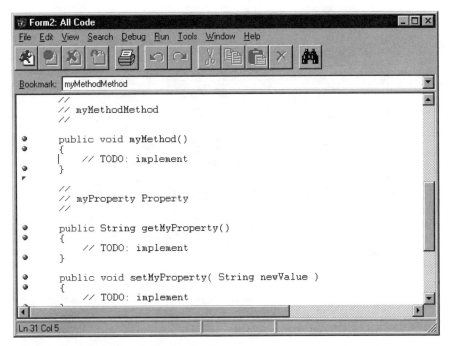

Figure 9.10   Code-editor window (method)

As with adding a property to a form, we will learn what code to place in these new methods when we take a closer look at classes (remember, a form is just a class) in chapter 13.

9.6.4 Adding events to forms

In the same way you add user functions, properties, and methods to a form, you can add a user event by invoking the Event Wizard, as shown in figure 9.11.

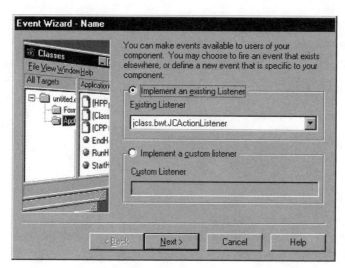

Figure 9.11
Event Wizard (Name)

There you may choose to trigger an existing event or define a new event. If you select "Implement an existing Listener" and click Next, you will see the page shown in figure 9.12, which indicates that you are not required to specify a data structure for the event (since the data structure for the existing event will be used).

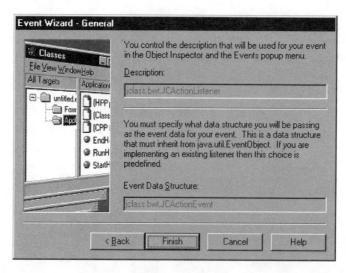

Figure 9.12
Event Wizard
(General)

If, on the previous page, you had elected to create a custom event, the second page of the wizard would resemble the screen shown in figure 9.13, and you would have been asked to define an event data structure. This is the structure that will be passed to the event when it is fired. You may enter a structure that you have created on your own or you may enter an existing structure.

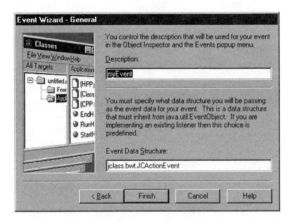

Figure 9.13
Event Wizard (General, page 2)

Clicking Finish will open a code-editor window showing the generated code for the event (see figure 9.14).

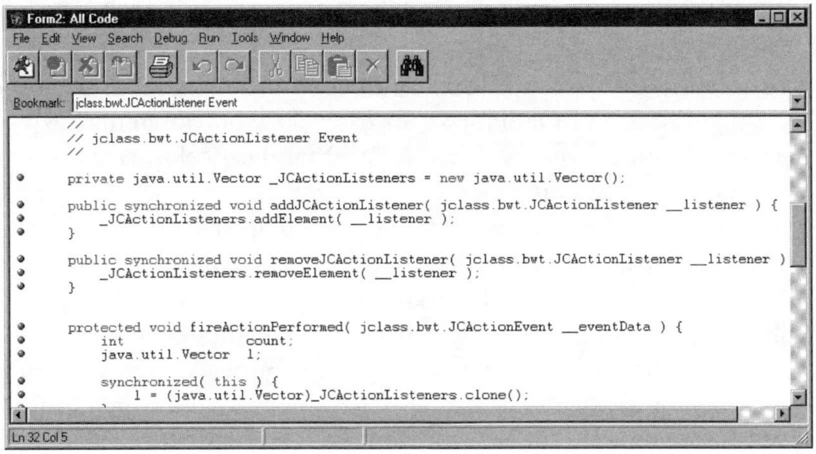

Figure 9.14   Generated code event

9.7   *Opening forms at run time*

When you begin program execution, the main form will be opened auto-matically. As your user interacts with the application, you will need to use code to open any other necessary forms. This is normally done by creating an object of the form type and invoking its `create` method, as follows:

```
Form2 myform = new Form2( );
myForm.create( );
```

9.8   *Destroying a form*

You must explicitly destroy all forms that you create at run time. You do this by issuing a `destroy()` call.

```
Formname.destroy();
```

In order to release the memory used by the form, you must also issue a `dispose call()`. Failure to do this may lead to memory leaks in your application.

```
Formname.dispose();
```

9.9   *The WindowDestroy event*

If the user clicks the Close button for a form (upper right corner), it gen-erates a `WindowDestroy` event on the form. It is there that you can handle processing to clean up data not needed after the form is closed or to destroy the form in memory—for example, you can generate a message asking "Closing Window. Are you Sure?" and cancel the close operation if users change their mind.

To prevent the form from closing, all you need to do is return `true` from the `WindowDestroy` event. This will prevent the window from being closed.

That's an overview of working with forms. Remember that the user interacts with your application through the components you place on the forms you design. Proper design and use of forms is essential to the suc-cess of your applications. Proper knowledge of how to manipulate forms and form classes in the development environment is crucial to getting the most out of PowerJ.

9.10 *Putting some of this to work*

In order to see how you can open and close forms in your programs at run time and how you can create and use a user-defined function, let's build a small application that does just that.

Start by creating a new Java 1.02 applet project. On the main form place three text field objects and two command buttons. Label one command button Open Window and the other Call Function as shown in figure 9.15.

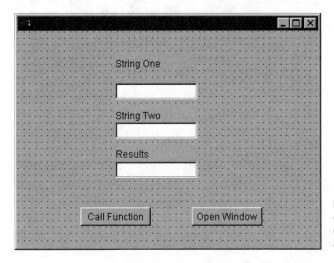

Figure 9.15
Open Window and
Call Function
command buttons

As you can see from our design, we are going to demonstrate two techniques in this application. The first demo will involve creating a user function that will accept as arguments the strings from the top two text boxes and will return the results of concatenating those two strings. The results will be displayed in the third text box.

The second demo will use the Open Window button to open another form. That form will be a simple modeless dialog, which does nothing but contain a Close button that will close the dialog when clicked.

The next step in creating this application is to create our user function. To do this, open the Classes window, select the form name, and then click Class...New...User Function from the menu. This will open the user function definition dialog, where you can prototype the function (see figure 9.16)

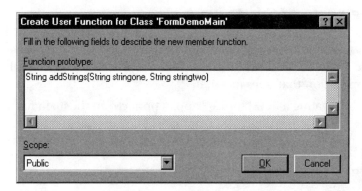

**Figure 9.16
User function
definition dialog**

The prototype for our function is as follows:

```
String addStrings(String stringone, String stringtwo)
```

This means that we are creating a function that accepts two strings as arguments and returns a string as a result. The name of the function is addString.

Once you have defined the function as needed, click OK and a code-editor window will open for us to write the code we need to make the function work. The code to add the two strings is simple.

```
String resultString;  //declare a variable to hold the result
resultString = stringone + "" + stringtwo; //add the arguments, putting
a blank in between
return resultString; // return the result
```

Now you have to write the code in the action event of the Call Function button that will retrieve the text typed into the first two text boxes, call the addStrings function, and place the result of that function call in the third box. It doesn't matter if you use the Reference Card or just write the code in the code editor yourself (I did), as long as the result looks something like this:

```
Stringtext1;
String                        text2;
String                     result;
text1 = textf_1.getText();
text2 = textf_2.getText();
result = addStrings(text1,text2);
textf_3.setText(result);
return false;
```

After you have the code in place, all you need to do is run the application, type something in the first two text fields, and then click on the Call Function button. The results will look like the screen shown in figure 9.17.

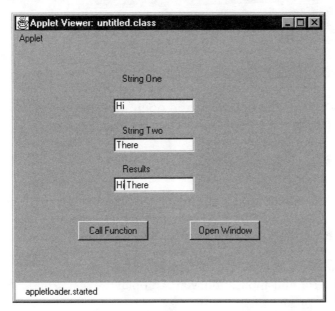

Figure 9.17
Applet Viewer

9.11 *Opening another window*

Now let's write code for the Open Window button that will open another window. Before we can do that, we have to create another window. You already know how to do that, so I'll just say that we will create a window of type modeless dialog using the Form Wizard and give it the name modelessdlg. On that form place a single command button and label that button Close. Make the form appear similar to that shown in figure 9.18.

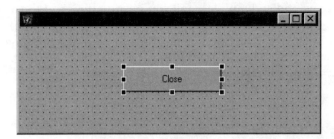

Figure 9.18
Close button form

Now, go back to the first form and open the code-editor window to the action event of the Open Window button. The code you want there is as follows:

```
modelessdlg mdlg = new modelessdlg();
mdlg.crate();
```

If you run the application at this point and click the Open Window button, the dialog will open. But the Close button on the dialog will not work. You need the following code in its action event to make it do so:

```
destroy();
```

Now if you run the application, you can open the dialog and close it by using its Close button.

Although these are very simple examples of user functions and dialog windows, the techniques you have just learned will be useful to you as you learn to write more complex applications.

9.12 *Summary*

In this chapter we learned how to create and use the different types of PowerJ forms. We learned how to use the Form Wizard to add forms to our projects. We took a look at what code is used to open and close forms at run time. We went on to learn how to add functions and methods to a form and how to call those in code.

10

Working with targets and projects

In this chapter we will learn about the following:

- Target Wizard
- Different kinds of targets and what each is used for
- How to add targets to projects
- Compiler settings for our targets
- Differences between debug versions of targets and release versions

175

This chapter looks at the use of targets and projects in PowerJ. Here is where you will learn how to organize your application components, build your application, and organize projects.

10.1 What are targets?

A target is an applet, a Web application, a stand-alone Java *EXE*, a Java library, or a *DLL*. The type of target corresponds to the type of project you initially create. PowerJ builds targets from the source files included in your project.

Every PowerJ target is stored in its own separate directory. By default, PowerJ creates target folders in the projects folder under the main PowerJ directory, but you can override that if you want. The default name for a target directory is based on the name of the target itself—for example, if your target is named *todo.EXE*, the default name for the target folder is todo. When you first save a project, PowerJ allows you to specify the directory that will hold the project files. It is at that point you are permitted to change the names from the default values.

10.2 What are projects?

A project is composed of one or more targets—for example, your project may contain both a Java application and a Java applet. You can view all of the targets that comprise your project by opening the Targets window, available under View on the main PowerJ menu bar. The Targets window is shown in figure 10.1.

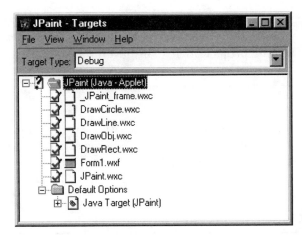

Figure 10.1
Targets window

PowerJ creates a project file for each project. The project file is a text file listing all the targets that belong in the project. Project files have the file extension *.wxp.*

By default, PowerJ places the project file in the same folder as the first target created for the project, but you can save the project file in a different folder if you want. You will never have to edit a project file directly, because PowerJ will make all changes necessary as you work within your project.

When you start PowerJ, it automatically creates a new project. At that point the project name is "untitled." The "untitled" project is stored in the temporary folder that you specified when you installed PowerJ. You should always save the project with its own name as soon as possible after it is created.

10.3 Starting new projects after PowerJ has started

You can start a new project at any time during a PowerJ session by selecting File...New Project from the PowerJ menu bar.

10.4 Opening an existing project

You will often want to open an existing project during a PowerJ session. You do this by clicking File...Open Project from the PowerJ menu bar. A standard file dialog window will open, and you will be able to navigate to the directory that contains the project upon which you wish to work.

You may only have one project open at any given time.

 Note

You may also use Windows Explorer to navigate to the project directory and then double-click on the desired project file. This will load PowerJ with the desired project instead of a new project.

10.5 *Closing projects*

When you close PowerJ, it automatically closes the open project. You may also close a project by clicking File...Close Project. PowerJ will always check to see if there are any unsaved changes in the project and will prompt you to save the changes before allowing the project to be closed.

10.6 *Running your project's targets*

When you want to run a target program for testing purposes from within PowerJ, all you need to do is click the Run icon from the PowerJ toolbar. When you run a target, PowerJ compiles your source code and links the result into an executable program. PowerJ displays a dialog box with a progress bar showing the compilation progress.

If the compile completes without errors, PowerJ will start executing the program and the main form window will be displayed. However, if PowerJ finds errors in your code, it will open a code-editor window displaying the line of code where the first error was found. Error messages will be displayed to inform you of the nature of the error. Error messages are designated by a red X in the lefthand margin of the editor window and are displayed in red text (in the default color scheme). You can move from error to error by using the menu items Next Error and Previous Error from the Search menu item on the code-editor window's menu bar.

You can also view errors in a different way, by using the error log shown in figure 10.2.

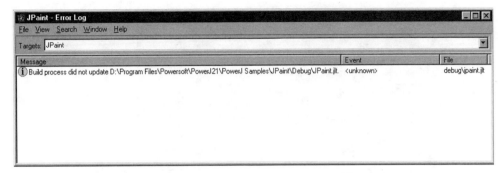

Figure 10.2   Error log

The icons next to the message indicate the severity of the error; an exclamation mark indicates an error that prevented completion of the build and an "i" indicates a warning of problems, but the problems are not severe enough to stop the build.

10.7   *Run options*

By default, PowerJ sets run options according to the type of program you are executing—for example, the default options for an applet specify that PowerJ should start the applet viewer and execute the applet from within the viewer, while the options for a Java application specify that the application should be run with a Java console.

You can change the default behavior for running a program by specifying appropriate run options. The run options are available from the File menu of the Targets window. Run options are specified using the run options dialog, as shown in figure 10.3.

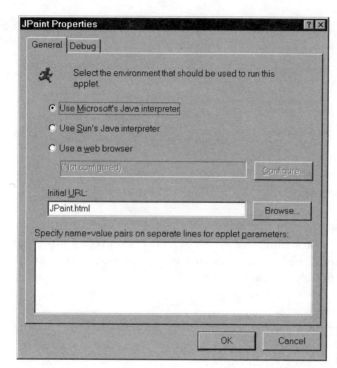

Figure 10.3
Run options dialog
(General tab)

On the General tab of this dialog you can set the environment that should be used to execute the program, while on the Debug tab, shown in figure 10.4. You can set whether or not you wish to run with the debugger turned on or off.

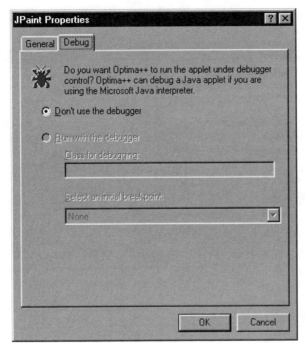

**Figure 10.4
Run options dialog
(Debug tab)**

Different types of targets allow different types of run options. To become familiar with the options for the different targets, open the run options dialog for each of the different types and review the possible settings.

10.8 *Debugging your program*

PowerJ offers a variety of debugging methods. These will be discussed at length in chapter 11.

10.9 *Target versions*

PowerJ creates two different versions of each target: the debug and release versions. These are stored in two separate directories beneath your main project directory. The folders are called, appropriately, Debug and Release. These folders hold only the compiled code of the targets, not the source code from which the target is compiled. The source code is always stored in the main project directory.

To save disk space, you may delete all the contents of the Debug and the Release folders. Do this by clicking Clean in the Run menu.

Note

PowerJ will recreate these files each time the program is executed. Normally, PowerJ only creates those files whose source code has changed since the last compile. For that reason deleting all the files in the Release and Debug directories will increase compile time.

10.10 Project backups

At times, PowerJ will create backup files of your project. Backup files are identified by having a tilde (~) character in the middle of the file name extension—for example, the backup file for *Form1.wxf* is named *Form1.w~f*. If you are sure you do not need them, these files can be safely deleted.

Note

These temporary files are used by PowerJ when recovering a project that was not properly saved when a PowerJ session was terminated. Deleting these files will affect PowerJ's ability to recover from that type of crash situation.

10.11 Working with projects

A project can consist of more than one program; it can control multiple executables and libraries. Since each program, as well as library is contained in its own target, you will need to know how to add targets to projects and how to add files to targets.

10.11.1 Adding new targets to your project

As you assemble your multiprogram project, you will need to add targets. You can either add targets that already exist as part of another project or you can create new targets.

Creating new targets

You create a new target using the Target Wizard. Open the Target Wizard by clicking File...New...Target from the PowerJ menu bar. The first page of the Target Wizard is shown in figure 10.5. This is where you select the target type.

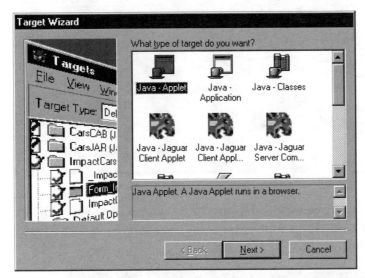

Figure 10.5
Target Wizard

Depending upon the type of target, the next pages of the wizard may appear differently. Clicking Next will take you to the second page of the dialog, as shown in figure 10.6, where you will elect whether or not to use the PowerJ framework in your program. If you do not elect to use the framework, you will not be able to take advantage of all of PowerJ's features, such as the Reference Card and drag-and-drop programming.

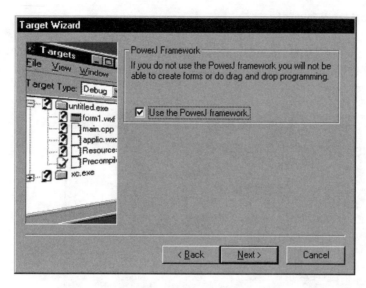

Figure 10.6
Target Wizard
(page 2)

Next, you will be asked to specify the Java version you wish to use (see figure 10.7). This is where you specify the version of Java you will use to create the target.

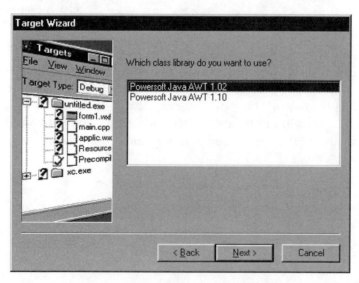

Figure 10.7
Target Wizard
(page 3)

Next you are asked to specify the directory that will contain the target files (see figure 10.8).

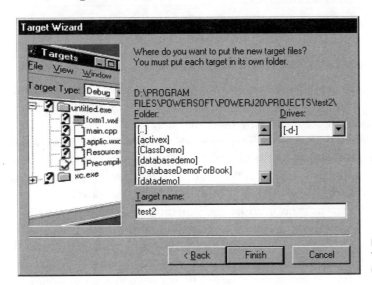

Figure 10.8
Target Wizard
(page 4)

Clicking Finish will create the target and display a blank Form Design window for the target's first form. The type of the form will be that specified for targets of that type in the startup options.

Adding an existing target to a project

You can also add existing targets to your project. To do this, click File...Add File. This will open a standard file open dialog. Navigate to and select the file you want (target files have *.wxt* extensions) and click OK.

PowerJ will ask if you want the current target to depend upon the new target. Click Yes if you want the current target to be rebuilt any time the new target changes; click No if changes in the new target will not affect the current target.

10.11.2 Adding source files to targets

Targets consist of source files. Source files can be of the following types:

- Java source code files
- Java class files

- Image files (e.g., *.GIF* files)
- Library and *DLL* files
- Managed class definitions
- Forms
- Existing targets

You can add files to targets in a number of ways. You may use the Files window, the Targets window, or the File menu on the PowerJ menu bar. Each method behaves in the same manner.

To add a file using the Targets window, simply click File...Add File from the Targets window menu bar. You will be prompted to select the file and may be asked to specify whether you want to copy the files to the new target directory or leave the files in their original location. If you choose to leave the files in their original location, any changes you make to them in this project will affect other projects that use the files from that location, and any changes you make to them in other projects that use the files from that location will affect this project. Alternatively, if you choose to copy the files to the current target directory, any changes made to them there or to the original files will have no effect on the other.

10.11.3 *Adding classes*

You add new classes to a target by using the Class Wizard. You can open the Class Wizard by clicking File...New...Class from the Targets window menu bar, from the Classes window menu bar, or even from the main PowerJ menu bar. The first page of the Class Wizard is shown in figure 10.9.

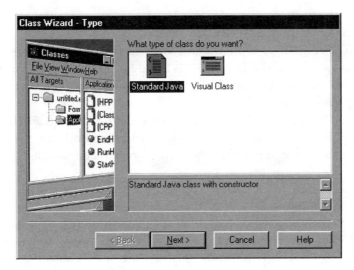

Figure 10.9
Class Wizard

Here you select between two different kinds of classes: the Standard Java Class or the Visual Class. The Visual Class is visual at design time but not at run time, while a Standard Java Class is any other type of class. The following steps will add a Standard Java Class to your target.

First, select Standard Java Class as the class type and click Next. This will take you to the second page of the Class Wizard, as shown in figure 10.10.

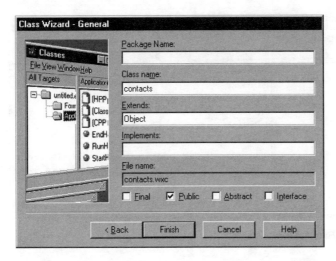

Figure 10.10
Class Wizard (page 2)

Here, you specify a name for the Java package that will contain the class, the name of the class, the name of the class from which this class will inherit (in the Extends text field), and the name of any interface this class implements, as well as whether the class is public, abstract or interface. We will discuss these choices at length in chapter 13, when we discuss creating and using classes in PowerJ.

Once you click Finish, PowerJ will create the class files and add them to the target. You can use the Classes window to add methods and properties to the class, as discussed in connection with forms in chapter 10.

Note

You will often add classes that already exist to a target. You do this when another project has a class you wish to use in your new target. To add a class that already exits, just add the file containing the class to the target.

10.11.4 Deleting targets and files

You can delete targets and source files from a project by using the Files window, as shown in figure 10.11. Just right-click the file you wish to delete and click Delete from the pop-up menu. Deleting a target or source file from a project does not remove the file from the disk.

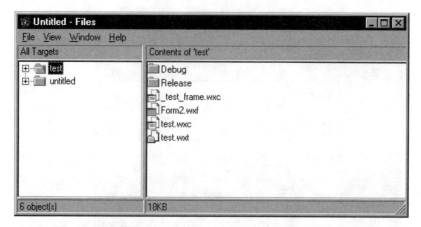

Figure 10.11   Files window

Note

You can also delete classes from the Classes window and delete files from the Targets window. Follow the same procedure as outlined in the previous paragraph.

10.11.5 Building targets

Before your application can be executed, it must be built. You build a target by clicking Build under the Run menu of the main PowerJ menu bar. The target will be built using the build options currently specified for the target.

Build options

You access the build options through the Targets window. Simply expand the default options tree and right-click a file. Select Properties from the pop-up menu to invoke the target properties dialog, as shown in figure 10.12.

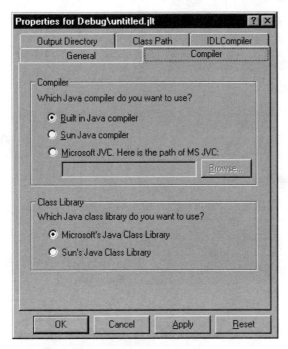

Figure 10.12
Target properties dialog

The Compiler tab is where you select the Java compiler to use when building your program. You may select from the PowerJ built-in compiler, the Sun compiler, or the Microsoft compiler. You also can select whether to use the Microsoft Java Class Library or the Sun Java Class Library as the base set of classes for your project. Remember that all the interface components will be inherited from this set of base classes and there are some differences between them. The Sun classes represent "pure" Java, while the Microsoft classes contain extensions to the Java language. Consequently, using Microsoft classes may affect the portability of your code and negate one of the main advantages of Java.

The Class Path tab, shown in figure 10.13, allows you to select the directories to search for class files, and the Output Directory tab allows you to specify the folder in which you want the compiled class files to be stored when you build the file (see figure 10.14).

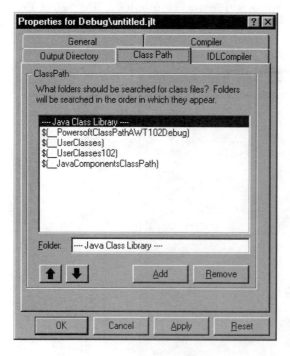

Figure 10.13
Class Path tab

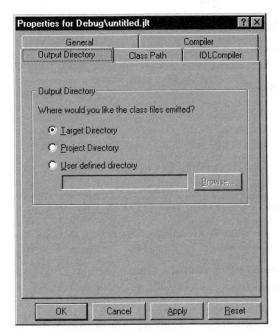

Figure 10.14
Output Directory tab

If you have changed the properties of a target away from the default and want to change them back to default options, right-click the file and click Use Default Build Options.

10.12 Debug versus release versions

PowerJ stores two different versions of your target files: the debug version and the release version. During the normal course of development, you will be working with the debug version. Debug versions contain debugging information, which is stored within the files when compiler optimizations are turned off.

When you are ready to create a version of the target for end users, you should build a release version. There is no debugging information stored in the files of the release version when compiler optimization is turned on. This results in the faster execution time desirable in the release version.

You specify which version you are building by using the Targets window, as shown in figure 10.15.

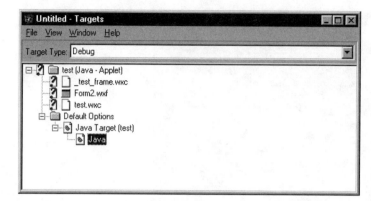

Figure 10.15
Targets window

Simply select Debug or Release from the target types drop-down list.

10.12.1 Separate build options for debug and release versions

The debug and release versions of a target can have different build options. These build options are managed separately, so if you change the build options for one version, you normally will have to change the build options for the other version. To do this, you set the builds option for one version and then change the target type and set the build options again.

10.13 Source control systems

Source control systems are applications that enable you to manage your source code files. Mostly, they are used in multideveloper environments to prevent one developer from overwriting changes made to files by the other developers. They also provide some version control functions that enable you to roll back changes made to the application from one build to the next. You select your source control system by using the Options dialog under the Tools menu. The choices are on the Source Control tab, as shown in figure 10.16.

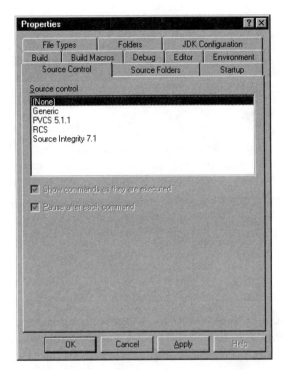

Figure 10.16
Source Control tab

PowerJ provides these source control functions:

- Check in
- Check out
- Get the latest revisions of files
- Undo check out operations
- View the checked-in/checked-out state of files
- Open a new source control project
- Set source control options

In addition to its native source control functions, PowerJ can also work with these third-party source control systems:

- PowerSoft ObjectCycle (version 1.0 and later)
- INTERSOLV PVCS (version 5.1 and later)

- MKS RCS (version 6.2 and later)
- MKS Source Integrity (version 3.2 and later)
- Any system that supports the Microsoft Source Code Control (SCC) interface.

10.13.1 ObjectCycle

PowerJ ships with a version of ObjectCycle, which is PowerSoft's own source control system. Since PowerJ ships with ObjectCycle, you will most likely use that as your source control system. You may use one of the third-party systems listed in the previous section. If you do, consult the manual of your third-party system for details on installing and configuring it to work with PowerJ.

You should be familiar with your source control system before configuring PowerJ to use it.

10.14 Summary

In this chapter we discussed how to use the Target Wizard to add targets to our projects. We looked at different types of targets and what they are used for. We discussed what different compiler settings may be useful for different target types and the difference between debug and release versions of the targets, as well as how to create each.

11

Debugging applications

In this chapter we will learn about the following:

- How to start the PowerJ debugger
- How to set stop points in our code
- How to run the application to our stop point
- How to use the debugger to step through the code
- How to examine the values of variables in our code
- Useful debugger windows

Of course, we all write perfect code the first time—every time, so we have no need for a debugger. But, for some reason, the folks at PowerSoft decided to include one in PowerJ anyway. This chapter takes a look at the PowerJ debugger and its use (just in case you ever need it).

11.1 *The art of debugging*

Debugging is impossible to teach. There are no rules for debugging that can be learned and then applied to find each and every bug. Every bug is unique and will fall to its own unique solution.

However, having said that, there are some approaches to debugging that are better than others. Most modern development environments allow you to examine your code, line by line, as the code is being executed. You can examine the values stored in each variable and see how the code is branching through your logic.

This chapter examines the PowerJ debugger and shows you how to use it. It is not to be considered a text on how to debug. Each reader will find his or her own debugging style.

11.2 *Setting breakpoints*

A breakpoint is a point in your executable code where you want to stop the normal execution of your program. While your program is stopped at a breakpoint, you can examine objects and variables used by the program. You can also change the value of variables and perform other, more advanced debugging tasks, such as examining the actual assembly code your computer is executing.

You set breakpoints in the code-editor window. To set a breakpoint, double-click the icon in the lefthand margin of the code editor at the line where you want to place the breakpoint. (Another way to set a breakpoint is to position the cursor on the line of code where you want program execution to pause and right-click. Then click Toggle Breakpoint.) A stop sign icon will appear in the left margin, indicating that a breakpoint has been set. Figure 11.1 illustrates a code-editor window with one breakpoint.

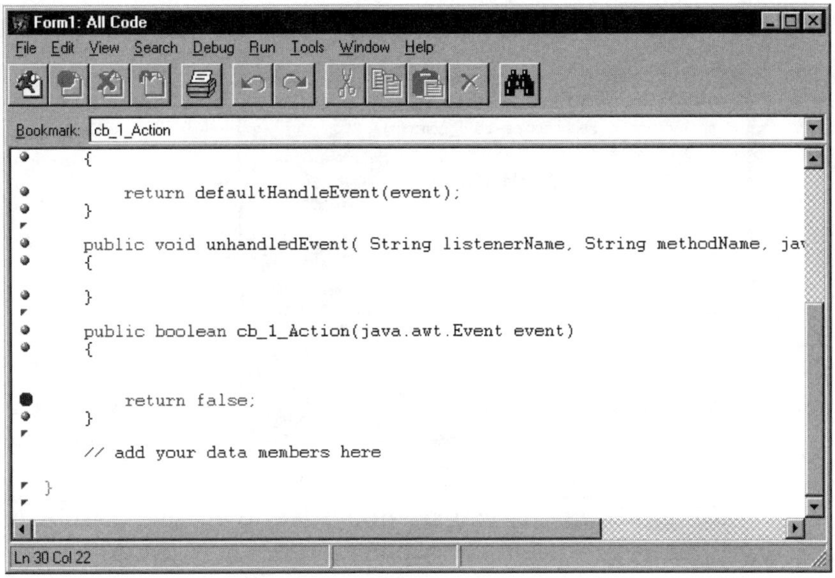

Figure 11.1   Code-editor window with one breakpoint

11.3 *Rules for setting breakpoints*

There are some simple rules for setting breakpoints. First, you can't set a breakpoint on a blank line or on a comment. If you set a breakpoint on a function prototype, the break will occur when the function is called. If you set a breakpoint on the closing brace that marks the end of the function, the break will occur when the function returns. If you set a breakpoint on any other line, the break occurs before the line is executed.

11.4 *Advanced breakpoint options*

PowerJ allows you to specify advanced breakpoint options, which define the behavior exhibited by the debugger when a breakpoint is encountered. You can specify these options by invoking the Breakpoints window, under the Run menu item on the main PowerJ menu bar. The Breakpoints window is shown in figure 11.2.

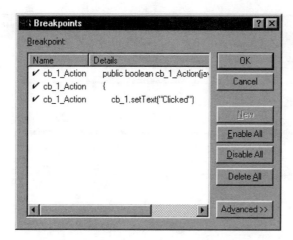

Figure 11.2
Breakpoints window

Using this window you are permitted to enable, disable, or delete breakpoints. An enabled breakpoint is one that is active—in other words, program execution will pause when the breakpoint is encountered. A disabled breakpoint is still present, but program execution will not pause.

Note

When the script editor is open, disabled breakpoints will be shown with a gray stop sign in the lefthand margin. The advantage of disabling breakpoints rather than deleting them is that you can always enable them again by using the Breakpoints window instead of searching through a code-editor window for the proper line.

Right-clicking a breakpoint in the list will display a set of operations that can be performed on that breakpoint. You may disable the breakpoint by selecting Disable from that menu. You may also disable the breakpoint by clicking on the check mark next to it. This will remove the check mark, signifying that the breakpoint is disabled. A disabled breakpoint has a gray stop sign icon in the code-editor window.

Clicking the Advanced button displays the advanced breakpoint options (see figure 11.3).

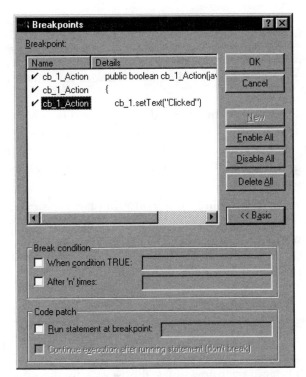

Figure 11.3
Advanced breakpoint options

The advanced options you may set here include creating a conditional breakpoint (one that will stop execution only when a certain condition is true), setting the debugger to stop after the line containing the breakpoint has been executed *n* number of times, setting an alternative line of code to execute in addition to the line at the breakpoint (use this to automatically alter the contents of a variable), and whether or not to continue execution after running the alternative code (the debugger will not stop program execution in that event).

11.5 *Running in the debugger*

To start running in the debugger, simply start your program in the normal way—by clicking on the run icon on the toolbar. When the program starts, it will execute normally until a breakpoint is encountered.

When a breakpoint is encountered, the behavior of the debugger will vary, depending upon the options that are specified for the breakpoint.

- If there is no condition set for the breakpoint, program execution is halted and the code editor will be displayed with the cursor located on the breakpoint.
- If a breakpoint has a condition specified, the condition is evaluated. If the condition is met, program execution is halted and the code editor will be displayed with the cursor located on the breakpoint. If the condition is not met, the program will continue to execute as if there were no breakpoint.
- If there is a code patch (alternative code) in place, it is executed. If you specified that execution should continue after the code patch, the program will continue as if there were no breakpoint. If not, then program execution is halted and the code editor will be displayed with the cursor located on the breakpoint.

11.6 Debug mode

When program execution is suspended, a Debugging window is opened with the cursor positioned on the line containing the breakpoint. You will notice that the Debugging window looks almost exactly the same as the code-editor window, but with a different set of toolbar icons and menu items. These new icons and menu items represent how you access the debugger features.

The red stop sign icon, which marked the line containing the breakpoint in the code-editor window will now have a yellow pointer in it indicating that this is the next line of code to be executed. The Debugging window is shown in figure 11.4. It is at this point you have complete access to the debugger features.

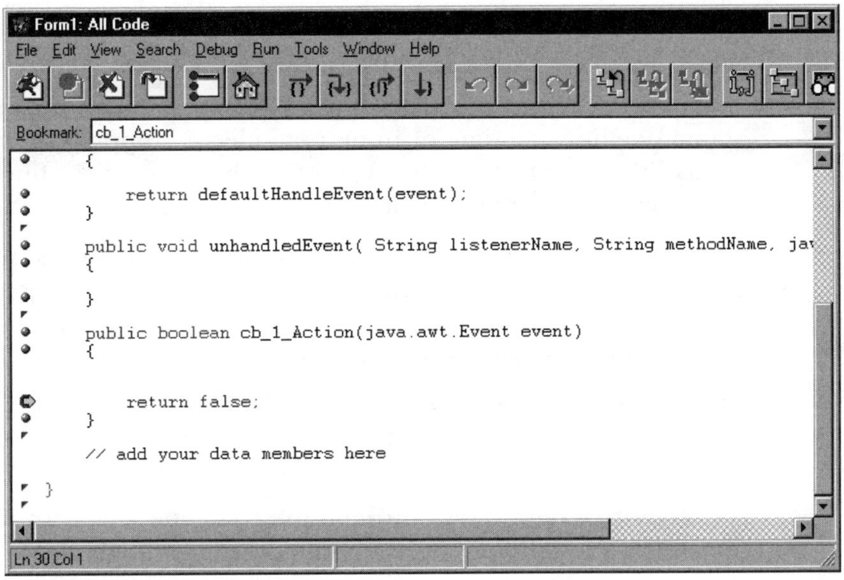

Figure 11.4   Debugging window

11.7 *Stepping through the code*

Although there are many wonderful and powerful features of the PowerJ debugger that make it a great tool for examining the details of your application, you will find that the main use of the debugger is in executing your code line by line to probe for errors in logic and values stored in variables. PowerJ allows you to perform this task using the main Debugging window.

When your application is suspended at a breakpoint, several icons and menu choices on the Debugging window become available to you. These choices include the following:

- Run: Continue the program's execution run normally from the point it was suspended. If the program hits another breakpoint, it will halt execution again.

- Restart: Start the program again from the beginning. This will reset all program objects and variables to their initialized state.

- Terminate: Stop program execution and return to the PowerJ design mode session.

- Stepping options: Stepping options allow you to execute the program one line at a time or in discrete pieces, stopping again after every line or on the next breakpoint, so that you can see the results of the execution of that single line.

You can step through the program in several different ways. You can elect to run to cursor, which will execute every line of the program between the current breakpoint and the cursor position. Just click on the line you want to run to and select Run to Cursor.

Likewise, Skip to Cursor moves the execution point to the line where the cursor is located but does not execute any lines of code in between the current breakpoint and the cursor location.

The Step Over action steps through the code one line at a time and executes each line but does not step line by line through any function calls that you step over.

The Step Into action behaves exactly like Step Over except that it does step line by line through any function calls that you step into. You can use Step Into to step through nested function calls (those functions called as parameters to another function).

The Step Out action executes the rest of the current function and stops when the function returns.

The Step Next action executes until reaching the next line of source code. It is typically used to allow loops to execute without stepping through each line of the loop *n* times.

11.8 *Examining values in variables*

Examining the values stored in variables at a particular moment in program execution is another part of debugging that PowerJ makes easy. If you want to see a value in a variable you can see in the Debugging window, just point to it with the cursor. The value will appear in a tooltip-type pop-up.

If you want to monitor a particular variable throughout your program's execution, you can do so using the Watches window.

11.8.1 *The watches window*

When you want to monitor a particular variable (or variables) throughout the execution of your program, you can add it to the Watches window, shown in figure 11.5.

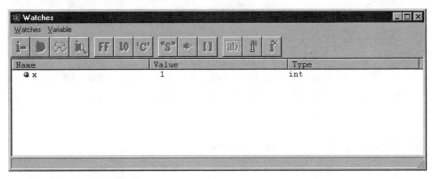

Figure 11.5   Watches window

You can add variables to watches by right-clicking them in the Debugging window and clicking Watch. You can also add variables to the Watches window by clicking Watches...Add from the Watches window menu bar. This will open the window shown in figure 11.6, where you can type in the variable name you want to watch.

**Figure 11.6
Adding variables**

Once a variable has been added to the Watches window you can see the value of the variable change throughout the execution of your application. You can also modify the value contained in the variable at any time by right-clicking the variable name in the Watches window and clicking Modify. This will open the Modify dialog, shown in figure 11.7.

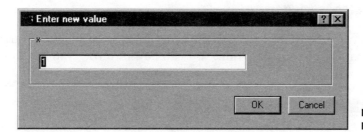

Figure 11.7
Modify dialog

Once you have modified the value stored in a variable, the new value will be used in all further operations using that variable (until it is changed by normal program execution).

11.9 *Other debugger windows*

There are a number of other Debugging windows that can be opened from the Debugging window, while program execution is halted, to enable you to view information about the current status of your program. Although we will discuss several of them here, some of these windows— such as the Hardware Registers window, the Threads window, and the Assembly window, are beyond the scope of this book, and we will not give many details about them. When using the Hardware Registers window and the Assembly Code window, you should take care to be certain of what you are trying to accomplish, since interacting with the computer at this level can lead to unfortunate results.

The following sections will discuss some of the other debugger windows you may find useful. You can access these windows under the Debug menu on the Debugging window's menu bar.

11.9.1 *The locals window*

The first option under the Debug menu is the Locals window. This window will display all the local variables defined in the function that is currently executing. The Locals window is shown in figure 11.8.

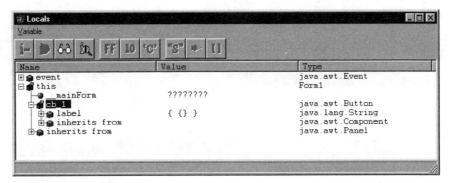

Figure 11.8   Locals window

The Locals window uses a familiar tree view to display information about the objects in your application. Each line in the Locals window gives the name and value of a local variable. Each different type of variable is marked with a different symbol, as follows:

- Objects are marked with boxes: red for member objects defined in the current class and blue for base classes.
- Simple values such as integers are marked with dark-yellow balls.

The Locals window shows only those variables currently in scope—in other words, it will show variables that have been defined for the current form or function. Depending upon the type of variable, you can view the contents of the variables either as pointers or strings.

The Locals window variables menu

You can perform a variety of actions upon a given variable in the Locals window by invoking some of the options found under the Variables menu. Not all of these options will be available at a given time, depending upon the type of variable currently highlighted in the Locals window.

Modify.   This allows you to enter a new value for the variable. From this point forward in program execution, the new value will be used.

Inspect.   You may more closely inspect a variable by opening the variable Inspect window. The Inspect window is shown in figure 11.9.

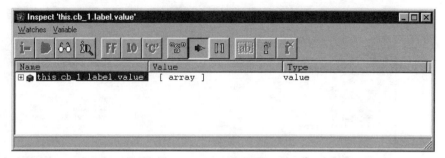

Figure 11.9   Inspect window

You can also open an Inspect window for a variable by using the right mouse button to click on the variable in the code editor and choosing Inspect Variable from the context menu. This window is very similar to the Locals window itself, except that it displays information for only one variable.

Show.   The Show window displays a section of memory. The type of window used by Show depends upon the type of memory requested. These types are as follows:

- Pointer memory displays the memory pointed to by a pointer, using a Memory window, shown in figure 11.10.

Figure 11.10   Memory window

- Variable memory displays the memory containing the variable, using a Memory window.

- Pointer code displays the memory a pointer points to, using a code editor or an Assembly window.

Type. This choice will show a cascaded menu, which allows you to choose the display type for the variable. You can, for example, choose to show the variable contents as a string or as a pointer to the memory address where the variable is stored.

Class. This choice will show a cascaded menu, which allows you to specify the kind of information you want to see when the Locals window displays class objects.

11.9.2 *Call stack*

The Call Stack window, shown in figure 11.11, displays the sequence of function calls leading up to the function that is currently executing. The last function listed is the currently executing function. The second last function is the one that called the last function, and so on.

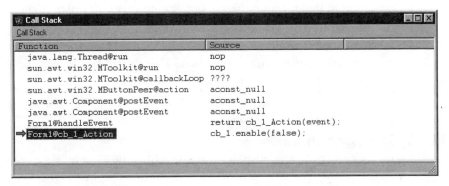

Figure 11.11 Call Stack window

The call stack window variables menu

You can traverse the call stack by using the following commands, which are available from the Debug menu of the code-editor window.

Up call stack. This displays information about the next function up the call stack. If possible, PowerJ opens a code-editor window to display the function (if PowerJ has the source code for the function available to it). If not, PowerJ shows an assembly code version of the function, as well as the hardware register values.

Down call stack. This displays information about the next function down the call stack.

Bottom call stack. This returns to the bottom of the call stack (to the currently executing function).

When you traverse the call stack in this manner, all open Debugging windows will change their contents to that of the function currently being displayed.

Call Stack window menu items. The Call Stack window has a single menu item, which contains some functionality for working with the call stack. The following items are all found under the Call Stack menu on the Call Stack window menu bar:

- Toggle breakpoint: This choice sets a breakpoint at the instruction immediately following the point where the entry called the next routine on the call stack. This means that the breakpoint is encountered as soon as execution returns to that function. If there is already a breakpoint at that location, toggle breakpoint turns off the breakpoint.

- Run to Cursor: This choice continues program execution up to the instruction immediately following the point where the entry called the next routine on the call stack. This means that execution stops as soon as it returns to the specified function.

- Up call stack to cursor: This choice moves up the call stack to the routine you have clicked.

11.9.3 *The assembly window*

The Assembly window displays the assembly language being executed by your program. The Assembly window is shown in figure 11.12.

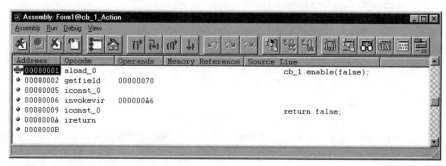

Figure 11.12 Assembly window

If your program is stopped at a breakpoint, the Assembly window marks the breakpoint with a red stop sign, overlaid with a yellow arrow.

The assembly window menu bar

The Assembly window has a menu bar that contains items you use to alter the way the Assembly window displays your program's instructions and to interact with your program. These menu items include the following:

Show address. This choice allows you to look at another code location. The dialog shown in figure 11.13 is displayed to allow you to enter the address of the location you wish to view.

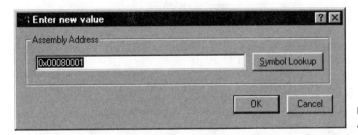

Figure 11.13
Adding variables

The run menu. The Run menu of the Assembly window uses the same methods of stepping through your code as does the Run menu of the script-editor window.

- Run to cursor: This resumes program execution and stops at the current cursor location.
- Skip to cursor: This resumes program execution by skipping the lines between the current execution point and the current cursor location. Use this to bypass code that you do not want to execute.

11.9.4 The registers window

The Registers window displays the contents of the computer's hardware registers at the time execution was suspended. The Registers window is shown in figure 11.14.

Figure 11.14
Registers window

You may change the contents of a hardware register by double-clicking the name of the register you want to change. The dialog shown in figure 11.15 will appear.

Figure 11.15   Adding variables

Enter the new value and click OK.

Note

When working with registers, you are interacting directly with your computer's hardware. Unless you are sure of the value you want to enter, you may obtain unexpected results when program execution is resumed.

11.9.5 *The threads window*

The Threads window displays information regarding the execution threads of your program (see figure 11.16).

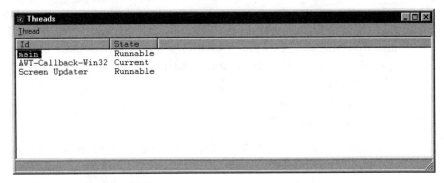

Figure 11.16   Threads window

The threads window menu bar

The Threads window contains three menu choices.

Freeze.   This choice freezes execution of the selected thread.

Thaw.   This choice undoes a freeze operation.

Make current.   This choice switches the debugger to the currently selected thread.

11.9.6 *The memory window*

The Memory window allows you to view the contents of specific memory addresses. The Memory window is shown in figure 11.17.

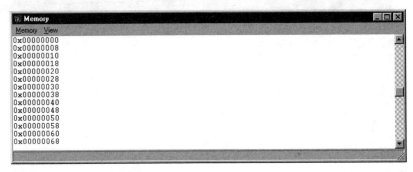

Figure 11.17   Memory window

The beginning of each line in the Memory window gives a memory address, in the form `segment:address`. The rest of the line shows the contents of the next 16 bytes, beginning at the address.

Data formats.   By default, the Memory window displays memory byte by byte. Each line in the window shows 16 bytes in hexadecimal format and then the same bytes as ANSI characters. If a byte value does not correspond to a printable character, it is shown as a thick vertical bar in the ANSI display.

You can use the Type menu item to change the display type of the Memory window.

Changing memory values.   You can use the Memory window to change any value shown in the window. This is called patching the memory location. Just double-click the value you want to change and enter the new value in the dialog box. You can also use the Memory...Modify menu item.

Showing a different address.   The Memory...Show Address menu item allows you to look at a different area of memory. Enter the address of the area you want to look at in the dialog and click OK.

11.9.7   *The stack window*

The Stack window is just a memory window that displays memory for the current stack only. The stack is where PowerJ programs store function arguments, local variables, and function call information. The Stack window is shown in figure 11.18.

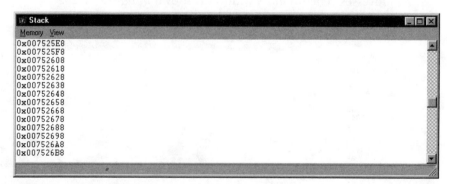

Figure 11.18   Stack window

Since the Stack window is a Memory window, refer to section 11.9.6 for more information on its use.

11.10 *Breaking without breakpoints*

Even if you haven't set any breakpoints, you can stop execution at any time by issuing a break command. Simply select Break from the Run menu. Break will halt program execution, but you will have no control over where the program is halted. You will have to examine the code in the editor window to determine whether execution was halted at a useful point. To resume execution select Run from the Run menu.

11.11 *Summary*

In this chapter we looked at the PowerJ debugger in detail. As stated, debugging is more of an art than a science. This chapter exposed you to some of the tools you can use to debug your programs but made no attempt to teach you how to debug. For that, you need to practice using the tools to step through code and examine data elements within many different applications until you get a handle on why things work the way they do in a computer.

We also learned how to set breakpoints in our code and how to run the application so that it would stop when we encountered a breakpoint. We looked at how to step through the code line by line and how to jump from breakpoint to breakpoint. We also learned how to examine the values of variables in our code and how to place watches on these variables. Finally, we looked at several useful debugger windows and how they are used.

Part III

Extending PowerJ—classes, templates, databases & more

PowerJ can be extended and enhanced in numerous ways. In the chapters that follow we will learn how to alter the PowerJ environment to suit your programming needs. We begin with a look at how to create and use Templates in chapter 12 and then move on in chapter 13 to learn how to create classes, a fundamental part of object-oriented programming.

Most business applications are data driven. They exist to move and manipulate data. PowerJ provides you with tools to make database programming easy and we examine those tools in chapter 14.

The most extensive use of Java programs to date has been to write programs for deployment on the Internet or intranet. In chapter 15 we examine some tools that can integrate the Internet into your PowerJ programs.

An easy way to extend an environment is through the use of third party tools. In Java these tools are referred to as Java Beans and PowerJ supports their use. PowerJ also supports limited use of ActiveX controls and we look at both Beans and ActiveX in chapter 16.

It's always nice to be able to write programs that manipulate graphics (games, games, games....) and chapter 17 presents the basics of graphics in Java.

We wrap up in chapter 18 with a look at how to build and deploy your application and in chapter 19, give you some ideas about how to move on to more advanced concepts on your own.

12

Defining and using templates

In this chapter we will learn about the following:

- How to create reusable interface elements called templates
- How to use templates on forms

In addition to using the standard components to develop applications, PowerJ allows you to create your own custom components consisting of one or more of the standard components built together into a visual interface. These custom components are called templates. When you save a template, you also save all code associated with the components that make up the template. This allows you to create custom templates to ease programming tasks that you perform frequently.

12.1 *The advantage of templates*

The advantage of templates is that they come complete with the code in all event handlers in which you had written code at the time the template was created—for example, you might create a template containing a button labeled OK and a button labeled Cancel and write the code in the action events that make both the buttons work. When you place that template onto a form, PowerJ places the two buttons on the form with all the code already in place. You can then use that template whenever you want to display both an OK and a Cancel button on a form, without writing additional code.

 Tip

When you are creating templates for use in multiple applications and in multiple forms, you must take care to write generic code. You must avoid hardcoding items such as form names. If you do not do this, the code is not portable across forms.

12.2 *Creating templates*

To create a template, just place the objects you want the template to contain on a Form Design window, write all the code necessary to make them work, and then right-click inside one of the selected objects and click Copy to Template. The dialog shown in figure 12.1 will appear to prompt you for a name for the template.

Figure 12.1
Naming the template

You must enter a name for the template and you may also enter a description of the template. The description can be useful to other developers, who may use the template in the future. Not everyone will be able to tell from the given name exactly what the template does.

Notice the "Component palette image" section at the bottom of the dialog. This represents the icon that will appear on the component palette representing the template. You may use the default icon or click Edit Create using the Watcom Image Editor, as shown in figure 12.2.

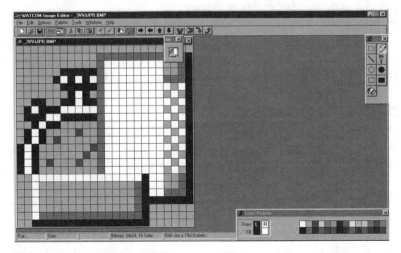

Figure 12.2   Watcom Image Editor

Clicking the Browse button allows you to select an icon from any image file on your machine. After you click OK, you can view the template icon on the component palette's Template tab (see figure 12.3).

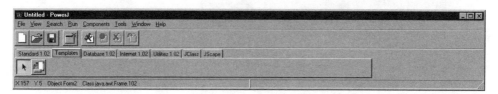

Figure 12.3   Template tab

12.3 *Creating templates from entire forms and targets*

You can create templates from entire forms. Just click in a blank area of the form and then click Copy to Template. The next time you click File...New Form, the form template will be listed as a selection.

You can also create templates from entire targets. Just right-click the target name and click Copy to Template. The next time you select File...New Target, the template will be listed as a selection.

12.4 *Using a template on a form*

You use your template on a form just as if it were any other component available on the palette. Just click its icon and then click on the Form Design window where you want to place the template.

12.5 *Deleting templates*

To delete any template, just right-click its icon (on the component palette, Form Design Wizard or Target Wizard) and select Delete.

12.6 *Storage of templates*

You may want to change the location where template files are stored to a location where other developers may have access to them. To change the location where templates are stored, click Tools...Options to open the options dialog (see figure 12.4), and switch to the Folders tab. Select "Let me specify a folder" and then enter the folder name in the edit field or browse for the new location.

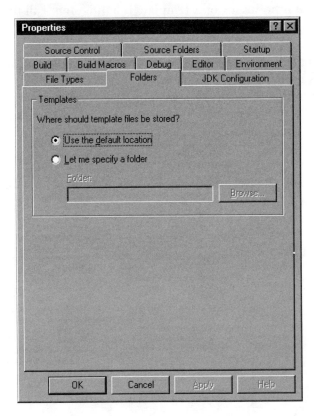

Figure 12.4
Options dialog Folders tab

12.7 *Templates do not use inheritance*

When you create and use a template, you are not using inheritance. Templates are simply copy-and-paste copies of the original. If you make changes to the original template (and resave it), none of these changes will automatically be available in the forms in which the template is already used. You will have to open each form that uses the template and make the same changes there. (Or you can delete the template components on the form and replace the form with the new template. Be careful though—this will delete any change you had made to the template on that form.)

Whether to use inheritance or a template is a judgment call that you need to make based upon a thorough understanding of a particular application. In general, if you anticipate that the original code will be changed from time to time, and you want these changes to be automatically available to all forms in all applications using the object, then you must use inheritance. If the reverse is true, then a template is easier to create.

12.8 *Summary*

In this chapter we learned how to create templates and how to use them on our forms. We also learned when we should consider using templates and when we should consider using classes.

Using classes in PowerJ

13

As an object-oriented language, almost everything you do in Java and PowerJ is class based. When you create a form using the Form Wizard, you are inheriting from an ancestor class of the type of form you choose. When you place a button on your form, you are creating an instance of the button class. These objects are all part of the Abstract Windowing Toolkit (AWT), which forms the set of base classes for Java programmers.

Although the AWT contains base classes for every user-interface element that you will routinely use, there will be times when you will want to create your own classes. An example of creating a class would be if you developed a standard search window and wanted the search window to be used in many different applications. In this instance, you could either create a template or a fully extensible class. If you wanted changes made to the interface to be immediately available to programmers using the interface, then you would define it as a class. If not, then you would most likely create a template. We discussed templates and their uses in the previous chapter.

If you were creating a visual user-interface type of class, you would not use the Class Wizard. Rather, you would create the class as a form (remember, forms are just classes) and make that form available for inheritance. This chapter does not deal with that type of class.

Another reason for creating classes is to encapsulate business logic and data. In this case the class does not contain any visual elements, only properties and methods. The class may interact with a database and with visual elements on a form through the use of its methods. This chapter teaches you how to create these nonvisual classes.

13.1 *Types of classes*

There are two types of classes you can add to your PowerJ targets: the Visual class and the Standard Java Class. Visual class is a bit of a misnomer in that the class is not actually visible at run time. Rather, the class consists of nonvisual components placed on a form. However, when you open the class at run time (by opening the form), you will not see a visible representation of the form. It will be invisible to the end user.

So why make an invisible Visual Class? Quite simply, it's a programmer's timesaving device. Suppose you want to obtain information from a database for user settings when the Java application is first started. There are several ways to do this. One would be to write the interaction with the database entirely in code and store the values you retrieve in member variables of a normal Java class. You would create `get` and perhaps `set` methods and use them to retrieve or alter the values in the variables at run time. If, during the course of the application, you needed to save the information back to the database, you would be required to write all the code necessary to handle the database interaction.

But if you create a Visual Class using the standard components, you can bind the controls to the database and take full advantage of PowerJ's ability to interact with the database using transaction objects and query objects (see chapter 14). Then, when the application is started, you can open the invisible form containing the objects, have that form automatically retrieve the information, and use `get` and `set` methods to interact with the information on the form. When it is necessary to save the information, you once again take full advantage of PowerJ's database capabilities.

13.2 Adding classes

You add classes to a target by using the Class Wizard. You can open the Class Wizard by clicking File...New...Class from the Targets window menu bar, from the Class window menu bar, or even from the main PowerJ menu bar. The first page of the Class Wizard is shown in figure 13.1.

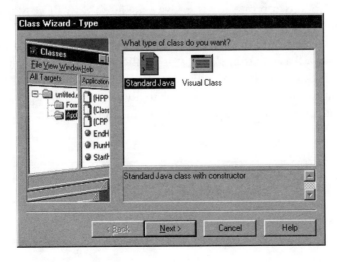

Figure 13.1
Class Wizard

Here you select between two different kinds of classes: the Standard Java Class or the Visual Class. The following steps will add a Standard Java class to your target:

First, select Standard Java as the class type and click Next. This will take you to the second page of the Class Wizard, as shown in figure 13.2.

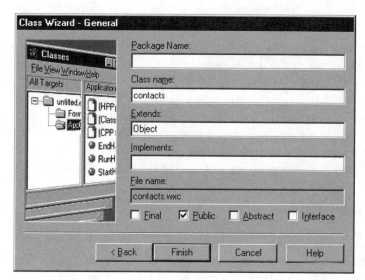

**Figure 13.2
Class wizard
(page 2)**

Here, you specify a name for the Java package that will contain the class, the name of the class, the name of the class from which this class will inherit (in the Extends text field), and the name of any interface this class implements, as well as whether the class is public, abstract, or interface.

Once you click Finish, PowerJ will create the class files and add them to the target. You can use the Classes window to add methods and properties to the class, as discussed in chapter 10. You will then have access to your class through the Classes window.

Note

To add a class that already exists, just add the file containing the class to the target.

13.3 *Creating a contacts class*

Now that we have an overview of how to create a class, let's put that knowledge to work by creating a class that will store information about a contact. This type of class would be helpful when writing a contact management application (as shown in the next chapter).

The first step in creating our class is to use the Class Wizard to create the skeleton of the class. Just follow the steps outlined in section 13.2 to create a class called contact information. Have the class inherit from object and make it a public class. The completed Class Wizard dialog should resemble the screen shown in figure 13.3.

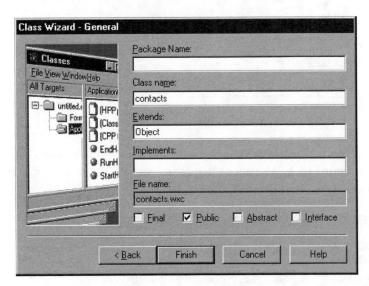

**Figure 13.3
Class Wizard
dialog**

Click Finish when you have all the information completed. You will see an open code-editor window for the entry of data members for the class. You can dismiss the code editor for the time being. Instead, open the Classes window and you will see the new contact information class ready for you to create properties and methods. Since the purpose of this class is to store contact information, the best way to accomplish that task might be to hold that information in the form of properties at the class level. These properties can then be accessed through get and set methods.

PowerJ makes implementing this functionality a snap. Just right-click on the class name in the Classes window and click Insert and then Property. You will see the dialog shown in figure 13.4.

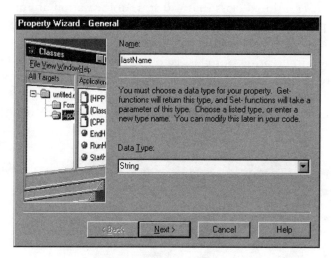

Figure 13.4
Property Wizard

Let's create a property that will hold the last name of the contact, as shown in figure 13.4. When we click Next, we will be asked to specify how we want to access that property (see figure 13.5).

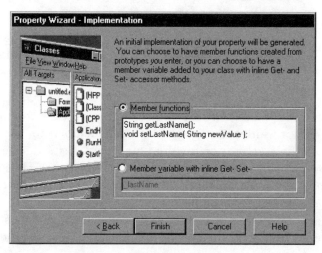

Figure 13.5
Property Wizard
(page 2)

Select "Member functions" and click Finish. You will then see a code-editor window open to the member functions of the class ready for you to write the code to implement those functions (see figure 13.6).

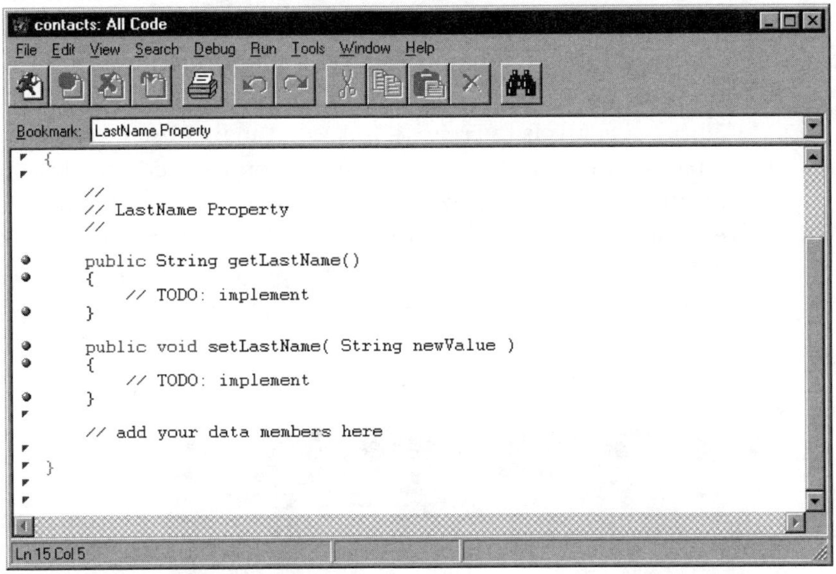

```
contacts: All Code                                    _ □ ✕
File  Edit  View  Search  Debug  Run  Tools  Window  Help

Bookmark: LastName Property

{

    //
    // LastName Property
    //

    public String getLastName()
    {
        // TODO: implement
    }

    public void setLastName( String newValue )
    {
        // TODO: implement
    }

    // add your data members here

}

Ln 15 Col 5
```

Figure 13.6   Code-editor window

To make the methods work, you must use the following code:

```
String getLastName()
    {
        // TODO: implement
        return lastName;
    }

void setLastName( String newValue )
    {
        // TODO: implement
        lastName = newValue;
    }

// add your data members here
    String lastName;
```

This creates a data member to hold the `lastName` property value and implements `getLastName()` by returning whatever value is stored in `lastName` when the method is called. It also implements `setLastName` by storing the value passed as a parameter to that method in the data member `lastName`. You would repeat this process for each property you wish to store in the class. In a real-world application, it might be better to store all contact information as an array of strings and get it all at once. Determining whether to store the information as a single data element or as part of an array would depend mainly on how the information is to be accessed. If you will access elements individually, then an array is extra overhead.

All that remains is to create a form that makes use of this class. If you started a new project for this class before you defined the class, then you already will have a blank form. If not, then either add a blank form to the current target or start a new project and add the class file to the target using the Class Wizard. Once you have a project ready to write this demo application, you want to create a form that has two text fields and two command buttons. The buttons should be labeled Set and Get and should resemble those shown in figure 13.7.

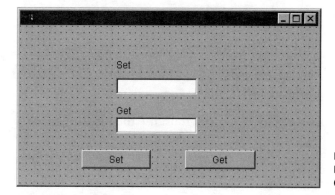

Figure 13.7
Form with Set and
Get buttons

The application will function in the following manner to demonstrate how to use the member functions of the contact information class to set and get the property values.

- The user enters a last name in the Set text box and then clicks the Set button. This copies the string from the text box into the `lastName` property of the contact information class.

- The user presses the Get button and the value is retrieved from the contact information class `lastName` property and displayed in the Get text box.

The code for this in the Set button's action event is as follows:

```
public boolean cb_set_Action(java.awt.Event event)
    {
        java.lang.String              text;
// Get the text from the text box and store it in lastName property
        text = textf_1.getText();
        contact.setLastName(text);
        return false;
    }
```

In the Get button's action event:

```
public boolean cb_get_Action(java.awt.Event event)
    {
        java.lang.String              text;
// Get the value in lastName and place it in the text box

        text = contact.getLastName();

        textf_2.setText( text );

        return false;
    }
```

You must also create an instance of the class as a data element of your form.

```
// add your data members here

//Create an instance of our class

contactinfo contact = new contactinfo();
```

Once you have this code in place, you can run the application. When you enter text in the Set box and click the Set button, and then click the Get button, you will see that the value has been copied into the last-Name property from the first text box and then copied back into the second text box.

Of course, full-featured classes for real-world applications will be much more complex than this. They will include business logic that validates the data sent to and from the class, as well as other code specific to the class. For these types of classes, much care must be taken to design the data members and methods for maximum efficiency.

You will find that proper use of classes is essential in object-oriented programming, and you will use classes often. The class is the main encapsulation device and also provides the basis for inheritance (you can inherit from and extend your classes as necessary).

13.4 Summary

In this chapter we learned how to use the Class Wizard to add new classes to our project and how to add existing classes to our projects. We discussed how to create data elements and methods for our classes and how to write code to manipulate the data elements. Finally, we learned how to use class in our programs by creating an instance of the class and then using its methods.

Using databases

14

In this chapter we will do the following:

- Learn how to use PowerJ to develop database programs
- Learn about JDBC and the JDBC-ODBC bridge
- Learn how to use the database objects (transaction, query, and data navigator)
- Learn how to use the Form Wizard to create a database form
- Learn how to work with bound controls
- Create a sample database application

This chapter discusses how you can use PowerJ to work with JDBC and ODBC databases (accessed by the JDBC-ODBC bridge). We will learn how to set up a transaction to connect to the database, set a SQL query on that transaction, and display the results using bound controls.

You will find the database components on the Database tab of the PowerJ components palette (see figure 14.1).

Figure 14.1   Database components

The components are, from left to right, Query Object, Transaction, and Data Navigator.

14.1 *Security issues for databases*

If you are creating a Java applet to a browser over the Internet, you will learn that the Java security model places several restrictions on what you can and cannot do. You cannot read or write information to a client's local drive (including a database), execute another program on a local machine, or make a network connection to any other source besides the server from which your applet was loaded.

For these reasons it is difficult to create database operations in an applet. This has changed somewhat for Java 1.1, which will allow some of these operations if you create a signed applet. You can also write applets that violate these restrictions and run them inside an applet viewer. Applets that run inside such a viewer are not restricted.

Since these topics are beyond the scope of this book, we will concern ourselves with writing Java applications with the idea that the skills you learn here will apply to applets should you write them.

14.2 *Methods of connecting to databases*

PowerJ offers three basic methods for connecting to and querying a database: JDBC, the JDBC-ODBC bridge and Sybase's jConnect. These are discussed in the following sections.

14.2.1 What is JDBC?

JDBC is a standard that establishes a methodology for connecting to and querying a database from within any Java application or applet. If you want to read about the inner workings of JDBC, you can find the full specifications at *http://splash.javasoft.com/jdbc.*

Drivers wanted!

A JDBC driver is a set of Java classes that implements the JDBC interfaces needed to connect and query a database. JDBC drivers are not provided by PowerJ, even though some are included in the box. Rather, they are provided by the various database vendors or other third parties. When a JDBC driver is installed on your machine (either manually or by downloading across a network), the classes register themselves with a JDBC driver manager. The application or applet then asks the JDBC driver manager for a driver to connect to a specific database. The JDBC driver manager scans through its list of registered drivers and returns the first one that is capable of making the connection to the requested database type.

All Java classes and interfaces are packaged together in sets called (appropriately) packages. The core classes and interfaces that ship with Java all have package names that begin with java, as in *java.awt* or *java.lang.* The *java* package name is reserved exclusively for core classes.

An applet is a Java application that is downloaded from a Web server and that runs inside a Web browser. Applets have special security restrictions that other Java applications do not—for example, applets cannot read or write to the local file system. They can open network connections but only to the Web server from which they were downloaded. Classes that have a package name starting with *java* cannot be downloaded across the Internet. They must be installed locally on your system. This last restriction creates special problems for JDBC.

Problems with packages

JDBC is an official part of the Java 1.1 specification. This means that the JDBC interfaces and the JDBC driver manager are packaged with Java 1.1. The package name is *java.sql.* So, when you install Java 1.1, the JDBC interfaces are installed locally, and that makes them available for an applet to use. JDBC was developed after Java 1.02 was released, and that means that the *java.sql* package is not part of Java 1.02. This is what causes the problem. Since the *java.sql* package cannot be downloaded and used by an applet, because of the security restrictions mentioned previously, it is unavailable for applets that use Java 1.02.

If your applet uses JDBC, you have two options. You can force users to install the JDBC drivers locally on their machines, or you can rename the *java.sql* package so that the classes it contains can be downloaded.

The first option is generally unusable if you are building applets that you want to deploy across the Internet, since it means that only a small number of users will be able to use the applets (only those who have the *java.sql* package installed). For that reason most developers are using the second option.

Many vendors have been taking the set of JDBC interfaces defined by *java.sql* and redefining them in a different package (*jdbc.sql*). Then they develop JDBC drivers that use the interfaces defined in *jdbc.sql* instead of *java.sql*. An applet developer can then put the applet, plus the *jdbc.sql* interfaces and the driver classes, on the Web server, where they can be downloaded and run on users' machines.

This split between Java 1.1 and 1.02 means that most driver vendors create two different versions of the drivers: one that works with the *java.sql* package (so that Java 1.1 users can use the driver) and one that works with *jdbc.sql* (so that Java 1.02 users can use the driver). The driver that uses *java.sql* will only work in Java 1.1 browsers but will require less download time, since the *java.sql* package is already installed on the user's machine. The driver that uses *jdbc.sql* will work on all browsers but will require more time to download (even using Java 1.1, since the driver doesn't use the built-in *java.sql* package).

This problem will disappear when Java 1.1 becomes the predominant Java version in use.

14.2.2 *What is the JDBC-ODBC bridge?*

The JDBC-ODBC bridge is a Java package containing classes and drivers that allow a Java application to access ODBC data sources. These drivers are not included with PowerJ but are downloadable from many sources on the Internet.

14.2.3 What is Sybase jConnect for JDBC?

The Sybase jConnect drivers that ship with PowerJ provide a method of connecting a Java applet or application to a machine running either Sybase SQL Server or the OpenServer software. Using the OpenServer software, you can make a connection to the Sybase SQL Anywhere database.

14.3 Using databases in PowerJ

PowerJ includes components that make writing database-enabled applications much easier. These components are found on the Database tab of the PowerJ component bar. These components are discussed in the following sections.

14.3.1 Transactions

A transaction object specifies the information required for connecting with a given database. The transaction object has properties that identify the database, as well as the password and user identification used when accessing the database. The transaction object also manages SQL transactions with the database. All interaction with the database must be via a transaction object.

If a form's code interacts with a database, you must place a transaction object on the form (or on a parent of the form). When you place a transaction object on a form, an icon appears on the form to show that the object is there and to give you access to its properties; however, this icon will not be visible at run time.

If your program only interacts with one database, you typically need only one transaction object in the entire program. If you connect to more than one database, you can manage the connections by placing one transaction object on the form for each database to which you connect.

After you place a transaction object on a form, you should set the properties for the transaction using the object's Properties dialog, shown in figure 14.2. The important properties are found on the Connection page.

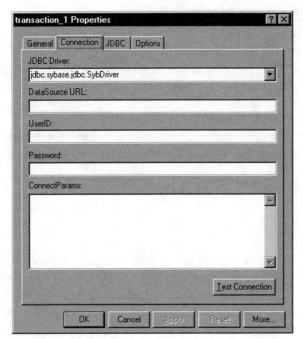

Figure 14.2
Property dialog

14.3.2 JDBC driver

Here you can select the JDBC driver used to interact with your database. Drivers that are currently available are displayed in the drop-down list.

Note

To access an ODBC database, use the driver named
sun.jdbc.odbc.JdbcOdbcDriver
This driver is often called the JDBC-ODBC bridge, because it performs the translations needed to execute JDBC operations on an ODBC database.

14.3.3 DataSource URL

This is a URL specifying the location of the database, if the database is a JDBC database. To connect to an ODBC database, the URL takes the form *jdbc:odbc:odbcdatasourcename*, where *odbcdatasourcename* is the name of the ODBC database as it is set up in the ODBC settings of the target machine. Other database types will have URLs specified in different formats. Consult the documentation that comes with your database for more information.

14.3.4 UserID

This specifies the userID that the program will use to attempt to connect to the database. If you do not specify a userID, the user may be prompted for a userID when your program attempts to connect with the database. Whether or not the user is prompted depends upon the configuration of the particular database.

14.3.5 Password

This specifies the password the program will use to attempt to connect to the database. So that others cannot see the password, if they look at the property dialog of the transaction, PowerJ displays an asterisk (*) in place of each character you type. If you do not enter a password here, the user may be prompted for a password when your program attempts to connect with the database, depending upon the configuration of the particular database.

14.3.6 ConnectParams

This provides additional information needed for connecting to the database. What this information contains depends on the type of Database Management System (DBMS). Consult the manuals that come with your DBMS for further information.

14.3.7 AutoConnect

If this option is checked, PowerJ automatically attempts to connect to the database when the form is created. If it is not checked, your code must explicitly issue its own commands to connect to the database. How to make a connection in code is explained in section 14.5.

14.3.8 AutoCommit

If you check this option, each database operation is committed as soon as it is completed.

14.3.9 TraceToLog

If this option is enabled, the transaction object automatically records actions in the program's debug log. You can later look at this log to determine what may be causing problems with your database-related activities.

Note

TraceToLog only has an effect in debug mode.

14.4 Setting transaction properties at run time

You can also set the transaction properties at run time using methods on the transaction object. Suppose, for example, that your program obtains the userid and password from a user input dialog window rather than having them hardcoded at design time. In that situation you would use the following code to set the transaction object's properties with the userID and password obtained from the dialog:

```
String userid;
String password;
transaction_1.setUserid( userid )
transaction_1.setPassword( password );
```

14.5 Making the connection

If you check AutoConnect on the transaction's property dialog, your program will automatically attempt to connect to the database when the form that contains the transaction object is displayed. If AutoConnect is not checked, you must write code that connects to the database at run time, using the connect method of the transaction object as follows:

```
transaction_1.connect( this );
```

This code connects to the database using the information stored in the transaction object's properties. If you have not specified a userID and password for the connection, the program may prompt the user to enter a password and userID (depending upon the type of database in use).

At times, you may need to determine if the transaction object is currently connected to a database. You would do this to prevent errors from occurring if you attempted to execute a database command against an unconnected transaction object. The following code will perform that task:

```
boolean connected:
connected = transaction_1.getConnected();
// IF connected is True then the transaction is connected
```

14.6 *Disconnecting from the database*

The `disconnect` method of the transaction object disconnects an existing connection, as follows:

```
transaction_1.disconnect();
```

14.7 *Transaction management*

PowerJ transaction objects provide you with all the methods you need to perform transaction management tasks. If you are running with Auto-Commit set to false, you will be responsible for handling all transaction management tasks. The `commit` method of the transaction object commits changes to the database:

```
transaction_1.commit();
```

The following `rollback` method of transaction cancels any changes made to the database (if those changes have not yet been committed):

```
transaction_1.rollback();
```

The `commit` and `rollback` methods have no effect if AutoCommit is true, because there can never be an uncommitted transaction against which they will work.

 Tip

When you are developing a program that uses databases, it is very tempting to specify the database administrator's userID at design time (DBA). That way you, the developer, have full access to rights to the database. But this is not generally a good idea. If the program will be used by nonadministrators, and their IDs will be used at run time, your code is not being developed and tested under the conditions in which it will ultimately run.

14.8 *Query objects*

A query object encapsulates a query on a database. All programs that work with databases make extensive use of query objects. Transaction objects handle the task of maintaining the connection to the database. All actual interactions with the database are other than connections, which are handled by query objects.

When you place a query object on a form, an icon appears on the form to show that the object is there and to give you access to its properties. This icon will not be visible at run time.

You can specify SQL queries by typing in the query as a text string using the Query tab of the query object's Properties dialog, as shown in figure 14.3, or by constructing the query using the PowerJ query editor. The query editor is discussed in detail in section 14.10.3.

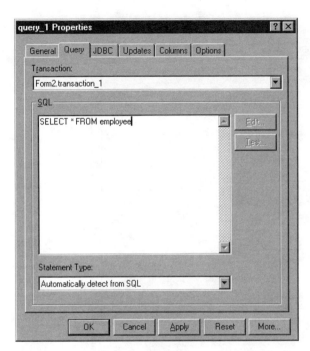

Figure 14.3
Query tab

14.9 Relationships with transactions

Every query object must be associated with a transaction object. The transaction object specifies the database on which the query will act. The query object is most often placed on the same form as the transaction object. It may also be placed on a "descendant" form of the form containing the transaction object—in other words, the form containing the query may be a child of the form containing the transaction object.

14.10 Query properties

After you place a query object on a form, you must set the properties for the query using the object's Properties dialog. Most of the important properties are on the Options tab, shown in figure 14.4.

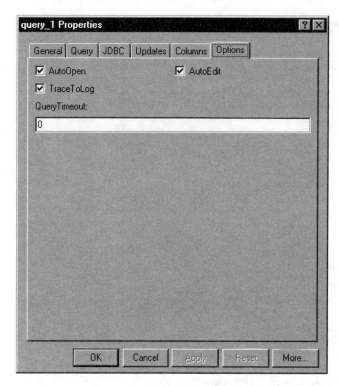

Figure 14.4
Options tab

The properties with which we are most concerned are discussed in the following sections.

14.10.1 Transaction (located on the query tab)

This is the transaction object associated with the database that you want to query. The drop-down list will display all the transaction objects defined on the current form. All interactions with the database using this query object will be transmitted via the connection maintained by the stated transaction object.

14.10.2 SQL

This is the SQL statement you want to execute on the database. You may leave this blank at design time, and then fill in an appropriate SQL query at run time. At design time, you can use the query editor to construct the desired statement, or you may write the statement by typing it in the text box. Experienced database users will probably prefer to type in the SQL rather than construct it using the query editor.

14.10.3 *The query editor*

The query editor helps you build the SQL statement that is associated with a query object. The query editor can be opened at design time, once you have placed the query object on a form and have bound the object to a valid transaction object. To open the query editor click Edit on the query object's Properties dialog. The query editor uses the information specified in the transaction object to connect to the database and display its contents.

The query editor is shown in figure 14.5.

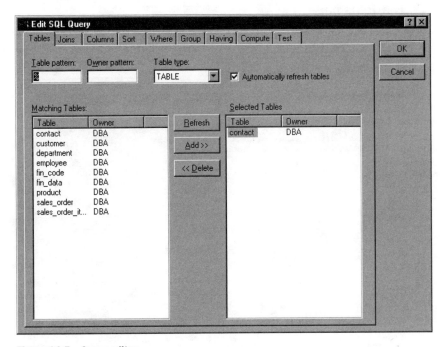

Figure 14.5   Query editor

The query editor has several pages that allow you to construct almost any SQL statement.

The tables page

The tables page (shown in figure 14.5) allows you to specify which database tables should be included in the query. This corresponds to the FROM clause in the SQL statement being constructed. All tables listed in the Selected Tables list will be included in the FROM clause. To select a table, click on the name of the table in the Matching Tables list, and then click Add. Double-click the name of the table in the Matching Tables list. This will copy the table from one list to the other.

The table pattern further controls which table names are displayed in the Matching Tables list. The Owner pattern text box lets you restrict entries based on the owner name. If you change the Table pattern or the Owner pattern, you must click Refresh to get the list of tables that match the given pattern.

The Joins page

The Joins page is where you state the manner in which the selected tables will be joined. The types of joins available will vary according to the type of database in use. (See figure 14.6.)

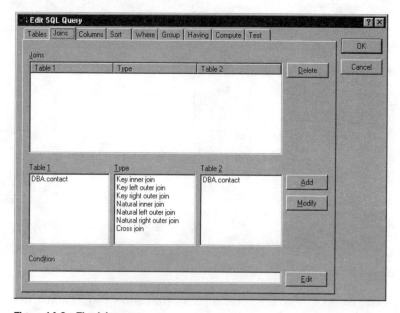

Figure 14.6   The Joins page

To specify a join, just click a table from the Table 1 list, and then click a type of join from the Type list. Then, select a table from the Table 2 list, and, finally, click Add. This will construct the join and place it in the Joins box.

The columns page

The Columns page is where you select the columns that will be included in the query's result set. This is what generates the SELECT clause in the SQL statement being constructed. (See figure 14.7.)

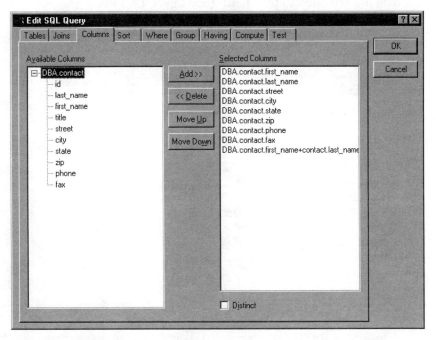

Figure 14.7   Columns page

The Available Columns list displays columns as a tree view, with the top levels of the tree shown by the tables selected from the database. Drilling down on these levels displays the columns contained within each table. All columns listed in the Selected Columns list are retrieved by the query.

To select a column, click on the name of the column in the Available Columns list and then click Add, or double-click the name of the column in the Available Columns list.

You can change the position of an item in the Selected Columns list by clicking on the item and then clicking Move Up or Move Down. (*Note,* this changes the column number in the query.)

The sort page

The Sort page is where you determine how the database should sort the results of the query. This generates an ORDER BY clause in the SQL statement, which means that the sort is done on the server side before the data are returned to the client. (See figure 14.8.)

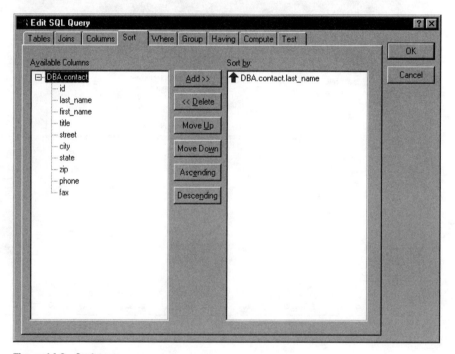

Figure 14.8 Sort page

The "Sort by" column lists the sorting items in order of priority and whether the sort on each item should be ascending or descending.

The direction of sorting is shown by the arrow beside the sorting item: An up arrow indicates an ascending sort, and a down arrow indicates a descending sort. You can change the direction of the sort by double-clicking the arrow.

You place columns in the "Sort by" list in the same manner you select tables and columns: by either selecting the column and clicking Add or by double-clicking the desired column.

The where page

The Where page allows you to specify limiting criteria for the query. This will reduce the rows returned by the query by returning only those that match the stated criteria. The criteria given on this page will be used in constructing the WHERE clause of the final SQL statement. (See figure 14.9.)

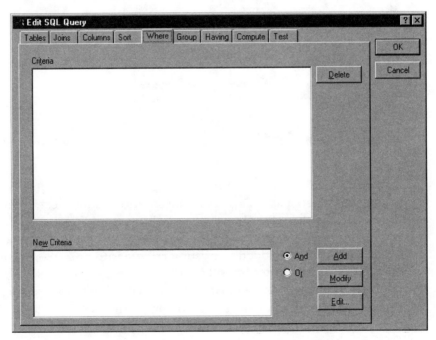

Figure 14.9   Where page

All the criteria on the Where page must be connected with AND or OR operations.

You can specify a where clause in one of two ways. First, you can simply type in the clause as a string, using normal SQL format, such as "WHERE lastName = Smith" or you can specify a criterion using the criterion editor, shown in figure 14.10.

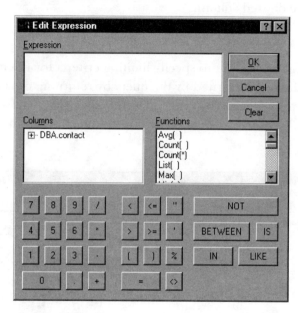

Figure 14.10
Criterion editor

To add a new criterion function using the criterion editor, just click Edit on the Where page. This opens the criterion editor. Next, create your criterion using the editor by selecting Columns and Functions. Click OK when done. When you have returned to the Where page, click And if the new criterion will be added to existing criteria with an AND operation, or click Or if the new criterion will be added to existing criteria with an OR operation. Finally, click Add to add the new criterion to the existing list.

You can modify an existing criterion by clicking on the criterion in the Criteria list, and then clicking Modify. This will copy the criterion to New Criteria, where you can edit it as a string or edit it using the criterion editor.

The group page

The Group page is where you select columns, by which rows will be grouped, in a GROUP BY clause in the final SQL statement. The Available Columns list shows the columns from the selected tables. To specify a column to be grouped, you add the column name to the "Group by" list by clicking on the name of the column in the Available Columns list and then clicking Add or by double-clicking the name of the column in the Available Columns list. (See figure 14.11.)

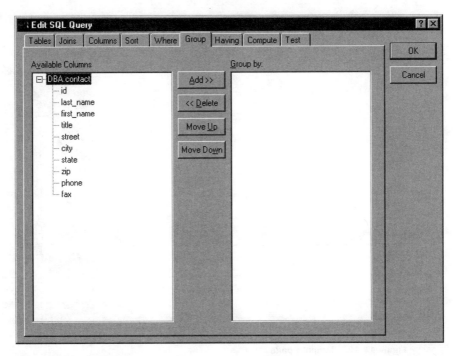

Figure 14.11   Group page

The having page

The Having page is where you set up group restrictions. This page creates a HAVING clause in the final SQL statement. The Having page looks and works similar to the Where page.

The compute page

The Compute page is where you add new columns to the result set, basing those columns on calculations performed upon existing database columns. To create and add a computed column, click the Edit button. This will open the Edit Expression dialog, which we discussed in connection with the Where page. After you have created your expression, click

OK and you will see it in the New Computed Column portion of the Compute page. Highlight it and click Add to add the column to the query. (See figure 14.12.)

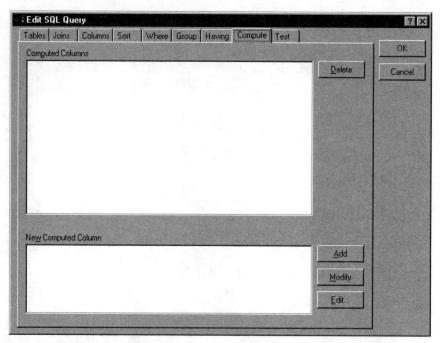

Figure 14.12   Compute page

The test page

The Test page allows you to test the results of your query by executing it to select a limited number of rows from the database. To test the query, click the Test button on this page to send the query to the database. The query editor only retrieves 20 rows from the database, which is enough to show sample results of the query and to determine whether it is working as desired. (See figure 14.13.)

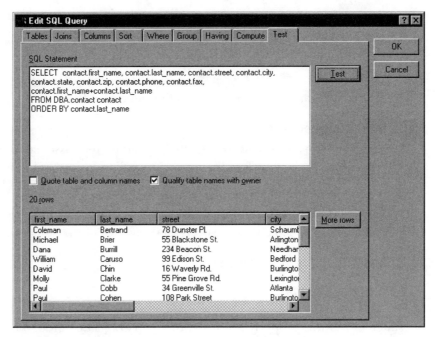

Figure 14.13   Test page

14.10.4 *Parameters for queries*

SQL queries may use the question mark (?) as a placeholder in statements such as this:

```
SELECT * FROM employee WHERE manager_id = ?
```

These placeholders are called parameters. The parameters must be filled in with actual values before the statement can be executed at run time.

Note

When a query contains such parameters, you cannot use the Auto-Open property for the query (since the parameters must be filled in before the query can be opened). You must fill in the parameter values and execute the query in code.

To specify values for a parameter, you use the `setParameter` method of the query object. This method assigns a value to a specified parameter in the query—for example:

```
query_1.setParameter( 1, DataValue( 500 ) )
```

sets the first parameter in the query to the value of 500.

14.10.5 Stored procedures

You can use stored procedures in the SQL statement associated with a query. To do this, you enclose the procedure call in braces, as follows:

```
query_1.setSQL( "{call test_output(?,?)}" );
```

This code calls a stored procedure named `test_output` and passes it two parameters, which must have been set using the `setParameter` method.

14.10.6 Additional query properties

PrimaryKeyColumn

This specifies the name of the primary key column used in the SQL statement. If this property is not set, the query object cannot go into edit mode. Databases require primary keys to be set before they can perform insert or update operations.

AutoOpen

This causes the query to be automatically opened when the query object is created. When the query is opened, it executes the associated SQL statement, and moves the cursor to the first row retrieved.

AutoEdit

This makes the query automatically go into edit mode if the user makes a change in a row. If this is not checked, your code must explicitly put the query into edit mode if you want to modify an existing row. By default, AutoEdit is false.

TraceToLog

If this is checked, the query object automatically records important actions in the program's debug log. You would then use this information to determine what caused a database-related problem.

TraceToLog only has an effect in debug targets.

14.10.7 *Setting query properties at run time*

You can set query properties at run time using methods provided on the query object—for example, you can create dynamic SQL applications by allowing the user to write SQL statements in a text area and then using the setSQL method of the query object to set up the query object with the user-provided SQL statement, as follows:

```
String userStatement;
userStatement = texta_1.getText();
query_1.setSQL( userStatement );
```

You can also set the transaction object to which the query is connected by using the following setTransactionObject:

```
query_1.setTransactionObject( transaction_1 );
```

Tip

You might change transaction objects if you want to use the same query object to query two different databases.

14.10.8 *Run-time-only properties*

Some properties of the query object can only be set or read at run time. These include the following:

AutoRefresh

Setting this property using setAutoRefresh forces the query to automatically refresh the contents of all bound objects after any update or delete operation.

Opened

The getOpened method returns true if the query is open. You can use this to determine whether any changes made to the database since the query was opened can be retrieved using the refresh method or whether the query must be reopened.

ReadOnly

The getReadOnly method returns true if the statement is not open or if the query is currently read-only.

14.11 Executing the query

The open method of query executes a query on a database and retrieves the result set—for example:

```
query_1.open();
```

executes the SQL statement in query_1 on whatever database is associated with the query object (through the transaction object).

Tip

If you have turned on the AutoOpen property for the query object, your program automatically executes open when the query object is being created.

14.11.1 Result sets

Opening a query will execute the query's SQL statement. Some types of statements do not obtain data. If a statement does obtain data from the database, the data obtained are called a result set. A result set contains zero or more rows of data, and each row contains one or more columns.

14.11.2 Row numbers

The first row of the result set is numbered 1, and the first column in every row is numbered 1.

14.11.3 Retrieving the result set

When you use open to execute a SELECT statement in code, the data are not returned to your program immediately. To obtain the data, you must use methods that retrieve the data. The easiest way to do this is to use one or more bound controls. Bound controls are discussed in section 14.14.

If a query object has bound controls associated with it, these controls will display values from the current row. If you want to change the contents of the control to another row, you can use one of several methods.

14.11.4 Getting the current row

From time to time you may need to determine the current row of the query. The query object offers a number of methods to assist in determining your exact position in a result set. The methods isFirstRow( ) and query_1.isLastRow( ) will allow you to test whether the current row is the first or last row of the result set. The functions return true if the current row is the first or last, respectively. The methods query_1.getBOF( ) and query_1.getEOF( ) permit you to test whether you are at "beginning of file" (before the first row in the result set) or "end of file" (after the end of the first row in the result set).

The method getCurrentRow returns the number of the current row.

```
int row;
row = query_1.getCurrentRow();
```

14.11.5 *Moving through the result set*

The move methods of the query object change the position of the cursor to a new row in the result set. When you do this, the data shown in any bound control will change to reflect the new values in the new row. The move methods of the query object are as follows:

move(row, validate, notify)

This method moves the cursor to the row number contained in the row parameter.

moveFirst(validate, notify)

This method moves the cursor to the first row of the result set.

moveLast(validate, notify)

This method moves the cursor to the last row of the result set.

moveNext(validate, notify)

This method will move the cursor to the next row of the result set.

movePrevious(validate, notify)

This moves the cursor to the previous row of the result set.

moveRelative(offset, validate, notify)

This method will move the cursor forward or backward, depending on the value of the offset parameter—for example, if offset is +3, moveRelative()

moves three rows forward from the current row, and if offset is –3, `moveRela-`
`tive` moves three rows backward from the current row.

Any `move` method will return `false` if it results in the cursor moving to
"beginning of file" or "end of file" (before the first row in the result or
after the last). This might happen if you move to a row that lies outside
the actual number of rows in the result set.

If the `validate` parameter of the `move` method is set to `true`, the
method triggers a `ValidateData` event on all bound controls before moving. In the `ValidateData` event you may stop the `move` operation by using
the following code:

```
event.setCancel( true );
```

You can use this to cancel the `move` when the user has entered invalid
data in the control. This will prevent the invalid data from being sent to
the database and causing an error condition. The `ValidateData` event
handler can prevent the `move` operation until the user enters a valid value.

The `move` methods will always execute an `update` before leaving the
current row. If the `notify` argument of the `move` method is `true`, the
`update` action notifies all bound controls that they should refresh themselves. Otherwise, you must issue a `refresh` of the query object before the
new values will be visible to the user.

14.12 Closing the query

The `close` method of the query object closes an open query.

```
query_1.close();
```

Closing a query frees up the memory used to hold the result set of the
subject query.

14.13 Direct SQL

The `execute` method of the query allows you to execute a SQL statement
directly.

```
query_1. execute( "delete from dba.employee where lastname="Smith" );
```

Commands executed in this manner must not return a result set, so it is only appropriate for commands such as `delete`, `insert`, and `update` (which do not return results).

14.14 *Bound controls*

A bound control is an object on a form whose value is automatically updated by query operations—for example, you can bind a text box to a query object and this would have the effect of making the text box always show the value of the bound column in the current row. If you move the position of the query cursor to a different row of data, the text box will automatically change to show the value in the same column of the new row.

The following objects can serve as bound controls:

- Text boxes (text fields, text areas, masked text field)
- Labels
- Check boxes
- Lists
- Choices

If the user changes the value of a bound control, this normally changes the corresponding value in the database. This is true unless the query is in read-only mode.

If AutoCommit is turned on for the transaction object, any changes are immediately made permanent (committed) in the database. If AutoCommit is turned off, the changes will not become permanent until you commit the transaction using the `commit` method of the transaction object. Until you call `commit`, you can cancel changes using the `rollback` method of the transaction object.

If updates are not allowed on a database, the user will not be permitted to change the values in bound controls. If you intend to use an object as a bound control, you must check the bound control check box on the Database page of the object's Properties dialog (see figure 14.14).

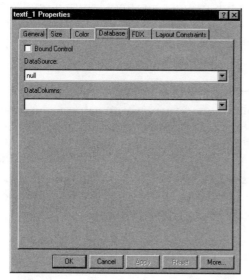

Figure 14.14
Checking bound control

Note

If you do not check the Bound Control property at design time, you cannot use the object as a bound control at run time.

14.14.1 Setting the DataSource and column

Before you use an object as a bound control, you must also set the DataSource and DataColumns properties for the bound control object. This is what binds the control to a particular column in a particular query. At design time, you can set these properties using the Database page of the object's Properties dialog. You can also set these properties with `set` `methods` at run time (but only if you checked Bound Control at design time). You usually perform this task in the Create Event handler for the form containing the bound control. This makes the form open with data displayed.

Note

If you have checked AutoOpen in the query object properties, you cannot set properties in the Create Event handler for the form, because the query object is opened before the form's `create` event is triggered (it is opened when the query object is created).

14.14.2 *The DataSource property*

The DataSource property is what connects the query object to the control. To specify the DataSource property at design time, fill in the DataSource box on the Database page of the bound control's Propertis dialog. The drop-down list displays the query objects located on the form. Just select the query to which you want the control to be bound.

To set the DataSource property at run time, use `setDataSource`.

```
textf_1.setDataSource( query_1 );
```

14.14.3 *The DataColumns property*

The DataColumns property is what binds the control to a particular column in the query. You can set the column using its name or its number.

Note

For code readability, you should always use the name of the column.

To set the column at design time, you use the drop-down list of columns on the Database page of the Properties dialog. To set the column at run time, you use `setDataColumns`.

```
textb_1.setDataColumns( "lastname" );
```

14.14.4 *Getting specific values*

The `getValue` method of the query object gets a value from the current row. This method is one way to obtain values from the query object without using bound controls. You call the `getValue` method as follows:

```
DataValue dv = query_1.getValue( column );
```

`Column` in the preceding line of code is the number of the column whose value you want. The result of `getValue` returns a `DataValue` object, which is a defined type that encapsulates all the datatypes that can be returned from a database. The DataValue class has methods that convert the values into other types.

```
String s = dval.getString();
```

Consult the Reference Card to learn about the other conversion methods available on the `DataValue` object.

14.14.5 When to use bound list boxes

You can use bound list boxes and choice controls to display all the values of all the rows from one column of the queries result set. This is different from other bound controls that can only display values from the current row.

In list mode, a list box displays all the values in all the rows for the bound column in the current result set. Each item in the list box corresponds to a row in the result set. In addition to the regular bound control properties discussed previously, there is another property you can use to specify the manner in which the list behaves when an item is clicked. This is the `DataTrackRow` property, which, if set to `true`, means that the selected item in the list box always corresponds to the column value for the current row. If you select a different value, the result set changes to a row containing that value—for example, if the user selects the first item in the list, the first row in the result set becomes the current row. If `DataTrackRow` is set to `false`, the selection of an item has no effect on the current row of the result set.

14.15 Making changes to the database

There are several different ways to make changes in a database:

- Delete existing rows
- Add new rows
- Modify the values stored in existing rows

14.15.1 *Making deletes*

You can use the query object to make this change if you follow these rules. First, the query object must be open. Updates must be enabled for both the query object and its associated transaction object. Once these properties have been set, your program can make changes to the database.

You can use the `delete` method of the query object to delete the current row, as follows:

```
boolean validate, notify, success
success = query_1.delete(validate,notify)
```

In the code above, if the `validate` argument is `true`, bound objects will receive a `ValidateData` event before the deletion occurs. If `notify` is `true`, bound objects are updated to show that the row has been deleted without your having to issue a `refresh` call.

14.15.2 *Adding rows*

You can use the `add` method of the query object to add new rows to the database. The `add` method creates a blank row into which you can set the new values. After the new values are in place, you issue an `update` call to send the new values to the database. The following code adds a row to the database:

```
query_1.add( false, false );
textb_1.setText("Smith");
textb_1.setText("Jones");
query_1.update( true, true );
```

The `add` method accepts two parameters: `copyValues` and `append`. If `copyValues` is `true`, `add` sets initial values for the new row by copying each column from the current row; otherwise, the new values are left blank. If `append` is `true`, `add` will put the new row at the end of the current result set; otherwise, the row is placed directly after the current row.

The update method

You issue an `update` call to send the changes made in the result set of the query to the database. The update method accepts two parameters: `validate` and `notify` targets.

If `validate` is `true`, each bound control will receive a `ValidateData` event in which you will have a chance to cancel the update before any invalid data are sent to the database. If `notify targets` is `true`, `update` will trigger a `DataAvailable` event to refresh the bound controls.

14.15.3 *Modifying existing data*

Modifying existing data works in exactly the same manner as adding new rows, except that you issue an `edit` call instead of an `add`:

```
query_1.edit();
textb_1.setText( "Smith" );
textb_1.setText( "Jones" );
query_1.update( true, true );
```

Tip

If the AutoEdit property is set to true, you will not have to call `edit` explicitly. The query object will automatically go into edit mode when the user changes the value in a bound control or uses `set-Value` to change a value. You still have to call `update` after making the changes. If AutoEdit is `false`, you must call `edit` explicitly before making changes.

If you execute a `move` after setting new values, the `move` method will automatically cause an update.

14.16 *Refreshing the result set*

If you are working with a multiuser database (and at other times) you may need to retrieve data from the database in order to present the user with an accurate view of the current data. The `refresh` method of the query object will retrieve the current data and display it in the bound controls. You call the `refresh` method as follows:

```
query_1.refresh();
```

After a refresh, the current row will be set to the same row that was current before the refresh, if that is possible (if the row no longer exists, then it will not be possible).

If the AutoRefresh property is set to `true` for the query object, your application will automatically perform a `refresh` operation after every `update` or `delete`.

14.17 Canceling updates

You use the `cancelUpdate` method of the query object to cancel any modifications you have made in the current row—for example, suppose you begin to edit the current row by calling `edit` and have changed the values in some bound controls. You can cancel the changes by calling `cancelUpdate`.

```
query_1.cancelUpdate( true );
```

This restores the contents of the bound controls to the previous values. If you pass `false` as the parameter to the method, it will not restore the previous contents to the bound controls.

You must call `cancelUpdate` before calling `update`. After you call `update`, you can't cancel the changes.

14.18 The data navigator

The data navigator provides a simple way for the user to move through a database without having to write a lot of code. When you place a data navigator on a form, it looks like a set of VCR buttons. Clicking these buttons automatically moves through the result set.

Data navigators work the same as bound controls—they are bound to the query object that retrieves data from the database on the form.

14.18.1 Vertical versus horizontal

If a data navigator is higher than it is wide, the buttons of the navigator are arranged vertically. If not, then the buttons are arranged horizontally.

14.18.2 Choosing the buttons

By default, all the available buttons appear on a data navigator. You can remove some of the buttons by turning off properties that appear on the Database page of the data navigator's Property dialog, shown in figure 14.15.

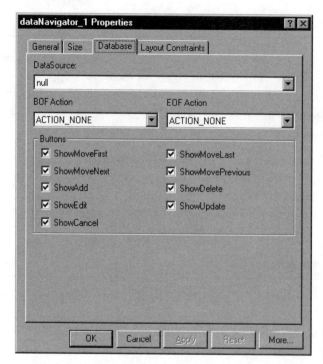

Figure 14.15
Data navigator's
property dialog

If you turn off ShowRefresh, the Refresh button will not appear on the data navigator. You can also remove or add the buttons in code at run time—for example:

```
dataNavigator_1.setShowRefresh( false );
```

makes the refresh button invisible.

The following code makes the refresh button visible:

```
dataNavigator_1.setShowRefresh( true );
```

14.19 Using database forms

The easiest way to create a database form is to select Database dialog from the Form Wizard. This creates a form containing a transaction object, a query object, a data navigator, and bound controls that display the columns contained in the query.

When creating a database dialog form, the Form Wizard will prompt you for information such as the userID and password for connecting to the database and the SQL statement(s) to be executed for obtaining information from the database. It will use that information to set the properties of the transaction object and query object—for example, you will be asked whether the dialog will be a single query or a master detail view (see figure 14.16).

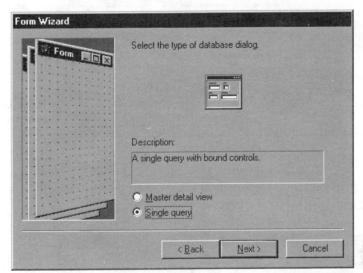

Figure 14.16
Form Wizard

Single queries show data from one SQL statement. Master detail queries show data in the form of a list of items you can select. When you select an item, the detail part of the query executes to display details (perhaps from other tables) about only that single item. You will then be asked to set some database information using the Form Wizard page shown in figure 14.17 (this information is used to set the transaction properties).

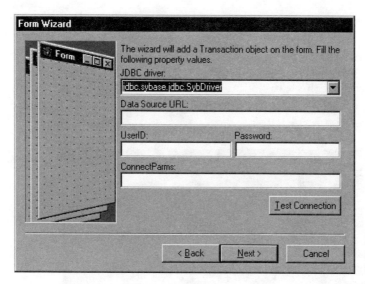

Figure 14.17
Form Wizard
(page 2)

You will be asked to specify the SQL statement that will retrieve the form's data (see figure 14.18).

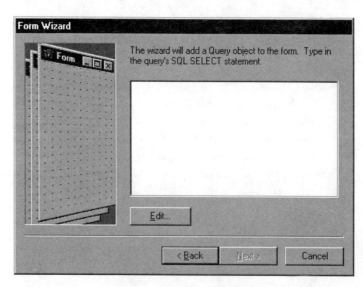

Figure 14.18
Form Wizard
(page 3)

You can either type in the SQL directly or use the query editor by clicking Edit. Finally, you will need to specify a presentation style (see figure 14.19).

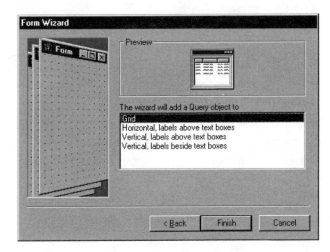

Figure 14.19
Form Wizard (page 4)

Clicking Finish will generate the form shown in figure 14.20.

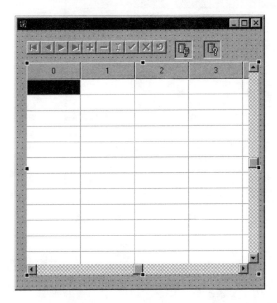

Figure 14.20
The completed database form

Of course, if you don't like the form's layout, you can move things around.

14.20 *Building a contacts database*

For our demo regarding using the database features of PowerJ, we will build an application that displays contact information from the Sybase SQL Anywhere sample database that ships with PowerJ. We will use that database, since we can be certain that all PowerJ owners have it.

This application will display the name of a contact and his or her address and phone number. We will use bound text fields to display the data and a data navigator control to move through the result set. We will generate our form using the Form Wizard.

The first step in creating this application is to create a new application project. Once you have the project created, let's start the Form Wizard to help us in creating our database applet (see figure 14.21).

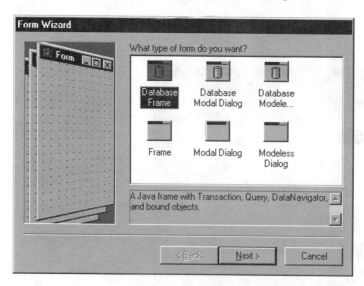

**Figure 14.21
Creating a
database applet**

Since this is an application, select Database Frame as the type of form and click Next. This will open the page that collects form class information.

You should change the name of the form to something meaningful to your project (see figure 14.22).

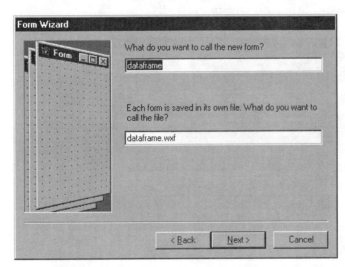

**Figure 14.22
Selecting a
form name**

Click Next to choose whether this is a master detail or single query form (see figure 14.23).

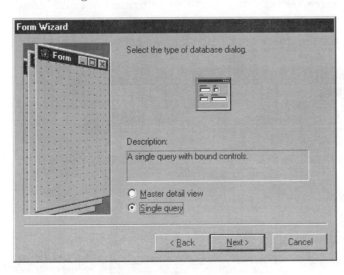

**Figure 14.23
Selecting master
detail or single
query form**

To keep it simple for our demo, select "Single query." You can experiment with "Master detail" later. Click Next and you will be asked to specify the database information (see figure 14.24).

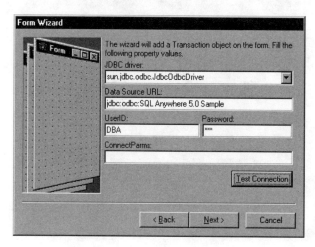

Figure 14.24
Specifying database information

For a SQL Anywhere database such as we are using, you use the *sun.jdbc.odbc.JdbcOdbcDriver* and specify *jdbc:odbc:SQL Anywhere 5.0 Sample* as the data source URL. Notice that this information corresponds to the properties of the transaction object. The logical next step would be to set properties for the query object (see figure 14.25).

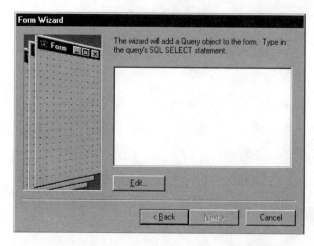

Figure 14.25
Setting query object properties

You can either click Edit to open the query editor and write your query, or you can enter it here as a text string. We will simply enter the string:

```
SELECT  contact.last_name, contact.first_name, contact.street,
 contact.city, contact.state, contact.zip, contact.phone, contact.fax
FROM DBA.contact contact
ORDER BY contact.last_name
```

After the SQL is entered, click Next and select a presentation style (see figure 14.26).

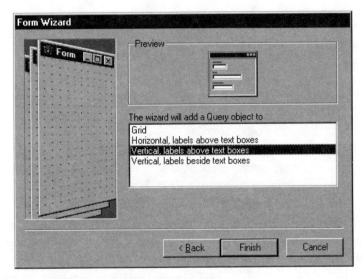

Figure 14.26   Selecting presentation style

Click Finish and the form will be generated (see figure 14.27).

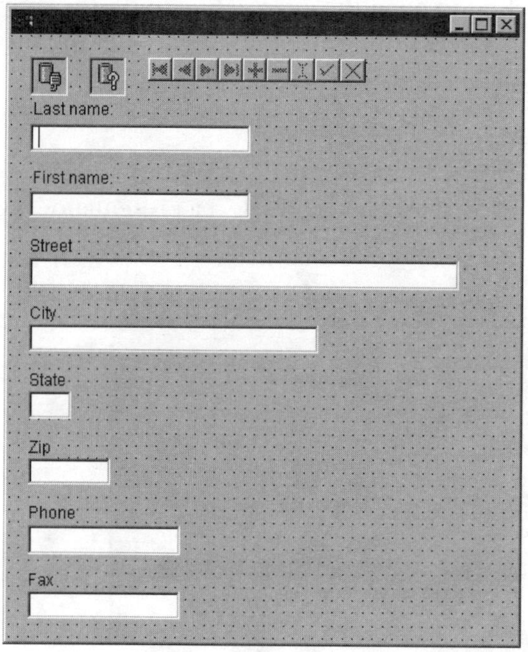

Figure 14.27
The completed contact
information form

Notice that the fields run off the bottom of the form and that the labels need to be resized on the name fields. PowerJ does this whenever it does not have room on the default form or label size. You will need to resize the form and move things around to make a better looking form.

When you have done that, it is time to test the application. However, before we can do that, we must make our new form the main form for the applet. By doing this, PowerJ will display the form when we run the applet without our having to write code to open it. We have to do this, because PowerJ always creates a form when you create a new project and that form is always the main form. Since we did not use that form, we need to switch our form to the main form. To do this, we open the Classes window and right-click on our form, then click Main Form. This will make the running man icon appear next to our form (see figure 14.28).

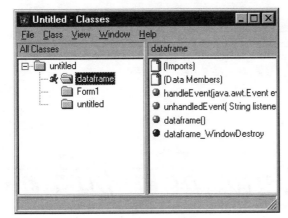

Figure 14.28
Classes window

Now, when we click the run icon on the toolbar, the application will start and our form will be displayed. You can use the data navigator to move through the database.

You can see that using bound controls in PowerJ allows you to quickly and easily build database applications. As you continue, you will find that it is easy to build much more sophisticated applications than those described in this chapter.

14.21 *Summary*

In this chapter we learned how to use PowerJ to create database aware programs. We learned how to connect to different kinds of databases using JDBC and the JDBC-ODBC bridge. We then discussed how to use the database objects—transaction, query, and data navigator—and how to use bound controls. We finished by creating a sample database application.

15

Building applications for the Internet

In this chapter we will do the following:

- Learn how to use the Internet components (socket, HTTP, FTP)
- Learn how to write server-side applications
- Learn how to write client-side applications
- Create a simple FTP application

The predominant use of Java as a programming language has been to develop applets and applications that are delivered to end users via an Internet or intranet connection. You can also write applets and applications that take advantage of the intranet and the Internet's TCP/IP transfer protocols to deliver other content to the end user.

This chapter deals with using PowerJ to write applications that make use of the Internet, such as incorporating the World Wide Web or providing File Transfer Protocol (FTP) functionality using socket facilities.

15.1 *Internet concepts*

Before you get started writing Internet applications, you should make sure that you have a fundamental grasp of the basics of the technologies involved. There are many books available on those topics, but I will attempt an overview here.

When you browse a Web site, there are two computer systems involved: the client system, where your Web browser runs to display the site's contents, and the server system, which supplies the content your Web browser displays. The client requests content from the server by specifying a URL (Uniform Resource Locator). Those of you who have used the Internet have seen URLs such as *http://www.crtvsoft.com /index.html*

When a URL begins with *http:*, the Web browser knows to obtain the content from the Web server on the target server using a protocol known as HyperText Transfer Protocol (HTTP). Requests made using the HTTP protocol are handled by programs called Web servers. On the other hand, if the URL begins with FTP, the browser knows to retrieve the content using the FTP protocol.

URLs usually refer to files on the server machine. In the URL above, the server system is *crtvsoft.com* and the file is *index.html*. When the client submits the request, the *crtvsoft.com* Web server locates the file *index.html* and sends it to the Web browser on the client system. The file probably contains text data in the form of HyperText Markup Language (HTML) code. The HTML code tells the Web browser how to format the content for display on the client.

URLs can also be used to pass a command or a program name to be executed on the server. Software invoked in response to a URL command is known as a Web service. There are two methods for submitting data to a Web service:

1 GET   The first method is GET. The GET command submits information from a form as part of the URL. The information is given as a sequence of query variables, with names and values specified in the URL itself as a "?" character. The "?" character marks the beginning of query variable definitions.

2 POST   The second method is POST, in which the Web browser will deliver information to the Web service as a collection of form variables passed as a block of data accompanying the URL. POST places no restriction on the amount of data sent, so it is most useful for large forms in which a lot of data must be transmitted.

15.2 *Internet programming components*

PowerJ provides standard components you can use to construct these types of applications. These components are: sockets, FTP, HTTP, and Internet. They can be found on the Internet tab of the PowerJ component palette (see figure 15.1).

Figure 15.1   PowerJ component palette

15.2.1 *Sockets*

A socket is the component you use to provide two-way connections between programs running over the Internet. When the client computer outputs data into the socket, the server computer receives the data from the other end of the socket. Transmission of the data is handled through the Internet (or some other proprietary communication channel).

Socket services are provided through a *DLL* (Dynamic Link Library) library named *WSOCK32.DLL,* which ships as part of your Windows environment. However, many Web browsers and their programs overwrite the existing *WSOCK32.DLL* with their own version. Different versions of the library may provide different services.

Sockets are represented by socket objects. So that you can access their properties, socket objects placed on a form are visible at design time, but they are not visible at run time.

Types of sockets

Sockets come in two types: blocking sockets and nonblocking sockets. Blocking sockets are used in synchronous applications. The effect of blocking depends on whether data are being sent or received.

Suppose that the client PC program sends data into a connected socket. The socket then blocks (stops taking data) until the data have been buffered for delivery by the *WSOCK32* library. (This does not mean that the data have been successfully delivered to the remote machine. The *WSOCK32* library has only made its own copy of the data and taken over responsibility for transmitting the copied data to the remote machine.) If an application calls a function to receive data from a blocked socket, the function does not return until the data are received. The application "waits" for the data, and the user can take no further action in the application until the data are received.

Nonblocking sockets are used in asynchronous programs. In an asynchronous program data may be output into a connected socket, and then more data may be output before the first transmission is acknowledged. The program does not have to wait until it receives data.

Socket properties

All sockets share the properties shown in figure 15.2, which you set at design time using the sockets Property dialog.

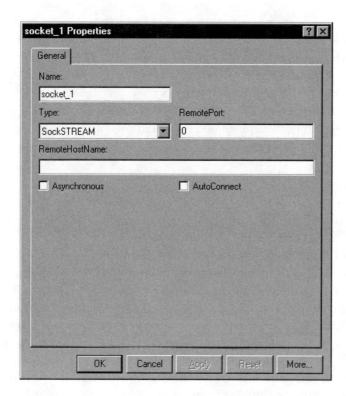

Figure 15.2
Sockets property
dialog

Type. This specifies the type of data that will be transmitted using the socket. The default is SockSTREAM, which indicates a connection-based streaming socket. SockDGRAM indicates a non-connection-based datagram (packet) socket, and SockUNKNOWN represents an unknown type of socket.

RemotePort. This specifies the port number on the remote computer. If you specify a port of zero, the socket connects to any free remote port.

RemoteHostName. This is the name of the remote computer. The name is in the form of a string giving the address of the remote computer in the standard Internet format.

Note

At design time, you should not enter a numeric IP address for the `RemoteHostName`. Use the domain name form instead (*crtv-soft.com*). If you want to identify the remote host using a numerical IP address, you can set the address at run time using `setRemoteInetAddress`.

Asynchronous. This determines whether the socket is blocking or nonblocking. By default, Asynchronous is unchecked and the socket is blocking. Most of your socket applications will be blocking.

AutoConnect. This forces the socket to try to make a connection to the remote system when it is created at run time.

Note

This only works if the socket's Asynchronous property is set.

If you do not select AutoConnect, you must call the `create` method for the socket in order to initialize the socket and make the connection.

```
socket_1.create( SockSTREAM ); // creates a streaming socket
```

Run time properties

In addition to the design properties, sockets have some properties that can only be set at run time.

RemoteInetAddress. This method is similar to `RemoteHostName`, but it expresses the Internet address as an array of four bytes. If the numeric form of the address is 207.222.202.114, `getRemoteInetAddress` returns an array of bytes holding the four values 207, 222, 202, and 114.

LocalHostName. This property holds the name of the system where the PowerJ program is running.

LocalPort. This sets a local port for the socket. If this property is set to zero, the socket can use any free port that is available.

BytesWaiting. If you are using a blocking socket, the `BytesWaiting` property tells the number of bytes of data that are waiting to be received

282 | **CHAPTER 15**
Building applications for the Internet

by your program. PowerJ provides appropriate `get` and `set` methods for interacting with these properties at run time.

Connecting to the remote system

You use the `connect` method to connect the socket to the remote system—for example:

```
boolean status;
socket_1.setRemoteHostName( "crtvsoft.com" );
socket_1.connect( );
```

will connect the socket to the *crtvsoft.com* system. The `connect` method returns `true` if the connection attempt succeeds and `false` if it fails.

Sending data

The `send` method writes data into the socket so that the data are transmitted to the remote application:

```
boolean status;
byte buf[];
status = socket_1.send( buf );
```

The `buf` argument specifies a buffer containing the data to send. The `send` method returns `true` if the operation succeeds and `false` otherwise.

Receiving data

The `receive` method reads data from the socket.

```
byte buf[];
int result;
result = socket_1.receive( buf );
```

Here, the `buf` argument specifies a buffer where `receive` can store the data read from the socket. Receive returns –1 if an error occurs, 0 if the remote system closes the connection, or the number of bytes received if everything worked properly.

Closing the connection

When your program is finished using a socket, you can use the `close` method to close the socket.

```
boolean success;
success = socket_1.close( );
```

Error trapping

Most socket methods return `false` if an error occurs during an operation. If this happens to you, use `getLastError` to determine what caused the error. The result of `getLastError` is an integer that indicates the cause of the problem. Possible error code values are defined in the SocketExceptionCode interface.

The `getLastError` method returns the most recent error that occurred on the socket. This means that you should check the last error after any socket operation that fails. If you try another operation on the socket and that operation also produces an error, the cause of the first error will be lost.

Resetting after errors

The `resetLastError` method cleans up after the last error detected. Whenever you recover from an error, you should use `resetLastError` to mark the socket as ready for another operation.

Socket events

If the socket is asynchronous, it may receive events. These events include the following:

SocketConnect.   This event fires when a connection request has been accepted by the remote system (meaning the socket is now connected).

SocketHostResolved.   This event fires when the socket support software has correctly translated the domain name of the remote system into its Internet address.

SocketDataArrival.   This event fires when data have arrived from the remote system and are ready to be read by the `receive` method.

SocketError.   This event fires when an error occurs during an operation on the socket. In this event you should use `getLastError` to determine what caused the error and take corrective action. Once the correction has been made, you can use `resetlastError` to mark the socket as ready to use again.

SocketSendComplete.   This event is triggered when all the data from a send operation have been delivered to the *WSOCK32* library for transmission to the remote system.

Server sockets

A server socket is used by network server applications to listen for incoming requests from client applications. This means that a server socket waits for incoming socket connection requests and then services each request by creating an appropriate socket on the server and making the new socket available to the program that will actually use it.

Server socket objects placed on a form are visible at design time, so that you can access their properties, but are not seen at run time. Server sockets support many of the same properties and methods as normal socket objects and these will not be discussed here. Server sockets do not support send, receive, or connect. Server sockets may not have the datagram type (WSockDGRAM).

Using server sockets

You use server sockets to wait for clients to attempt a connection and to accept connections when they are attempted. Before the socket listens for connection requests, you must set the LocalPort property so that the server socket knows where to listen. You use the accept method to wait for a connection request to be received and then to accept the request.

```
Socket socket = srvsocket_1.accept( );
```

If accept is successful, it returns socket object, which can then be used to communicate with the program that submitted the connection request—for example, you can execute the send method on this socket to send data down the socket to the remote system. The following code demonstrates how to use a server socket:

```
int portNumber;
socket.setLocalPort( portNumber );
Socket client = socket.accept( );
if ( client != null )
  {
      String msg;
      int received = client.receive( msg );

if ( received > 0 )
      System.out.println( msg );
  }
```

15.2.2 Internet objects

An Internet object is what you use to make a connection with remote servers on the Internet. So that you have access to their properties, Internet objects placed on a form are visible at design time, but are not seen at run time.

Internet object properties

Internet objects have properties that allow you to set the information needed to make the connection to the remote server. You access these properties via the Internet object's Properties dialog, shown in figure 15.3.

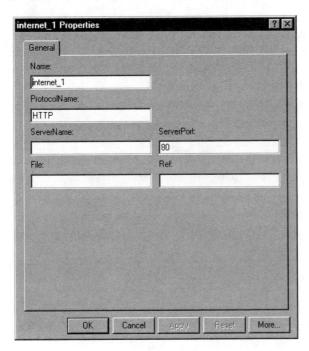

Figure 15.3
Internet object's
Properties dialog

The URL property of an Internet object specifies the URL to which the object will connect—for example, the following code initializes the URL:

```
internet_1.setProtocolName( "http" );
internet_1.setServerName( "www.crtvsoft.com" );
internet_1.setFile( "index.html" );
```

Internet objects also have properties named `UserName` and `UserPass-word`, which are used to specify any required login information needed by the remote server

Making the connection

The open method of the Internet object establishes the connection to the URL contained in the Internet object's URL property. The following code sets up the URL and then attempts to open a connection:

```
internet_1.setProtocolName( "http" );
internet_1.setServerName( "www.crtvsoft.com" );
internet_1.setFile( "Index.html" );
internet_1.open( );
```

Opening a URL creates an input stream to your program. If you open a URL that points to an HTML file, the data are delivered to your program using this input stream. You read the input stream using the `read-File` method of the Internet object.

```
byte buffer[];
int byteCount;
byteCount = internet_1.readFile( buffer );
```

The `readFile` method reads bytes into the specified buffer until the buffer is filled. `readFile` returns the number of bytes read.

Closing the connection

The `close` method of the Internet object closes a connection.

```
internet_1.close( );
```

15.2.3 HTTP object

The HTTP object is what you use to submit an HTTP request to a Web server. So that you have access to their properties, HTTP objects are visible at design time, but are not visible at run time.

Every HTTP object has an associated URL, which is constructed by setting the properties ServerName, ServerPort, File, and Ref. You can set some of these properties at design time using the Property dialog of the HTTP object (see Figure 15.4).

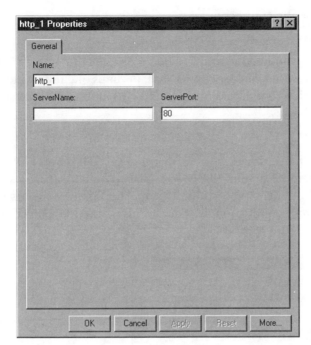

Figure 15.4
HTTP property dialog

Making the connection

The `connect` method of HTTP connects to the URL associated with the HTTP object.

```
boolean success;
success = http_1.connect( );
```

`connect` returns true if the connection was established.

The following code example will request an HTML page from a Web server:

```
boolean success;
success = http_1.openRequest( "http://www.crtvsoftIndex.html",
"GET","HTTP/1.0" );
success = http_1.sendRequest( );
http_1.closeRequest( );
```

You then read the results of the request as follows:

```
byte buffer[];
int byteCount;
byteCount = http_1.readFile( buffer );
```

Then you close the connection:

```
http_1.closeConnection( );
```

That's really all you need to know to begin using HTTP objects in your applications. Why would you use them? Well, perhaps one use would be to create an application that, based on a timer, reads and displays a different URL every few minutes.

15.2.4 *FTP objects*

FTP objects are what you use to perform common FTP on an FTP server running on the remote system. FTP objects placed on a form are visible at design time, so you have access to their properties, but are not visible at run time. You specify connection information using the FTP object's Properties dialog (see figure 15.5).

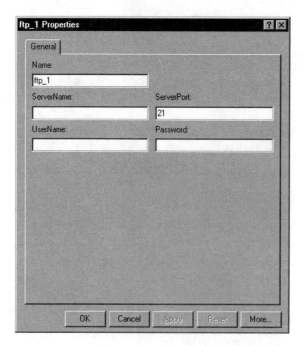

Figure 15.5
FTP Property dialog

Making a connection

FTP objects work almost like HTTP objects. You use the `connect` method of the FTP object to connect to the URL specified in the FTP object's URL property.

```
boolean success;
success = ftp_1.connect( );
```

Connect returns `true` if the connection was established.

Retrieving a directory

The `retrieveDirectoryListing` method of FTP retrieves the contents of a specified directory on the remote system.

```
String dirName;
Vector files;
files = ftp_1.retrieveDirectoryListing( dirName );
```

The result is a vector of file names held as `String` objects.

```
Vector files = ftp_1.retrieveDirectoryListing( "pub" );
```

retrieves the contents of the `pub` directory in the current directory.

Changing the directory

The `changeCurrentDirectory` method of FTP changes the current directory on the remote system. The following code will change the current directory to `pub2`. The method returns `true` if it succeeded:

```
String dirName;
boolean success;
success = ftp_1.changeCurrentDirectory( "pub2" );
```

Retrieving a file

The `retrieveFile` method of the FTP object retrieves a file from the remote system and copies it to a local file.

```
String remoteFile;
String localFile;
int transferType;
boolean failIfFileExists;
boolean success;
success = ftp_1.retrieveFile( remoteFile, localFile, transferType,
  failFileExists );
```

The parameters are pretty much self-explanatory according to their names. `failFileExists` may require some explanation. If `failIfFileExists` is `true`, `retrieveFile` terminates if the specified local file already exists. If `failIfFileExists` is `false`, `retrieveFile` overwrites the local file if it exists.

The `transferType` argument may have one of the following values, which specify the type of data file being retrieved. `retrieveFile` returns `true` if the file was retrieved successfully:

```
powersoft.powerj.net.FTPInterface.TYPE_ASCII
powersoft. powerj.net.FTPInterface.TYPE_BINARY
powersoft. powerj.net.FTPInterface.TYPE_EBCDIC
powersoft. powerj.net.FTPInterface.TYPE_IMAGE
powersoft. powerj.net.FTPInterface.TYPE_LOCAL
```

You make a `retrieveFile` call as follows:

```
boolean success;
success =
ftp_1.retrieveFile("rfc959.txt","mycopy.txt",powersoft.powerj.net.
  FTPInterface.TYPE_ASCII,false );
```

Sending files

You use the `putFile` method of the FTP object to send a file from the local computer to the remote computer.

```
String localFile;
String remoteFile;
int transferType;
boolean overwriteFile;
boolean success;
success = ftp_1.putFile( localFile, remoteFile, transferType, over-
  writeFile );
```

The parameters of `putFile` are the same as those for `retrieveFile`. The `overWriteFile` parameter performs the same function as `failFile-Exists` in `retrieveFile`. The `transferType` argument may have the same values as `receiveFile` to indicate the type of data file being sent. `putFile` returns `true` if it successfully transfers the file.

You use `putFile` as follows:

```
boolean success;
success = ftp_1.putFile( "myprog.zip", "yourprog.zip", TYPE_BINARY, false );
```

Closing the connection

You use the `closeConnection` method of the FTP object to close a connection to the remote computer.

```
ftp_1.closeConnection( );
```

15.3 Web applications

A Web application project target binds together a set of other targets into a single package.

15.4 Web projects

A Web project consists of a Web application target and any number of dependent targets. The dependents are targets such as Java applets and Web services, which PowerJ builds as separate "subtargets" of the Web application. The files associated with the Web application target represent all the files needed in a Web site to deliver the Web application to the end user.

15.5 Building the web application

When PowerJ builds the Web application, it also builds any dependent targets that need to be built. After dependent targets have been built, PowerJ copies the class files to a location specified for the Web application target.

15.6 Publishing the web application

The process of copying files from the Web application target folders to the staging Web site is called publishing. You can also publish a Web application to a production Web site, in which case PowerJ omits any files that are only needed for debugging.

15.7 Creating a web target

Before creating a Web application target, create the dependent targets that will make up the Web application and store them in a single project. Then use the Target Wizard to create a Web target. Part of the Target Wizard process will be to specify the dependent targets that will make up the

Web application. PowerJ creates a file named *index.html* to serve as the starting Web page for this target. The contents of this file provide a typical HTML skeleton for a Web page.

15.8 *Running the web target*

Running a Web target will enable a Web browser to browse the staging Web site.

15.9 *Web services*

Programs that reside on the server and are invoked through and interact with the Web server and Web browser software are collectively known as Web services. There are several methods of providing Web services and these are discussed briefly here.

15.9.1 *Common Gateway Interface*

The Common Gateway Interface (CGI) is a method used to pass a URL request to a Web service residing on the Web server and receive data in return. When you call a CGI program on a server, it writes data to its standard output and the Web server passes that data back to the Web browser that made the request. These data are usually in the form of HTML, which will be displayed as a Web page in the client's Web browser. As end users browse the Web, they do not know whether the content they are viewing is delivered to them from static HTML files or as the result of output from a CGI program running on the Web server.

CGI has a severe limitation in that there is no way to have the client and server interact dynamically. A new instance of the CGI program must be invoked each time the browser submits a URL. Performance becomes even slower if a database has to be accessed or if input fields have to be checked for validity, since this usually means more back-and-forth communication between the server and client. There is also a steep learning curve involved in CGI programming.

15.9.2 *Proprietary web services*

The Netscape Web Server Plug-in environment (NSAPI) and the Microsoft Internet Information Server environment (ISAPI) are two methods of providing Web services in addition to CGI.

These environments are provided through proprietary Web servers, which provide the special interfaces for executing the programs on the server side. This means that they are not "universal" like CGI. They will only work on servers that run the proprietary Web service software from Microsoft and Netscape. These Web services address some of the limitations of CGI programs. They allow back-and-forth communication between client and server by allowing a single instance of the Web service to remain in execution on the server side throughout the client session.

PowerJ supports writing CGI, NSAPI, and ISAPI programs. You just use the Target Wizard to create an appropriate target, and then write the application normally, following certain specifications.

All three types of Web service targets run on the server side. They interact with the client through the server's Web server software. These targets do not have forms associated with them. Since they do not interact with users on the server side, they do not need graphical interfaces. However, you can use visual classes to take advantage of PowerJ's bound controls and database abilities to provide database-related services to the clients.

15.10 *Let's build a sample application*

Now that we have reviewed some of the PowerJ Internet capabilities, let's try our hand at developing a sample applet that uses one of the components. For our sample we will use the FTP component to read a directory of files from the PowerSoft FTP site. A secondary goal of this application will be to show you how to use code from an existing class in your PowerJ projects.

To get started, create a new applet project and place an FTP object on its form. Once that is done, open the FTP object's Properties dialog (see figure 15.6).

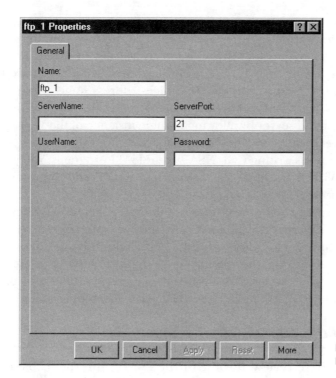

Figure 15.6
FTP property dialog

Here you want to enter the information needed to connect with the FTP server. For this example we will connect to the PowerSoft FTP server using an anonymous connection. To do that specify *ftp.powersoft.com* in the Server Name and *anonymous* and your e-mail address in the Username and Password fields, respectively. Leave the port set to the default 21. In a real-world application, you would get these values by prompting the user with a dialog and then storing the values in the FTP object using the appropriate get and set methods previously discussed. However, here we will simply hardcode them.

We also want to place a list box on the form to contain the directory information we will receive from the remote computer and two command buttons to open and close the connection. Our form should resemble that shown in figure 15.7.

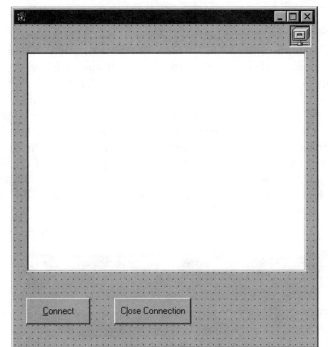

Figure 15.7
Sample application form

Now that we have our basic design down, let's write some code to make the application work. The first step is making the connection. We want to do that when the user clicks the Connect button, so open a code-editor window for the action event of that object and place the following code there (it doesn't matter if you type it in or use the Reference Card):

```
boolean                        result;
result = ftp_1.connect();
if (result)
   {
      cb_1.enable( false );
   }
```

This code makes the connection with the FTP server and, if the connection is successfully established, disables the Connect button to prevent it from being clicked again.

Note

This sample application is a little more complicated than others in this book. Fortunately, PowerSoft shipped some fairly neat samples with PowerJ. One of these samples is a full-featured FTP client. When I was writing this application, I needed to develop a class that would parse the directory listing. Rather than write this from scratch, I merely added the class file containing the method Power-Soft used to do this into my project. In order to get the following code to work, you must do the same. Simply add the *FTPDirectory-Listing.wxc* file from the FTPClient sample application under your PowerJ Samples directory to your project using the Files window (see figure 15.8).

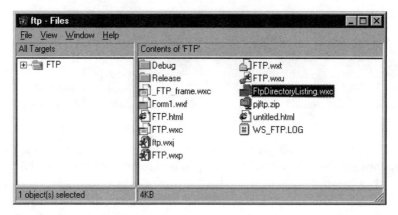

Figure 15.8   FTP Files window

Now write the code in the Close Connection button's action event to disconnect the connection and re-enable the Connect button so that we can connect again if necessary.

```
boolean                        result;
result = ftp_1.closeConnection();
if (result)
   {
      cb_1.enable(true)
}
return false;
```

Now it's time to retrieve the directories and list them in the list box. We want to do that as soon as the connection is established, so we want to return to the action event of the Connect button and place this code inside the `if` statement, which is executed if the connection is properly established. The code in that button's action event should look like the following code segment when you are finished:

```
booleanresult;
java.util.Vector          directoryListing;
java.util.Vector          parsedDirectoryListing;
int                i;
String                 currentDirectory;

result = ftp_1.connect();
if (result)
    {
        cb_1.enable( false );
        /* get current directory from powersoft ftp component */
        currentDirectory = ftp_1.retrieveCurrentDirectory();
        /* get directory listing from powersoft ftp component */
        directoryListing = ftp_1.retrieveDirectoryListing( currentDirec-
            tory );
        /* create an instance of FtpDirectoryListing. This object will
            allow parsing of raw listing to files and directories */
        FtpDirectoryListing myDirectoryListing = new FtpDirectoryList-
            ing();
        myDirectoryListing.setrawDirectoryListing (directoryListing);
        /* clear directory listbox before populating */
    lb_1.clear();
    parsedDirectoryListing = myDirectoryListing.
        getparsedDirectories();
    lb_1.addItem( ".." );
    for (i=0;i<parsedDirectoryListing.size();i++)
        {
        lb_1.addItem( (String)parsedDirectoryListing. elementAt(i) );
        }
}
return false;
```

This code is a little more complicated than other segments in this book, so an explanation of what it does is in order. The main purpose of the code is to create a connection to *powersoft.com* via the FTP object placed on the form. Once the connection is successful, the code reads the directory listing from the FTP server and stores it in a vector of directory names:

```
java.util.Vector                 directoryListing;
```

It uses the FTP object's `retrieveDirectoryListing` method as follows:

```
currentDirectory = ftp_1.retrieveCurrentDirectory();
directoryListing = ftp_1.retrieveDirectoryListing
  ( currentDirectory );
```

All this is fairly straightforward. The tricky part is next. The directory listing needs to be parsed into useful directory names that can be presented to the user in the list box. To do this we need code that loops through the vector of directory listings and stores the parsed directory names in another vector, which can then be looped to place the names in the list box. The code that does the parsing resides in a class called `FTPDirectoryListing` and is a method of that class called `getParsedDirectories`. For an explanation of that class, see the Note regarding object-oriented programming at work on page 296. The following code segment passes our unparsed directory listing to the `FTPDirectoryListing` class and receives a parsed listing in return:

```
FtpDirectoryListing myDirectoryListing = new FtpDirectoryListing(); //
  this creates an
                                     // instance of the
                                     //class
myDirectoryListing.setrawDirectoryListing(directoryListing);
parsedDirectoryListing myDirectoryListing.getparsed
  Directories();
```

Once we have the parsed listing in return, all we need to do is loop through the listing and add each item to the list box.

```
for (i=0;i<parsedDiredtoryListing.size();i++)
  {
      lb_1.addItem( (String)parsedDirectoryListing.elementAt(i) );
  }
```

Now, if you run the application and click Connect, your window will display the directory listing from *powersoft.com* (see figure 15.9).

Figure 15.9
Directory listing

Of course, this is just a barebones implementation of an FTP object that demonstrates some of its use. To make this demo fully functional, you would have to add file listing and transfer capabilities and the ability to connect to servers other than *ftp.powersoft.com*. For a good example of how to do those things, take a look at the FTP client sample application that ships with PowerJ.

All of the Internet programming objects work on the same principles. Learn them by creating small applications that demonstrate part of their use (as we did) and then build more complicated applications based upon the knowledge you have gained.

15.11 Summary

In this chapter we learned how to use PowerJ to write Internet applications using the Internet components (socket, HTTP, FTP). We learned about different ways to write server-side applications and how to write client-side applications to interact with them. We finished up by writing a simple FTP program.

Using JavaBeans and ActiveX

16

In this chapter we will learn about the following:

- JavaBeans
- How to add JavaBeans to the PowerJ IDE
- How to use JavaBeans in our programs
- ActiveX controls
- How to use ActiveX controls in our programs

Most modern development environments can be judged by what they include in the box, and PowerJ is no exception. PowerJ ships with everything included for you to write almost any type of Java application without the necessity of additional tool purchases on your part. But for those times when you need to extend the PowerJ components to include something that was left out, or for those times when you want to develop reusable components on your own, PowerJ makes it easy for you to do so by incorporating the ability to use JavaBeans and ActiveX controls.

This chapter takes a look at how you use JavaBeans in PowerJ and how you use ActiveX controls to extend the Java language.

16.1 JavaBeans

JavaBeans is a component that can be used in the same way as the standard components that ship with PowerJ, such as command buttons and list boxes. JavaBeans is really nothing more than a Java class definition (a.class file), which conforms to the JavaBeans standard for specifying properties and methods. This means that certain programming rules must be followed by the programmer. One rule requires that properties for the class be accessed using `get` and `set` methods.

16.2 JavaBeans versus ActiveX

JavaBeans serves the same purpose as Microsoft Windows ActiveX components in that it is a custom-written object designed to be reusable in many different applications. However, since JavaBeans is written in Java, it can be used on any system that supports Java—not just on Windows systems, and that gives JavaBeans an advantage over ActiveX. Also, ActiveX controls do not have to follow the Java language rules. They can take any actions on the client computer that the programmer wishes. This reintroduces the security problems that Java was designed to avoid.

16.3 Using JavaBeans in PowerJ

PowerJ allows you to use existing JavaBeans in your PowerJ programs by adding it to one of the component palettes. After JavaBeans is added to the palette, you can use it as if it were a standard PowerJ component.

16.4 Placing JavaBeans on the palette

You use the Java class Component Wizard, to place JavaBeans on the component palette. This wizard is different from the Class Wizard discussed previously. To open the Class Component Wizard, click Add Java Component under the Components menu on the PowerJ menu bar. This will open the first page of the Component Wizard, shown in figure 16.1.

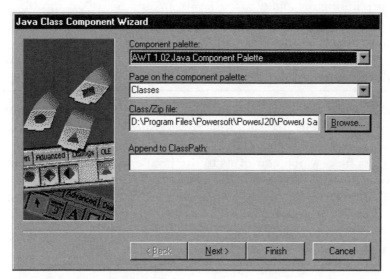

Figure 16.1   Java Component Wizard

On this page you specify the tab page where you want the component to appear, as well as which component palette you are using (this should correspond to the Java version palette that was used to develop Java-Beans). You also specify the file that contains the class definition. When you have specified this information, click Next. That will open the second page of the wizard, shown in figure 16.2.

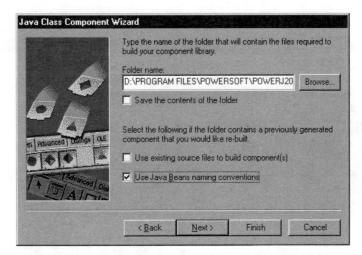

Figure 16.2   Java Component Wizard (page 2)

Make sure the "Use JavaBeans naming conventions" option is checked. Clicking Next will show you this dialog, where you can specify the location of any other class files needed to run the Java component (see figure 16.3).

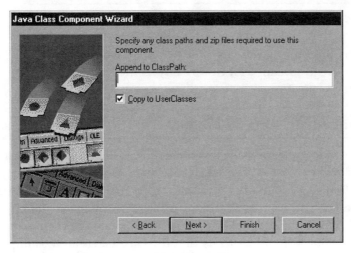

Figure 16.3   Java Component Wizard (page 3)

Click Next to open the last page of the wizard (see figure 16.4), where you specify an icon file for JavaBeans, either by clicking Browse and choosing an existing icon file or by clicking Edit and designing your own. When all the information is correct, click Finish.

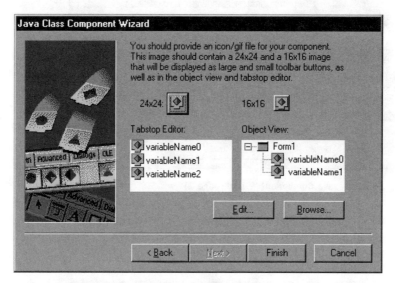

Figure 16.4   Java Component Wizard (page 4)

PowerJ will build JavaBeans and place its icon on the proper palette. You then use JavaBeans as if it were any of the standard components by placing it on your form.

16.5 *Creating JavaBeans in PowerJ*

To create your own JavaBeans with PowerJ, you simply create a class using the Class Wizard.

The first step in creating JavaBeans is to create the class. You do this the same way you would create any other class by using the Class Wizard, as discussed in chapter 15. You create the class in the normal manner, except that you must specify that the class be created using `get` and `set` methods.

You then add properties and methods to the class to make it function as desired.

16.6 *Setting properties*

PowerJ maintains property dialogs for JavaBeans classes. These property dialogs summarize the information gathered by the wizard that created the item. If you define a method in a JavaBeans class, the property dialog for the method summarizes the information gathered by the Method Wizard when you first created the method.

You can use the property dialogs to change information about Java-Beans classes, properties, methods, and events. If you want to change the Reference Card categories where a method appears, you can open the property dialog for the method and make a change on the appropriate page of the property dialog.

16.7 *Using ActiveX controls in PowerJ*

Microsoft has developed a class of components based upon their OCX technology. These components are known as ActiveX controls. Although these components are not written in Java, PowerJ does allow you to use them as if they were. ActiveX controls used to be known as OCXs, due to their *OCX* file extension. These controls are based on Microsoft's Object Linking and Embedding (OLE) technology. Not all ActiveX controls will work with PowerJ.

ActiveX controls are very similar to native PowerJ components. Their interface is also implemented as properties, methods, and events. As is the case with most OOP-based components, ActiveX controls are not used within the applet's window. Instead, they are embedded in a Web page along with a Java applet written in PowerJ. You access the ActiveX control in your Java applet by calling the control's methods and setting its properties.

When the ActiveX control triggers an event, the event is relayed to your Java applet using Visual BASIC script. This process is handled automatically by PowerJ so that you can call methods and respond to events in the same way you do with native Java components. In general, you will not be able to tell the difference between a Java-based component and an ActiveX control.

16.8 *Server-side versus client-side*

ActiveX controls come in two flavors. ActiveX server components are used by a Web server to perform server-side operations. You can use ActiveX server components on a Web server to access databases or to handle business logic. ActiveX controls are used to build client-side applications in the same way other components are used in PowerJ.

16.9 *Adding a control to the component palette*

To use an ActiveX control in your PowerJ programs (see figure 16.5) you must add it to the component palette using the ActiveX Component Wizard.

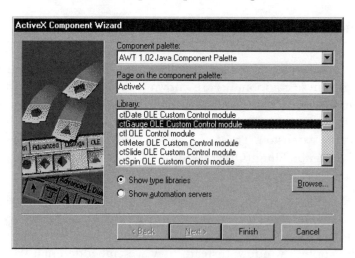

Figure 16.5   ActiveX Component Wizard

Here you select the control that you want to include in your project and which component page you want the control to appear on. When you have provided that information, click Finish and the ActiveX component will be added to the component palette on the ActiveX page.

Adding an ActiveX component in this way creates a native interface to it, and the methods and properties of the control are added to the PowerJ Reference Card, which makes them available for drag-and-drop programming. Figure 16.6 shows the Reference Card open to the methods of the Microsoft ActiveMovie Control.

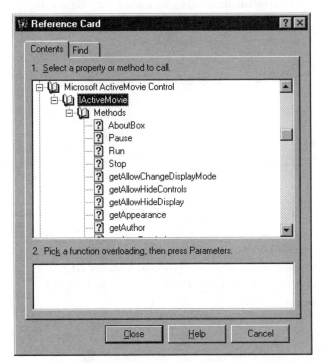

Figure 16.6
Reference Card

You have full drag-and-drop programming capabilities available for using your ActiveX control.

After the ActiveX control has been added to the component palette, you can use it as you would any native PowerJ component, except that ActiveX controls are not visible on PowerJ forms. ActiveX controls are embedded in a Web page and controlled by a PowerJ applet on the same page by calling its methods.

16.10 *Registering ActiveX controls*

Before you can use an ActiveX control, it must be registered in the system registry. Registration allows all programs (not just PowerJ applications) to use the control. Some controls provide an installation program that registers them for you. Otherwise, you must do so manually. PowerJ provides a test that helps you register your ActiveX controls. Just click Register ActiveX Control under the Tools menu (see figure 16.7).

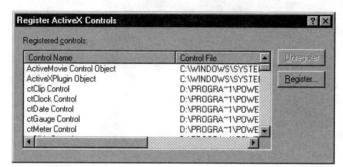

Figure 16.7
Registering ActiveX controls

This displays a list of all ActiveX controls currently registered. If the control is already registered, it will appear in the list of ActiveX controls. You should not register a control twice. Click Register if it is not listed and locate and select the control's library (the *OCX* file or *DLL* file containing the control). When you have found the library, click Open. This opens the file and registers the control.

Note

If you change the location of an ActiveX *OCT* file, you must unregister and reregister it

---

16.11   *Programming by proxy*

ActiveX components are placed on a Web page rather than on a Java form. To use an ActiveX component in your Java applet, place a component proxy on your Java form and use the proxy to call the component's methods.

Place the component you want to use on your Java form in the normal manner. The icon that appears will not be visible at run time.

The new ActiveX component is represented by a member variable at the form level. Since the ActiveX component resides on the Web page and not on the Java form, your Web page must call a method from your Java applet to provide your Java applet with access to the component. When you turn on the externally created property, PowerJ automatically creates a method for your form that allows the Web page to provide the form with a component. The Web page calls this method when it is loaded. PowerJ also generates Visual BASIC script to invoke the method that will attach the Java applet to a component.

Since the component resides on the Web page, PowerJ also generates an OBJECT tag in the default Web page for your applet.

```
<OBJECT ID="HTML_DVCF1_1" WIDTH=200 HEIGHT=100
 CLASSID="CLSID:042BADC5-5E58-11CE-B610-524153480001">
</OBJECT>
```

This tag will be replaced with the component's interface when it is viewed with an ActiveX-enabled Web browser, such as Internet Explorer 3.0 or Netscape Navigator equipped with the ActiveX plug-in. When the Web page is loaded by the browser, the component's method must be called to provide your applet with access to the component. PowerJ generates the following Visual BASIC script to call the component's method when the Web page is loaded:

```
<SCRIPT LANGUAGE=VBScript>
Sub window_onLoad
    document.applet.Set_MethodName ( HTML_MethodName )
End sub

</SCRIPT>
```

When the Web page is loaded, your applet is started, the ActiveX component is created, and the Visual BASIC script is executed, you can attach the ActiveX component to your applet's form.

16.12 Using the control from the applet form

Once you have placed an ActiveX control on your Java form and turned on its externally created property, you are ready to start using the ActiveX component with your applet. You treat an ActiveX control just like any native Java component. To perform the desired task, you call its methods and manipulate its properties. This section describes how to invoke methods, set and retrieve properties, and handle events.

You can invoke the controls methods the same way you call the methods of any PowerJ components. You also have the Reference Card and drag-and-drop programming available to help you write the code.

16.13 *Using the reference card*

Once you have added an ActiveX control to the component palette, its methods are available in the Reference Card. You access these methods and properties the same way you use the Reference Card to program any PowerJ component. Figure 16.6 illustrates a Reference Card open to the methods available on the ActiveX control we had just placed on the palette. If the control's vendor has provided it, you can access online documentation for the methods of the ActiveX control.

You can set properties of an ActiveX control the same way you call methods. Just as with standard Java components, you call the property's set method to change the value or the property's get method to retrieve the value.

ActiveX controls trigger events the same way native Java components do—for example, an event may be triggered when the user clicks the control or when a timer expires. PowerJ allows you to program the event handlers of ActiveX controls within your Java applet. Just right-click the component's icon and select the event you want (you may have to open the Object Inspector). A code-editor window will open so that you can write the necessary code.

Just as with any event handler, the code you write in the event handler is executed when the control triggers the event. Because the ActiveX control resides on a Web page and not on a Java form, the event must be relayed to the Java applet using Visual BASIC script. PowerJ automatically generates the Visual BASIC script required to call your event handler when the event is triggered—for example, the following Visual BASIC script in an HTML document relays the click event from an ActiveX control to your Java applet.

```
<SCRIPT LANGUAGE=VBScript>
Sub HTML_ControlName_Click( P0, P1 )
    document.applet.Call_ControlName_ClickEvent()
End sub

</SCRIPT>
```

If your applet is using an ActiveX control on a Web page, you must run the applet in a Web browser that supports ActiveX controls. Both Microsoft Internet Explorer version 3.0 and Netscape Navigator version 3.0 with the ActiveX plug-in offer support for ActiveX controls. (All examples in this book were tested under Internet Explorer 3.0, and should run under the recently released Internet Explorer 4.0 as well.)

Once you have configured the Web browser, you can run your applet, and PowerJ will open your applet's Web page using the web browser you have specified.

Because ActiveX controls are executed on the client machine, they have full access to the client computer. Most Web browsers inform users when an ActiveX control is instantiated and allow them to decide whether the control will be allowed to execute. When a Web page with an embedded ActiveX control is loaded, you will see a dialog box indicating that a potentially dangerous application is running. If you know that the control will not cause damage to your computer, you can allow the control to execute.

This raises serious security issues not normally associated with Java programming. For some time now, the programming community has been debating the propriety of the use of ActiveX controls. The results of that debate are not yet in and it will probably go on for quite some time. However, since the wide variety of ActiveX controls makes them extremely useful, it can be assumed that these controls will continue to be used in the foreseeable future.

16.14 Summary

In this chapter we discussed the concept of JavaBeans—a reusable Java component that we can add to the PowerJ environment. We learned how to use JavaBeans in our programs. We went on to learn the rules for creating classes of our own that can be used as JavaBeans. We then took a look at another type of reusable component—ActiveX controls. ActiveX controls (also known as OCXs) can be used in Java applets if the target browser supports them. We learned how to add an ActiveX control to the PowerJ IDE and how to use it in our applet. Finally, we looked at the HTML code that PowerJ generates to link the ActiveX control to the applet.

Creating and using graphics

17

In this chapter we will do the following:

- Learn how to create a graphics context
- Learn how to use the graphics object functions to draw graphics within our context
- Create two applications to demonstrate these techniques

Since the computing world is now a graphical world, it is important for any language or development environment to support means of creating and manipulating graphics. PowerJ fully supports directly creating graphical elements in your applications. This chapter discusses that support.

Support for graphics is provided by the AWT graphics class. This class is an abstract class representing an area where a graphical image may be drawn. Graphics is a platform-independent abstract class. The AWT library on a particular computer may define one graphics-derived class for drawing pictures on the monitor screen, another class for drawing pictures that will be sent to a printer, and so on. Any class derived from graphics must support the standard methods defined for the root class graphics. This chapter describes the methods that can be applied to any graphics object.

17.1 Creating a graphic context

When you want to draw graphics in a component, you must use the get-Graphics method against that component in order to get a graphics context—for example, if you want to draw a form, you call:

```
Graphics g = getGraphics();
```

which obtains a graphics context for the form. If you want to draw on a smaller part of the form, you can get another context to adjust that part of the form by using the create method of the graphics context itself—in other words, if you want to draw a picture in a part of a form, you use get-Graphics on the form to get a graphics context for the entire form, and then create on the first graphics context to get a new context for just the portion of the form you need.

```
Graphics g = getGraphics();
Graphics g2 = g.create( x, y, width, height );
```

One way to avoid the necessity of obtaining a graphics context is to use a paint canvas component, as discussed in Chapter 5.

17.2 Graphics properties

Graphics objects, as with any object, have a number of properties you manipulate to perform the desired task.

17.2.1 ClipRect

This is the rectangle that marks the boundary of the object's printable area. This is the area in which you can actually draw. It is most likely an area smaller than the entire graphics region.

If you want to reduce the size of the clipping area, you use the `clip-Rect` method—for example, suppose you have already drawn an image on one side of the graphics context and you want to avoid drawing over that image. You can reduce the clipping rectangle to exclude the area of the existing image, so anything you might draw in the future cannot touch that image.

17.2.2 Color

This sets the color currently used for drawing on the object. If you draw a line of any type on the object, the line will have the color specified by the color property.

17.2.3 Font

This specifies the font currently used when placing text on the object.

17.3 Watch your memory

You are responsible for handling memory management tasks on graphics objects you create. When you are finished using a graphics context, you must free up the memory that is used to maintain information about the context. This is done by calling the `dispose` method of graphics.

```
g.dispose( );
```

17.4 Drawing in a graphics object

The purpose of a graphics object is to allow you to draw. To assist you in this task, the graphics class defines a method for drawing on a graphics context. `DrawLine` draws a line, `drawOval` draws an ellipse, and `draw-String` writes out the text from a string object. These methods (and others) are discussed in the following sections.

17.4.1 Drawing lines

The `drawLine` method of graphics draws a line between two points:

```
g.drawLine( x1, y1, x2, y2 );
```

The draw line function, as used above, draws a line between points (x1, y1) and points (x2, y2). This line will have the color specified by the color property of the graphics object.

 Note

All points are measured in pixels.

17.4.2 Drawing rectangles

The `drawRect` method of graphics draws a rectangle:

```
g.drawRect( x, y, width, height );
```

X and Y specify the position of the upper lefthand corner of the rectangle. The edges of the rectangle have the color specified by the color property of the graphics object.

17.4.3 Filling the rectangle

The `fillRect` method fills a rectangle with the current color (as specified by the color property):

```
g.fillRect( x, y, width, height );
```

 Note

You do not have to use `drawRect` before using `fillRect`.

17.4.4 Clearing a rectangle

The `clearRect` method clears a rectangle by filling it with the current background color.

```
g.clearRect( x, y, width, height );
```

More than just rectangles

Of course, if we could only draw rectangles, our programs would be dull. For that reason, the graphics class supports several alternatives to the rectangle—for example, a 3D rectangle is a rectangle that appears to be raised above the level of other objects, or recessed into its container. The following methods draw such rectangles:

```
boolean raised;
g.draw3DRect( x, y, width, height, raised );
g.fill3DRect( x, y, width, height, raised );
```

In this code the `raised` argument is `true` if you want the rectangle raised above its surroundings and `false` if you want it recessed into its surroundings. In all other respects, these methods are similar to the methods for normal rectangles.

A round rectangle is a rectangle with rounded corners instead of sharp points. The amount of rounding is specified by two arguments: `arcWidth`, which specifies a horizontal distance from a corner of the rectangle, at which point the rounding begins, and `arcHeight`, which specifies a vertical distance from a corner of the rectangle, at which point the rounding begins.

You use the following methods to work with rounded rectangles:

```
g.drawRoundRect( x, y, width, height, arcWidth, arcHeight );
g.fillRoundRect( x, y, width, height, arcWidth, arcHeight );
```

These methods work in the same manner as normal rectangles, except for the additional rounding parameters.

17.4.5 Drawing ovals

The `drawOval` method of graphics draws an ellipse. In order to draw an ellipse, you specify that the rectangle will contain the ellipse, and `draw-Oval` draws an ellipse whose edge just touches the midpoints of each of the rectangle's sides.

The following methods draw ellipses:

```
g.drawOval( x, y, width, height );
g.fillOval( x, y, width, height );
```

The `fillOval` method fills the ellipse with the current color specified by the color property for the graphics object.

Note

To draw a circle, just make the bounding rectangle a square.

17.4.6 Drawing arcs

The `drawArc` method of graphics draws a portion of an ellipse. The ellipse itself is defined by the rectangle that bounds it (just like drawing ovals). The starting point of the arc is specified by an integer giving angles in terms of degrees. The zero degree mark is at the three o'clock position. Positive angles are measured counterclockwise, so a value of 90 indicates the twelve o'clock position. Negative angles are measured clockwise, so a value of –90 indicates the six o'clock position. The length of the arc is specified in terms of degrees, with positive values indicating counterclockwise rotations and negative values indicating clockwise rotations. The following code draws a 90-degree arc, starting at the three o'clock position and going to the twelve o'clock position:

```
g.drawArc( x, y, width, height, 0, 90 );
```

Of course X, Y, width, and height must be specified appropriately.

17.4.7 Drawing filled arcs

The `fillArc` method of graphics draws a pie shape or wedge. The edges of the pie consist of an arc, plus the two radius lines from the endpoints of the arc to the midpoint of the ellipse. The interior of the pie is filled with the color specified by the color property of the graphics object. The `fill-Arc` method is used in the same manner as the `drawArc` method.

The following code draws the same arc as described in section 17.4.6, but this code fills it with the color specified by the graphics color property.

```
g.fillArc( x, y, width, height, 0, 90 );
```

17.4.8 Drawing polygons

A polygon is any figure whose sides are straight lines. The point where two lines meet is called a vertex of the polygon. In order to draw a polygon, you specify the vertex points in the order they should be joined by lines.

The lines for the polygon are drawn in the order given, using the color specified by the color property for the graphics object.

The `drawPolygon` method of graphics draws a polygon. It has the following format:

```
int xPoints[];
int yPoints[];
g.drawPolygon( xPoints, yPoints, N );
```

In this code, N is the number of vertex points for the polygon. The first vertex of the polygon is (`xPoints[0]`, `yPoints[0]`), the next is (`xPoints[1]`, `yPoints[1]`), and so on.

17.4.9 *Filling polygons*

The `fillPolygon` method fills the interior of a polygon with the color given by the color property of the graphics object:

```
int xPoints[];
int yPoints[];
g.drawPolygon( xPoints, yPoints, N );
```

Remember that the lines are drawn in the order specified. This means that the order defines the shape. If you specify the points starting with point one and moving to point five in one order, you will see a polygon. Any other order will draw a different shape.

17.5 Text

Text is just another graphics object. There are several different methods for "drawing" (placing) text on a graphics context. The simplest is `draw-String`.

```
String str;
g.drawString( str, x, y );
```

This places the specified string, using (x, y) as the starting point for the baseline of the string. The baseline is the line on which the characters are drawn; characters may extend above and below this line.

17.6 *The image class*

The AWT Image class is an abstract class representing graphical images. These can be used as "pictures" on Java forms. Image is intended to be a platform-independent basis class.

The easiest way to create an image object is to load an image from a file or a URL. AWT supports *GIF* and *JPEG* images.

The `getImage` method creates an image object based on a *GIF* or *JPEG* file format:

```
Image img1 = tk.getImage( "some.jpg" );  // this loads an image from a
file
Image img2 =   tk.getImage( new URL("http://www.crtvsoft.com//
image0003.gif");
// loads an image from a URL.
```

The `getImage` method associates the name of the file or URL with the image object, but it does not load the image and it does not check whether the file or URL can actually be opened. The image will not be loaded from its source until the program actually tries to draw the image. At that time, the run-time environment will attempt to access the file or URL, and then load the image.

17.6.1 *Placing an image in a graphics context*

The `drawImage` method of graphics draws an image on a graphics context.

```
Image img;
g.drawImage( img, x, y, this );
```

The `x` and `y` arguments specify the upper left corner position for the image—for example:

```
g.drawImage( img, 0, 0, this );
```

draws the image in the upper lefthand corner of the graphics context.

Other versions of `drawImage` allow you to scale the image to fit a rectangle or to set a background color for the image. Consult the online Help for these functions.

17.7 *Creating an application*

Let's put what we have learned to use and create an application that draws some shapes on a form. To do this, create a new applet project and put three command buttons on it. Give the buttons labels: Fill Rectangle, Fill Circle, and Text. When you are finished, the form should resemble that shown in figure 17.1.

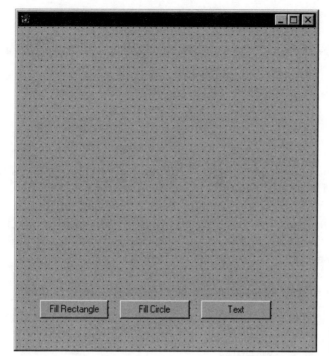

Figure 17.1
Form with three buttons

In the action event of the Fill Rectangle button, you will place the following code:

```
Graphics g = getGraphics();
Color c1 = new Color( 255, 255, 255 );
g.setColor(c1);
g.fillRect( 10, 10, 100, 100 );
g.dispose();
return false;
```

In the action event of the Fill Circle button, place this code:

```
Graphics g = getGraphics();
   Color c1 = new Color( 255, 255, 255 );
   g.setColor(c1);
   g.fillOval( 100, 100, 100, 100 );
   g.dispose();
   return false;
```

In the action event of the Text button, place this code:

```
Graphics g = getGraphics();
Color c1 = new Color( 0, 0, 0 );
g.setColor(c1);
g.drawString( "Isn't this Fun?", 300, 300 );
g.dispose();
return false;
```

When you run the application, you will get a display resembling that shown in figure 17.2 (after clicking all three buttons).

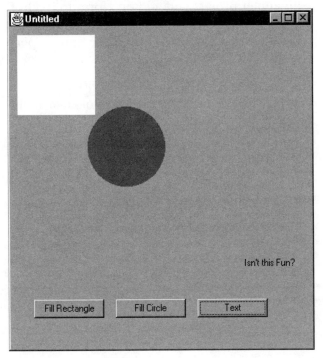

Figure 17.2
Running the application

Of course, you can use these graphics methods to create much more sophisticated applications such as games! But, that is beyond the scope of this book.

However, we can build another application that uses graphics. If any of you are familiar with my Introductory PowerBuilder course taught at Ziff-Davis University, you will be familiar with the Executive Decision

Maker application that we built. (The files for this application are now available at *http://www.manning.com/Hatton2*.) In the PowerBuilder version, we created several objects on the program's window and manipulated those objects' properties to simulate the flipping of a coin (how else do executives make decisions?).

The Executive Decision Maker application can be created in PowerJ using only the graphics class methods without using a single on-screen component (except for the command button to trigger the "decision"). Here's how we do this:

First, create an applet project and add one form to it. On the form place a single command button and label the command button Decide.

In the action event of the command button we want to perform the following tasks:

- Get two random numbers and store them in variables.

- Check to see if the first number is greater than or equal to the second.

- If the first number is greater than or equal to the second, draw a filled circle with a specified background color and inside that circle draw the text "Heads."

- If the second number is greater, then draw a filled circle with a different background color and the text "Tails."

The code should look like this:

```
    // Don't forget to import the Graphics, Math and Color classes
double          result;
double          result2;
result = java.lang.Math.random();
result2 = java.lang.Math.random();
if (result2 >= result)

    {

        Graphics g = getGraphics();
        g.clearRect(125, 125, 125, 125);
        Color c1 = new Color( 255, 0, 255 );
        g.setColor(c1);
        g.fillOval( 125, 125, 125, 125 );
        Color c2 = new Color( 0, 0, 0 );
        g.setColor(c2);
        g.drawString( "Heads", 170, 190 );
        g.dispose();
        return false;
```

```
        }

   else

      {

           Graphics g = getGraphics();
           g.clearRect(125, 125, 125, 125);
           Color c1 = new Color( 255, 255, 0 );
           g.setColor(c1);
           g.fillOval( 125, 125, 125, 125 );
           Color c2 = new Color( 0, 0, 0 );
           g.setColor(c2);
           g.drawString( "Tails", 170, 190 );
           g.dispose();
           return false;
      }
```

This code makes a determination, based upon the return of the random number generations regarding whether to display heads or tails and draws the appropriate graphics. (See figure 17.3.)

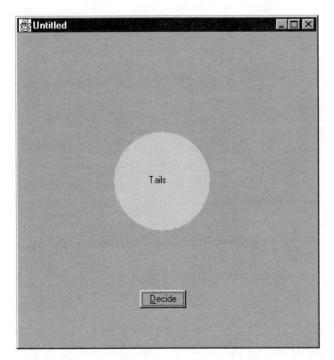

Figure 17.3
Final result

Of course, this application does nothing more than demonstrate that it is possible to build applications in Java that make use of classes other than the standard *java.awt* component classes to perform a task.

17.8 *Summary*

In this chapter we learned about Java graphics and how to use them in our applications. We learned how to create an instance of the graphics class and how to create a graphics context. We then learned how to use the methods of the graphics class to draw lines and other shapes within the graphics context. We demonstrated these techniques with two simple applications showing some of the things you can do using Java graphics.

Build options and running the application

18

In this chapter we will learn about the following:

- How to set build options for our programs
- How to compile the programs
- How to deploy the programs

The final step in creating a PowerJ application is to build the application into its executable form. This form depends upon the type of target, and the available options, which are controlled by the Targets window. To control the build process, PowerJ provides you with a number of properties. We have already seen some of these properties in chapter 10, where we reviewed PowerJ targets and projects. We will take another look at them here and then discuss how to distribute your PowerJ programs.

18.1 Build options

In the Targets window, you can use the right mouse button to click any of the file names displayed and obtain a Property dialog for the target (see figure 18.1).

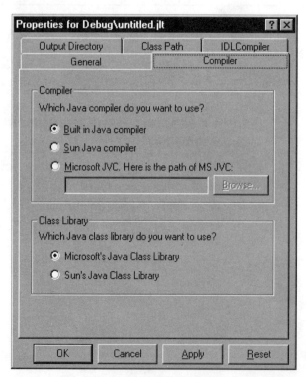

Figure 18.1
Target properties dialog

For a target, the Property dialog controls the way in which PowerJ attempts to build the target. This includes the specific options for building and linking the target and which folders will be searched for class files needed to link the target. On the Compiler tab of the Property dialog, shown in figure 18.1, you choose which Java compiler and class libraries you want to use in building your application. The Sun compiler and classes represent "pure" Java. The Microsoft compiler and classes have some enhancements and may limit the environments under which your application can run.

18.2 *The class path tab*

The Class Path tab is where you specify the places that PowerJ will look for class files. Class files include those that make up the core Java classes (*java.awt, java.lang,* and so on), as well as the PowerSoft classes. In order for your applications to run, these classes must be located where the run time environment can find them. Unless you have altered the locations of these class files from the choices you made when you installed PowerJ, you will seldom have any reason to use this dialog. (See figure 18.2.)

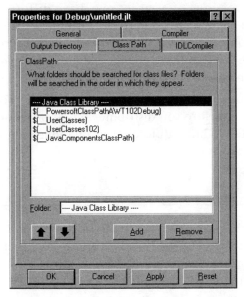

Figure 18.2
Class Path tab

18.3 *Debug versus release targets*

When you are debugging a target, PowerJ prepares a test version of the target under the Debug folder in the Target folder. Debug versions of a target are larger and slower than release versions, since debugging information is stored in them and compiler optimizations are turned off. When you are ready to create a version of the target for end users, you should build a release version. Release versions do not contain any of the debugging information provided with debug versions of the program. They are also optimized in various ways, making the executable file smaller and its execution faster.

To build a release version of your target, open the Targets window and click Target Type drop-down list; then click Release.

From this point on, PowerJ prepares release versions of your target. These are placed in the Release folder in the Target folder. If you later need to do more debugging on the target, you can use the Targets window to change back to the debug target type.

18.3.1 *Build options for debug and release versions*

The debug and release versions of a target may have different build options. Therefore, if you change the build options for one version of the target, you usually have to change the build options for the other version too. To do this, you set the build options, change the target type, and then set the build options again.

By using these build options, it is possible to take control of the type of code that PowerJ will create before you distribute your application to the end users. It is also possible to build different sets of application files for use in different environments.

18.4 *Restoring defaults*

The targets Properties dialog has a button that allows you to eliminate any changes you have made to a target's build options and restore them to the defaults. Feel free to experiment with various options with the confidence that you can always return to the default values if a problem occurs.

18.5 Deploying your Java applet to a Web server

Once you have a program written and tested, you must deploy it to a Web server so your user can access it. You can easily do that using the following steps:

18.5.1 Step 1. Create a release version of your project

Use the Targets window to change the target type from debug to release. Then build the release target by clicking Run...Build. This will create the Java class files associated with your applet. You must deploy release versions of applets since debug versions do some logging, which violates Java security.

18.5.2 Step 2. Add a Web application target

Adding a Web application target will generate all the files you need to distribute your application on the Web. To add a Web application target to your project, click File...New...Target in the Targets window. This will open the Target Wizard and will allow you to add the Web target. On the first page of the wizard, select Web application and click Next. Then complete the folders information on page two. Then click Next to go to page three of the wizard (see figure 18.3).

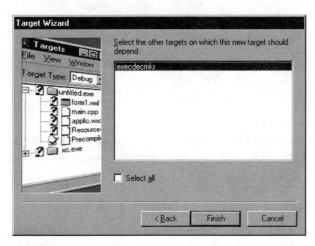

Figure 18.3
Target Wizard (page 3)

Here is where you select the targets that the new Web application target is dependent on. This means that when the Web application target is built, the targets it is dependent on are built first. When you have selected all the targets that make up your application, click Finish.

18.5.3 Step 3. Editing the HTML

Now that you have a Web target, an HTML page for the target is opened up in the code editor (see figure 18.4).

Figure 18.4
HTML page

You must edit this HTML page to include your PowerJ applet by inserting the following code between the <BODY> and </BODY> tags:

```
<applet code=appname.class width=300 height=300 id=applet>
</applet>
```

This code tells the page that it should load your applet and display it in a 300-by-300 box. Of course, you should adjust the size to fit your applet.

18.5.4 Step 4. Set the location to publish your Web Application

The next step is to tell your Web application where it should publish the files that make up the applet. Create an appropriate directory, and then open the Target window again. Right-click on the Web application target and select Run Options. On the Publish tab, choose "Copy the files to a folder" and specify the directory you created. (See figure 18.5.)

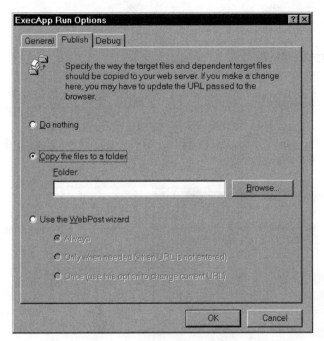

Figure 18.5
Run options

18.5.5 Step 5. Build the Web application

Now you must build the Web application. To do this, select Run...Build from the menu. Then choose the Web application target you have created. After your Web application builds, check in the directory you created and you will see that the *index.html* file and the applet's classes are all there.

If you want to run the application locally, you will need to create an environment variable so that your browser can locate the PowerJ class library. The environment variable should be set up as:

```
set CLASSPATH=powerjdir/java\lib
```

where `powerjdir` is the install directory you chose for PowerJ.

If you know the *index.html* file in a Web browser, you should now be able to view the page.

If you deploy your applet to a Web server not on your local machine, you must also deploy the PowerJ-specific classes along with it. These classes are found in the *\java\lib* directory in the main PowerJ installation directory.

That's all there is to deploying your applets.

18.6 *Using the newest Java*

You can adapt PowerJ to use the latest version of the Java classes—for example, Java 1.1.3 is currently the latest available. If, in the future, Sun releases Java 1.1.4, you can switch PowerJ to use that version.

To do this, open up the Options dialog from the Tools menu and navigate to the JDK Configuration tab (see figure 18.6).

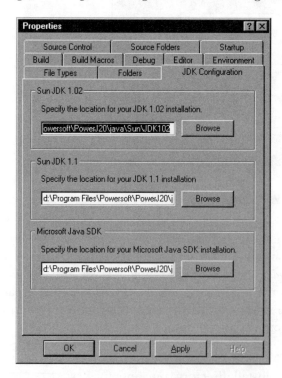

Figure 18.6
JDK Configuration tab

Here you can specify the locations of the various Java Development Kit components used by PowerJ. If a new version of a JDK is released, all you need to do is install the new files on your system and change the folders here to point to the new location. If you place the new files in a folder different from the default PowerJ installation, you will be able to switch back in the event some of your code does not work properly with the new version.

In this way, you can always use the latest version of Java without having to wait for PowerSoft to upgrade PowerJ.

18.7 Summary

In this chapter we learned how to use PowerJ to set build options for our targets and how to compile the programs so that they can be executed outside the PowerJ IDE. We then learned how to deploy the programs so that they can be used by our end users.

Where do we go from here? 19

In this chapter we will do the following:

- Learn where to look for more information
- Learn a little about the future direction of Java

Now that you know all about programming using PowerJ, you probably are wondering what to do next. This chapter will tell you a little about the topics we did not cover in this book and give you some direction on where to turn to find information as you become a more proficient Java programmer.

19.1 Java on the web

Java is primarily in use on the Internet, and there are many resources available there for you to use in learning the Java language. Some of these are listed in the appendix.

In addition to those listed herein, many other sites exist. You can use your favorite search engine to find such things as Java classes and objects and even entire applets and applications, which can be used on your Web sites. Most of these are free; the author merely wants recognition for his or her work.

19.2 Java publications

Most of the trade publications now include regular columns and features on Java programming. Visit your news stand and pick up copies of them.

19.3 Other Java books

Many books have been written on the basics of Java. As I stated at the beginning of this book, you do not have to be an expert in the Java language to write good PowerJ applications. You do need to be an expert in the Java language to write great PowerJ applications.

The appendix contains a bibliography listing some of the more useful books about the Java language.

19.4 Practice makes perfect

The best way to expand your Java skills is to practice. Use the O'Reilly Web Site package, which comes with PowerJ, to set up a Web site on your personal machine, and then practice writing Java applications and deploying them to that Web site. The more code you write, the more proficient you will become.

19.5 *Summary*

In this chapter we looked at some things you can do to continue learning about PowerJ and Java on your own, as well as the future direction of the programming world.

appendix A

Following are some Web sites and
other information you may find
helpful in learning the Java language
and PowerJ programming

Source code

All source code for the examples presented in this book can be obtained directly from the book's descriptive pages on the Manning Publications Co. Web site. The URL *www.manning.com/Hatton2* contains a hyperlink to the source code files.

Java naming conventions

Here are some rules that are in general use regarding naming conventions in Java programs:

- Constants are named with all caps with underscores separating the words, such as PI or INTEREST_RATE.

- Classes are named with the first letter capitalized, using uppercase letters to separate words, such as Applet.

- Methods are named beginning with a lowercase letter but use uppercase letters to separate words, such as setText().

- Variables are all lowercase with underscores separating words, such as interest_rate.

As with any programming language, you should try to give your variables descriptive names.

Java on the Web

CreativeSoft, Inc.—*http://www.crtvsoft.com*—Provider of online training and tools for users of PowerSoft development products including PowerJ.

Builder.Com—*http://www.cnet.com/Content/Builder*—news, information and tools for the Internet professional.

Java Home Page—*http://java.sun.com*—the home page for the creators of Java. Look here for the latest information and updates.

JavaSoft Home Page—*http://developer.javasoft.com*—online magazine type site for the Java developer

Java Language Tutorial—*http://porky.eecs.uic.edu/~rsteven/ java_indx.html*—a basic tutorial of the Java language.

OOPas Java Tutorial—*http://www.adb.gu.se/~fagrell/OO/Tutorial/ contents.html*—another Java language tutorial.

Java Bibliography

Here are some books that are good references for the Java language.

Flanagan, D. *Java in a Nutshell: A Desktop Quick Reference.* Sebastopol, CA: O'Reilly & Assoc., 1997.

Fraizer, C., and J Bond. *Java API Reference.* Indianapolis, IN: New Riders Publishing, 1996.

Holzner, S. *Java 1.1: No Experience Required.* Alameda, CA: Sybex, 1997.

Jepson, B. *Java Database Programming.* New York: John Wiley & Sons, 1996.

Naughton, P., and H. Schildt. *Java: The Complete Reference.* Berkeley, CA: Osborne McGraw-Hill, 1996.

Walnum, C. *Java by Example.* Indianapolis, IN: MacMillan Computer Publishing, 1996.

index